TRADE WITHOUT MONEY:
Barter and Countertrade

150.

TRADE WITHOUT MONEY:
Barter and Countertrade

Leo G. B. Welt

LAW & BUSINESS, INC.
(Harcourt Brace Jovanovich, Publishers)
New York   Washington, D.C.

Printed in the United States of America

Library of Congress Cataloging in Publication Data

Welt, Leo G. B. (date)
  Trade without money.
  Bibliography: p.
  Includes index.
  1. Countertrade. 2. Barter. I. Title.
HF1412.W443 1984   380.1   84-11263
ISBN 0-15-004374-0

*I wish to express my thanks to
Ethan Berger, Chris Brown,
Andrew Gordon, Geoffrey James,
and Jim Walsh. Their assistance
helped make* Trade Without Money
possible.

CONTENTS

Introduction 1

Chapter 1: The Importance of Countertrade in
International Commerce 5

What Is Countertrade? 5
The Prevalence of Countertrade 7
Economic Pressures for Countertrade 8
Lesser Developed Countries 10
The People's Republic of China 11
Reasons for Engaging in Countertrade 12
Western Motivations for Engaging in
Countertrade 13

Chapter 2: Forms of Countertrade 15

Variables in Countertrade Practices 16
Barter 17
Counterpurchases 18
Compensation 20
Evidence Accounts 25
Switch Trading 26

Chapter 3: Negotiating Countertrade 29

Preparing for Negotiations That May Involve
Countertrade 29
Negotiating the Commitment 30
Selecting Countertrade Goods 32
Linkage 33
Lists 35
Long-Term Arrangements 35
Choice of Products 36

Chapter 4: Contract Considerations 39

Separation of Contracts 40
Obligation to Purchase 42
Penalties 44
Pricing 44
Quality 45
Distribution 46
Transferability of Countertrade Obligations ... 47

Chapter 5: Case Studies 49

Case Study No. 1: The Subsidiary Trading
Company 49
Case Study No. 2: The Profit Center
Subsidiary 53
Case Study No. 3: Cooperation in Eastern
Europe—No Special Countertrade Unit 56

Chapter 6: Financing Countertrade 59

Guaranteeing Barter Transactions 61
Supplier Credits 62
Letters of Credit 64
Buyer Credits 66
Financing in China 66
Financing in CMEA Countries 68
Project Financing 69

Chapter 7: Government Attitudes Toward Countertrade 73

Uncharted Waters 73
Dispelling Myths 73
Lack of Consensus Among Governments 74
United States Concerns 75
The Case for Countertrade 77
The Case Against Countertrade 78
The Role of Western Governments in
Countertrade 79

Chapter 8: Creating a Countertrade Capability ... 81

Making the Decision to Countertrade 81
Considering the Countertrade Option 81
Forming a Countertrade Unit 82
The Autonomous Profit-making Center 83
The Direct Countertrade Organization 86
The Indirect Countertrade Organization 86
The Countertrade Purchasing Organization ... 87
The Countertrade Cooperative 87
Multi-faceted Countertrade Programs 88
Other Organizational Alternatives for
Countertrade 88
Trading Houses 89

Chapter 9: Countertrade in the Lesser Developed Countries 93

The Growing Attraction of Countertrade 93
The Evolution of Countertrade 95
The Main Types of Countertrade 97
How Lesser Developed Countries Encourage
Countertrade 100
Countertrade Practices in Individual
Countries 103
Special Countertrade Arrangements 113

Chapter 10: Countertrade in Eastern Europe 119

Negotiations 120
Import Priorities 121
Selecting and Obtaining Countertrade Goods .. 123
Product Quality 125
Pricing 127
Negative Files 129
Letter of Release 129
Future-Buying 129
Bulgaria 130
Czechoslovakia 134
German Democratic Republic 139
Romania 144

Hungary 149
Poland 155
The U.S.S.R. 161

Chapter 11: Countertrade in China **171**

The Role of Countertrade in China 171
Barter 173
Evidence Accounts 173
Processing Arrangements 174
Compensation 174
Joint Ventures 175
Joint Ventures and Resource Development 176
Joint Venture Regulation 178
Countertrade at the Subnational Level 180
Negotiating Countertrade 181
Why Countertrade is Limited 182

**Agreement Between The Government of the
United States and The Government of Jamaica
for the Barter of Bauxite for Agricultural
Commodities** **187**

Appendix A: Sample Countertrade Contracts **209**

**Appendix B: Trading Houses With Countertrade
Capability** **239**

Appendix C: Countertrade Risk Insurance **251**

**Appendix D: Government Procurement of
Imports** **253**

Bibliography **259**

Index **263**

TRADE WITHOUT MONEY:
Barter and Countertrade

INTRODUCTION

The evolution from a simple system of barter to a complicated system of banking occurred over a period of thousands of years. In the process the concept of money—that is, paying cash for goods—evolved, improved, and finally reached the stage where today money is one of society's most important tools.

But our present monetary system is far from perfect. And as the worldwide financial situation worsens, and business risks and uncertainties multiply, it is imperative that we explore improvements and alternatives to the economic assumptions and principles that we have developed over the past millenia. It is the purpose of this book to suggest one such improvement and alternative—countertrade: a term that covers a variety of business arrangements in which payment is made by something other than cash.

What I am proposing here is *not* that we turn the clock back 360 degrees to a primitive system of barter—Manhattan, after all, can no longer be traded for glass beads—but rather that we adjust the dial only slightly, and regard countertrade as simply a new twist on an ancient but practical way of doing business.

Countertrade, unfortunately, has been subject to misinterpretation by bankers, trade commissioners, and government officials. Too often, the term is understood only in its most narrow sense: as a form of barter that is employed principally in East-West trade. Today the direction has changed to a North-South emphasis. Countertrade, as defined here, is really a much broader concept: one that encompasses many forms of compensatory trade—including counterpurchase, buy-back, triangular trade and swap—so long as there is always some kind of asset transfer as a condition of purchase.

Although some members of the world trade community may not like it, countertrade is growing rapidly. Estimates

1

are that countertrade today amounts to one-third of world trade, or more than 700 billion dollars. The U.S. Department of Commerce believes that by the year 2000, one-half of all world trade will be under- taken via some form of countertrade. The companies that will benefit most from this growth will be those that are flexible enough to respond to the realities and demands of the marketplace.

In the pages that follow, I will clarify the different forms of countertrade and explain how the business community can take advantage of both present and future countertrade opportunities. I will describe how each of the major forms of countertrade may best be negotiated. Contract considerations will be discussed, with several case studies presented to illustrate the potential benefits of countertrade. Finally, attention will be paid to current government attitudes toward countertrade, as well as to the specifics of practicing countertrade in the Third World and Eastern Europe.

Countertrade, admittedly, is not the preferred way of doing business. Indeed, there are several problems with countertrade that cannot be ignored: countertrade requires more executive time, thereby increasing the cost of transactions. It creates additional legal work and distorts international trade. So, the obvious question is: why barter and countertrade?

The most compelling reason is that developing and socialist countries are currently unable to pay cash for the imports they need, because they cannot generate sufficient export income. The colossal foreign debt that plagues these countries is no closely guarded secret. It is estimated that their indebtedness currently totals nearly 820 billion dollars worldwide; and at its present rate of growth, will break the trillion-dollar threshold sometime around 1989.

Due to high interest rates on their loans, the developing countries are finding it increasingly difficult to make their interest payments. Many countries have been forced to reschedule their debts, seeking additional credit from the commercial banks in the industrial nations. Yet these banks, growing more and more nervous since August 1982, when Mexico announced it was on the brink of insolvency, have been tightening their lines of credit. International lending to developing nations dropped precipitously during 1983.

As a result, many of the debtor nations—most notably Brazil, Mexico and Argentina—have turned to the International Monetary Fund for assistance. But in order to be eligible for IMF aid, a debtor country must agree to strict guidelines that, while intended to improve international balance of payments and reduce trade deficits, can lead instead to any (if not all) of the following: sharp reductions of imports, shortages of hard currency, high inflation and growing unemployment. The inevitable result will be internal political instability. Throughout Latin America, where the crisis has been most severe, the signs are growing. Venezuela's government was voted out of power and Peru's lost heavily during a key election this year. Financial troubles were central issue in both cases. Brazil's foreign debt and how—or whether—to pay it is the most pressing issue polarizing that country. Trade unionists seeking wage increases may prove to be the most serious threat to Argentina's newly formed democratic government. Even Chile is feeling the debt crunch: the growing movement to unseat Gen. Augusto Pinochet grew this year in large measure to protest worsening economic conditions.

The developing countries are therefore caught in the horns of an explosive dilemma. If they try to meet the large interest payments on their loans from commercial banks, they will be spending a dangerously high proportion of their hard-currency earnings to do so. Brazil, for instance, is spending roughly 80 percent of its export earnings to service its foreign debt.

Moreover, there is growing domestic pressure on the governments of debtor nations not to pay the interest on these loans. In many cases, such as Argentina, the loans were negotiated by regimes that are no longer in power. The electorates of such countries are becoming less and less willing to sacrifice not only their local currencies, but also their jobs, to pay off the interest on debts incurred by a discredited government.

Equally chilling is the fact that the dangers of the debt crisis are by no means confined to debtor countries. Commercial banks in the developed world may be reluctant to extend additional credits to the debtor nations; yet they know that a default on the loans could lead to a collapse of the international banking system. Even the IMF is being challenged; on the one hand for its stiff guidelines that create unpleasant economic conditions in the debtor nations; on the other hand by the citizens of the creditor countries as shown by the recent struggle in the U.S. Congress over additional funding for the IMF. Taxpayers are unprepared to foot the bills for errors of judgement made by the banks. They are also distressed at the IMF's inability to solve the world's financial troubles.

Countertrade—trade without money—offers an escape from this precarious scenario. Countries that are rich in certain resources but short of cash can use countertrade to market their commodities and gain needed foreign exchange and technology. Jamaica has traded bauxite for needed food. Mexico and Brazil are exchanging oil for capital goods. Countertrade offers a way of paying for a developing country's ambitious program of industrialization without bankrupting its economy or destabilizing its government.

In short, the developing countries are looking toward countertrade as one of the ways to stay afloat in the current doldrums of international trade. Will government officials and members of the business community in the developed world respond to these needs? It is my hope that this book will help provide an answer in the affirmative.

In today's interdependent global economy, the U.S. must export to survive. We must meet the needs and conditions of developing countries for our exports, we must become flexible and plan for their countertrade demands. Members of the business community in Japan, Western Europe, and other parts of the world have already been responding to the realities of the marketplace. They have recognized that countertrade is a force in the world today that can be ignored only at the risk of losing sales to one's competitors. We, too, must be prepared to meet the countertrade challenge.

Chapter 1

THE IMPORTANCE OF COUNTERTRADE IN INTERNATIONAL COMMERCE

What is Countertrade?

When businessmen speak of countertrade, they are usually describing the practice in its simplest terms—trade without money. Although this description distinguishes countertrade from strictly cash-for-goods transactions, it fails to convey the variety and complexity of this mode of trade as it is practiced today.

For purposes of this book, "countertrade" means those modes of trade in which the seller is contractually obligated to purchase goods or services from the party, organization, ministry or country to which a sale is made. Also included under this definition are any commercial arrangements in which purchases are formally considered to offset sales. This includes such practices as evidence accounts and bilateral clearing arrangements as well as individual sales that involve an obligation to purchase.

In a typical countertrade transaction, the seller is a company from an industrialized nation and the buyer (who imposes countertrade obligations) is a trade organization in a communist or developing nation. The buyer will require the seller to take a percentage of the compensation in a form other than cash. The portion of payment in goods can range from five percent of the contract value or less, to 100 percent or greater. Countertrade transactions vary in complexity from seemingly simple direct barter of, for example, pig iron for oil, to extremely complex switches of credit among three or more nations.

However, only in rare instances today is countertrade actually conducted without the exchange of money. To use the analogy of farmers trading their goods, pure barter ("I'll trade you one pig for 20 bushels of corn") is not widely practiced. Rather, international countertrade today involves a countertrade of sales transactions ("I'll buy a pig from you for $20, but only if you agree to buy $10 worth of corn from me.") or a variation of this involving a buy-back of resultant product ("I'll buy a pig from you for $20, but only if you agree to buy $30 worth of pork from me when I slaughter the animal.").

International countertrade is a balancing act. By making sure that a foreign purchase is offset, at least partially, by a foreign sale, a buyer of Western technology, goods or services can limit the depletion of scarce hard currency on a transaction.

For these reasons, and others that will be discussed later in this chapter, developing and communist nations have found it attractive to impose countertrade obligations on Western imports as a solution to some of their most serious economic problems. Companies of the industrialized West, however, are generally less enthusiastic about this complicated and risky mode of business. In addition to the inherent difficulties of negotiations, drafting contracts, financing, risk management and, in some instances, disposing of counterpurchased goods, Western companies also balk at having to purchase goods not of the nature or quality they might otherwise purchase, and at often having to purchase these goods at inflated prices. Furthermore, since countertrade obligations do not always obey the laws of supply and demand, they can result in serious market disruptions. For instance, a manufacturer in the West will, in order to obtain a sale of his products in a developing country, concede to purchasing in return a specified, unrelated product. The Western firm will, subsequently try to sell a product for which there had, in fact, been no demand. The only purpose for selling the product is to dispose of the company's countertrade obligation.

Nevertheless, Western businessmen are overcoming their distaste for countertrade because they simply cannot afford to ignore the enormous markets in which countertrade has become a fact of life.

The Prevalence of Countertrade

Only five years ago, countertrade was an anomaly considered by international traders, particularly in the United States, as a primitive and archaic way of doing business. By 1981, 10 to 20 percent of the $1.2 trillion of international trade was being conducted through countertrade. Currently, some 50 percent of trade between the West and communist countries is tied to some form of countertrade.

Part of this increase is due to the direct correlation between world economic conditions and the use of countertrade. When the economic climate in the industrialized countries worsens, there is an automatic ripple effect on the economies of developing nations, whereby their export markets and, subsequently, their foreign exchange earnings are substantially reduced. In order to maintain some momentum in their development projects, developing countries continue to import technology and goods from the industrialized nations, by requiring the sellers to accept, in most instances, some form of countertrade. Of course, in times of economic prosperity, i.e. full foreign exchange coffers, when conventional methods of trade (cash for goods) are appropriate, the occasions on which countertrade obligations are demanded decrease. For Western exporters, moreover, favorable world economic conditions often help to effectively resist countertrade demands, simply by allowing manufacturers to consider alternative markets.

In the years ahead, however, countertrade will continue to be a fact of life regardless of short-term economic conditions in the West. Because of the economic policies pursued during the past decade by Third World and East European nations, whereby they maintained high levels of imports from the industrialized countries in the face of sharply increased energy costs, conditions that foster a need for countertrade will continue to prevail.

In addition, the practice of making countertrade demands on foreign imports is expanding geographically to the potentially enormous markets of the People's Republic of China and to the centrally planned economies of many developing countries in Africa, Latin America, and the Middle East.

Economic Pressures for Countertrade

Countertrade, especially in the form of pure barter, is certainly the oldest form of international trade known to man. Long before international monetary systems were developed, commerce was conducted through trading that took many of the forms of countertrade now in use, including barter, evidence accounts and bilateral clearing arrangements. Among the Mesopotamia clay tablets on which are inscribed the ancient Sumerian characters, one will find accounts of barter transactions.

Countertrade has been used to conduct international business when monetary systems break down under the pressures of war, extreme inflation, or other conditions that render trade in currency impractical or undesirable for a national economy.

The practice of countertrade first emerged on a large scale in this century after World War I. Germany used it during the Weimar Republic when its currency had become too unstable to use as a medium for foreign exchange and, by this method, helped nurse its war-ravaged economy back to health. Similarly, national economies of Europe reverted to barter and international clearing arrangements as a means to help recover from the devastation of World War II. In exchange for machinery components, for example, Germany was able to provide manufactured goods. France, in turn, was able to use its large agricultural base to provide food stuffs as payment for technology and equipment to rebuild its manufacturing industries.

The current era of countertrade is primarily a phenomenon of the past decade in the communist countries of Eastern Europe. With their non-convertible currencies, trade on a large scale with nations of the industrialized West is difficult under normal cash-for-goods terms. In addition, the central economic planning of these countries encourages policies that direct industrial and economic sectors to demand countertrade obligations on foreign imports. The reason is simple: inherent in centralized economies are production targets of all kinds, including exports. By requiring foreign trade organizations to demand countertrade in their contracts with Western companies, central planners are able to control the amount of imports relative to exports. The result of this control is a greater likelihood of meeting export target levels, enhancing prestige.

As the Soviet Union and other East European countries adopted ambitious industrialization plans in the mid-1960's, their need for capital goods from the West surged. With the expansion of trade relations with the West during the period of detente in the early and mid-1970's, these plans held the promise of increased exports to the industrialized world. The failure of their export capacity to keep pace with their foreign expenditures, coupled with the general slump of trade in the West, resulted, however, in serious balance of trade problems for most East European countries. By 1982, the combined hard currency trade deficit of the USSR and Eastern Europe had reached an estimated $12 billion.

With extremely lean hard currency reserves, East European countries turned increasingly to foreign credit in order to finance their deficits. The result was a five-fold increase in the net external debt of the countries in the Council for Mutual Economic Assistance from approximately $12 billion in 1973 to $58.5 billion by year-end 1978. By the end of 1981, Council for Mutual Economic Assistance (CMEA) net external debt reached $88 billion—an annual debt growth of 38 percent since 1973.

Although the imports of advanced plant and equipment (some 35 percent of total CMEA imports) and vital raw materials failed to bring about the desired increase in exports, CMEA countries have been unable to significantly cut back these imports. They are essential to the accomplishment of their much-publicized five-year plans, and are vital to the advancement of industrial modernization programs that have proceeded too far to abandon.

Faced with these grim economic conditions—serious trade imbalances with the West, soaring hard currency debts, the need for continued imports from the West, and a failure to increase hard currency exports—East European nations have had to limit hard currency imports to those of the highest priority, or those that are guaranteed to result in hard currency export earnings. Under these conditions, stern economic messages have come down to the foreign trade organizations of many CMEA countries to demand countertrade.

The same economic pressures that have led to the widespread practice of countertrade in Eastern Europe are increasingly having the same effect in developing countries and the People's Republic of China. For both non-oil exporting developing nations and China, aspirations toward industrial modernization are out of proportion to the ability to pay for it with hard currency. These countries' only recourse is to pay for hard currency imports with earnings from domestic exports. It is logical that they demand, when possible, import transactions that "pay for themselves," that is, foreign joint ventures and countertrade.

Lesser Developed Countries

Along with economic pressures, trends in industrial development in lesser developed countries (LDC's) have spurred demands for countertrade. Characteristic of these trends is a shift from agriculture and raw material production to the manufacture of light industrial goods, basic chemicals and steels, and relatively unsophisticated machinery. Total exports of manufactured goods from the developing world grew 11 percent annually from 1960-1975, according to World Bank figures, and are expected to grow steadily at a similar rate through the 1980's. This compares to a growth of the same product exports of only 7-8 percent in the industrialized West. Markets for these goods in the developing world, however, have not grown proportionately, and LDC's have not been able to capture needed market shares in the West.

At the same time, LDC's have suffered severe depletion of hard currency reserves caused by the enormous rise in oil prices. As a result, LDC's foreign debts have soared. At the end of 1978, the public hard currency debt of the 96 non-oil producing developing countries totaled more than $300 billion. This foreign debt is substantially higher than that of the Council for Mutual Economic Assistance countries for the same time period, although the debt growth for LDC's was considerably lower than CMEA's at 23 percent annually since 1973. Under these conditions, countertrade is the only available means for many LDC's to satisfy their hunger for industrial growth.

The People's Republic of China

The economic development plans adopted by the People's Republic of China in 1978 entice Western business with the promise of great export opportunities. The Chinese economy, however, as it emerges from years of relative isolation and policies of economic nondevelopment, is ill-prepared to pay for its ambitious modernization goals. A major challenge facing Chinese economic planners today is to find a means of acquiring foreign technology for modernization without incurring an unbearable burden of foreign debt. One way is the use of countertrade.

When China's pragmatic leadership set out on its course toward modernization in 1978, it envisioned the accomplishment of the "four modernizations"—agriculture, industry, national defense and science—by the year 2000. The first phase of this drive, the 1976-1981 five-year plan, included some 120 major projects, most of them involving imports or foreign participation.

By 1979, however, it became clear that China's meager hard currency reserves, and her limited capacity to generate hard currency through exports, due to an underdeveloped infrastructure and industrial production capacity, made it impossible to implement the 1976 five-year plan without relying heavily upon foreign credits.

Since the Chinese aversion to foreign debt, on ideological grounds, made this course unacceptable, Chinese leaders decided to shelve the five-year plan and to scale down, postpone or cancel a number of the major projects envisioned under the plan. At the same time, Chinese economic planners em-

barked upon a "readjustment period." Under this retrench-
ment, priority was given to projects that require less foreign
exchange, provide a quicker return on investment, and offer
potentially greater export earnings.

The decisions made in this readjustment manifest an attitude that, rather than falling into the foreign debt patterns
of Eastern Europe or the developing world, China will modernize slowly, and will tie foreign imports as directly as possible to exports to the West. Part of this attitude is a determination to countertrade. Indeed, many Western executives
who were involved in contract negotiations on projects that
were cut back in 1979, reported that Chinese officials made
it clear that the deals could only remain viable under countertrade terms. As China continues on its path of economic
readjustment, it must rely on projects that can be paid for in
resultant exports in order to achieve even its modest modernization goals.

Reasons for Engaging in Countertrade

From the standpoint of East- European countries, lesser
developed countries and the People's Republic of China, the
reasons for placing countertrade obligations on Western imports are often compelling. Many of these reasons have already been introduced in this chapter. For the sake of clarity,
a brief list of these reasons follows:

- *To preserve hard currency.* Countries with non-convertible currencies look to countertrade as a way of guaranteeing that expenditures of hard currency for foreign
  imports are offset by hard currency earnings, which
  are, generated by the foreign party's obligation to purchase domestic goods.
- *To improve balance of trade.* Nations whose exports to
  the West have not kept pace with imports are concerned with both the reality and appearance of trade
  deficits. Increasingly, these nations rely upon countertrade as a means to balance bilateral trade ledgers.
- *To gain access to new markets.* As communist and developing nations increase their production of exporta-

ble goods, they do not have sophisticated marketing channels to sell them to the West for hard currency. By imposing countertrade demands, foreign trade organizations utilize the marketing organizations and expertise of Western companies to market their goods for them.

- *To upgrade manufacturinq capabilities.* By entering into compensation arrangements, under which foreign firms provide plant and equipment and buy back resultant products, foreign trade organizations can enlist Western technical cooperation in upgrading or installing industrial facilities.

- *To maintain prices of export goods.* Countertrade can be used as a means to dispose of goods at prices that the market would not bear under cash-for-goods terms. Although the Western seller absorbs the added cost by inflating the price of the original sale, the nominal price of the counterpurchased goods is maintained, and the seller need not concede what the value of the goods would be on world supply-and-demand markets.

Western Motivations For Engaging in Countertrade

Western companies generally enter into countertrade contracts reluctantly. They would rather engage in straight cash transactions that are more simple and that pose fewer risks. However, some of the reasons they are willing to concede to countertrade demands include:

- *Sales opportunities.* In order to make a sale in the markets of the communist and developing worlds, it is often necessary to respond positively to countertrade demands. A company that is willing to engage in countertrade may gain a crucial competitive edge over an unwilling competitor.

- *Sources of supply.* In some cases, particularly in compensation transactions, countertrade can be used by a Western company to obtain a long-term, reliable supply of raw materials, component parts, or finished products that may be inexpensive because of low labor costs, or may be essential to the Western company's operations elsewhere in the world. The U.S. and Jamaica, for example, recently concluded a deal whereby the U.S. would supply Jamaica with surplus dairy products in exchange for bauxite. Jamaica found an export outlet for one of its main foreign exchange earners, and the U.S. was able to add to its stockpile of strategic raw materials.

- *To gain prominence in new markets.* Western companies sometimes employ countertrade to show good faith in certain markets, and to establish themselves as reliable trading partners, thereby enhancing the prospects for future sales.

Chapter 2
FORMS OF COUNTERTRADE

To the bewilderment of a businessman approaching the subject, terminology about forms of countertrade lacks standardization. As a result, the same words often mean different things depending upon the sources. Indeed, different sources of information—studies, reports or presentations—do not even agree on a single term for the practice of countertrade as a whole. One may find *barter* or *compensation* used as generic terms to refer to the general practice discussed here as countertrade. This discrepancy in terminology becomes even more confusing when discussing individual forms of the practice, with some transactions going by two or three different names and with a single term used to refer to quite different practices.

Perhaps the greatest reason for this lack of standardization is that the subject is relatively new. Although countertrade is the most ancient form of international trade, the particular types of countertrade now most widely in use have only emerged in the past decade. Compensation, for instance, has only come into practice since the end of the 1960's. Similarly, counterpurchase (although related to the older forms of countertrade) has not been practiced under its present contractual arrangements until fairly recently. As a result economic organizations have lacked the data needed to arrive at precise and comprehensive terms and definitions.

The problem of definition is exacerbated by the fact that, since countertrade transactions are formed according to the contingencies of commercial conditions surrounding each individual deal, they often defy simple categorization. A barter transaction, for instance, may have elements of counterpurchase or compensation in it.

Another reason for differences in terminology is that Eastern and Western parties in a transaction often choose to refer to a practice by different names. This is partially due to the difference in economic contexts between the two, but can also be an intentional decision to emphasize one or another aspect of a practice. In Eastern Europe, for example, policy planning people look more favorably on a compensation transaction than on a barter deal. Whereas barter involves a simple exchange of goods, compensation leaves room for technology transfer agreements and enhances national prestige. Thus a deal that is, in fact, a barter transaction, will be referred to as a compensation agreement.

Variables in Countertrade Practices

Before discussing the various types of countertrade, it may be useful to examine some of the characteristics by which countertrade practices are categorized:

1. *Relative duration*
   A countertrade transaction may take place within a matter of days, or may span two or more decades.
2. *Form of settlement*
   Hard currency may change hands, or only goods and services may be exchanged (pure barter).
3. *Relation of countertraded products*
   In some cases, counterdeliveries are in the form of products resulting from the original sale (compensation); in others, products exchanged are unrelated.
4. *Legal arrangements*
   The countertrade transaction may occur under a single contract, or under two or more legal instruments.
5. *Value relations of deliveries*
   Counterdeliveries, as a proportion of original sale, range from a small percentage to well over 100 percent.
6. *Size of a deal*
   Countertrade practices are used for transactions involving sums as small as a few thousand dollars, or as large as several billion dollars.

7. *Technology transfer motives*
Countertrade arrangements are sometimes employed by a communist or developing nation to acquire technology.

In the following definitions and explanations, the terms used are those used most commonly by current authoritative sources. Forms are described as models to illustrate their typical characteristics. Many individual transactions will generally fall into one category or another without embodying all of its characteristics, and one deal may incorporate more than one of the forms in a single commercial arrangement. By applying these definitions, however, the general varieties of countertrade can be identified.

Barter

In its classic form, a barter transaction is a simple exchange of goods, with no money changing hands, executed under a single contract. Typically, the entire exchange occurs over a relatively short period of time (under two years) and the products exchanged have no relation to one another. Although these deals are most commonly transacted between two parties, in more complicated deals they may involve several parties. Under some circumstances, an exchange of hard currency may enter into a deal to offset minor variations in the values of bartered goods, and a transaction may take place over a period of several years.

Barter was last employed as a widespread practice in East-West trade during the period immediately following World War II when, for instance, Austrian shipments of timber were used to pay for badly needed food from Hungary. In recent years, barter has become rare but not extinct; 1981 estimates of its prevalence range from "almost non-existent" to 10 to 15 percent of all countertrade transactions. Barter is used most commonly today between communist countries and poor developing countries, although Western companies occasionally involve themselves when potential partners can offer a profitable exchange.

In addition to the rarity of pure barter, many problems

that can arise from the legal arrangement of barter deals also discourage their use. One obvious difficulty is that of determining and agreeing upon the relative value of traded goods in such a non-cash transaction. Another crucial disincentive for conducting barter is the use of one contract to cover both deliveries and counter-deliveries. Western banks are rarely willing to finance or guarantee a transaction in which a creditor's proceeds are contingent upon another party's performance. Moreover, even if guarantees can be obtained from a willing financial institution, the complexity of covering contingency risks in a barter contract with guarantees is a disincentive in itself.

In a conventional cash-for-goods international transaction, the seller is guaranteed payment and the buyer is guaranteed that funds will not be released until the goods are received. Both of these guarantees are provided by a letter of credit issued by a bank to the seller on behalf of the purchaser. Since no actual payment in currency occurs in a barter deal, however, a letter of credit cannot be issued.

In the absence of letters of credit, participants in a barter transaction can obtain parallel bank guarantees in the form of standby letters of credit or performance bonds. These insure that, in the case of default, the defaulting party would compensate the performing party in hard currency. In most cases, however, it is easier simply to employ two separate contracts: one for the delivery and another for the counterdelivery of goods, and to have each party pay for the goods in hard currency with payment guaranteed by a letter of credit. This type of transaction is referred to as *parallel barter* or, more commonly, *counterpurchase.*

Counterpurchases

Under a counterpurchase agreement, a Western company sells goods to a foreign trade organization in a communist or developing nation and contractually agrees to make reciprocal purchases from that organization, or from another commercial body in the same country, within a designated period of time. Counter-deliveries in these transactions are generally not resultant products (they are not produced by, derived from, or related to Western goods delivered in the original sale), but are chosen from among a range of products offered by the purchaser in the first contract. The duration of the entire transaction is relatively short—from one to three years—and the commitment for reciprocal purchase, stated in currency or as a percentage of the original sale, varies from 10 to 100 percent, but is generally less than the full value of the original sale.

Counterpurchase is conducted under two separate contracts linked by a protocol. This makes financing a counterpurchase agreement similar to that of standard trade, since each of the agreements is an exchange of goods for hard currency. The separation of contracts also protects the original sale from encumbrances so that payment for the sale cannot legally be witheld if problems arise in the execution of the second contract.

The first contract in a counterpurchase arrangement is a standard cash-for-goods agreement not unlike any other contract for international sales. The second contract, however, is broader and more complex. Although it may call for the purchase of specified goods for a set price, more typically the second contract identifies a list of goods that may be chosen for purchase, and identifies a criteria for pricing rather than actual prices for the goods. In East-West trade, it is often stipulated that reciprocal orders must be placed with the Foreign Trade Organization (FTO) or, in China, with the Foreign Trade Corporation (FTC) to which the original sale was made. In many cases, however, goods may also be purchased from products offered by other trade organizations within the country. This practice is called "linkage," and normally requires authorization at the ministry level. Linkage is still rare in trade with China because coordination among industrial sectors for this purpose is not yet sophisticated enough to handle the procedure.

Since counterpurchase is a short-term commercial arrangement for the exchange of goods, it does not typically involve significant technology transfer from the West to the East. Rather, it is often employed by an Eastern or developing nation to acquire goods for which hard currency would not otherwise be allocated. In the case of CMEA countries, these are often products that are not included in five or ten year economic plans, or hold a low priority in the plan. The amount of counterpurchase demanded on a sale is in inverse proportion to the importance of the goods acquired under planned objectives.

Goods offered for counterpurchase may be raw materials, manufactured goods, semi-manufactured goods, or machinery, but typically and increasingly they take the form of finished manufactured products. These are products which have limited access to hard currency markets, often because of lack of demand or low quality.

Normally, a counterpurchase agreement allows the seller in the first contract to assign his counterpurchase obligation to a third party—a trading house or other foreign buyer. If the Western company can find no products for counterdelivery that it can use in its own operations or that it can market through its organization, it often transfers its obligation to a trading house, which will dispose of the goods for a commission or "discount." These discounts range from under five percent for disposal of easily marketed goods such as raw materials, to as much as 40 percent for hard-to-market manufactured goods.

Compensation

Compensation often called buyback, involves the sale of technology, or a plant with a contractual commitment on the part of the seller to purchase a certain quantity of products that are produced by or derived from the original sale. Because these transactions involve setting up entire production facilities, their values can run into hundreds of millions of dollars. The duration of the transaction, accordingly, is far more lengthy than for counterpurchase arrangements owing not only to the magnitude of the projects, but also to the time necessary to complete projects before they come on-stream to produce goods for counterdelivery. At a minimum, the period of the buyback obligation runs three to four years, and it is not uncommon for a compensation arrangement to last 25 years or longer.

The commitment to buy back goods, as a proportion of the original sale, is also typically greater than for counterpurchase, with counterdeliveries often totaling 100 percent or more of the value of the original sale.

As in counterpurchase arrangements, compensation is conducted with the use of two separate contracts linked by a protocol. The separation of legal instruments for deliveries and counterdeliveries serves the same function as in counterpurchase, but they gain added importance both because of the need to keep large payments for the transfer of technology and goods unencumbered, and because innumerable variables and contingencies inherent in the establishment of full scale facilities place added risks in the second, buyback contract of the deal. Similarly, the protocol that links the two contracts in a compensation deal takes on added importance by insuring that counterdeliveries are, in fact, produced with the technology and equipment delivered in the original sale.

Unlike counterpurchase, it is the first contract in compensation that is the most complex and poses the most potential problems. The Western seller in the deal is often setting up a potential competitor, and in the contract to transfer technology and equipment, he must pay special attention to clauses pertaining to the second party's right to transfer technology, its right to use the Western company's brand name, and its right to distribute in certain market territories. These considerations make compensation negotiations a complex and lengthy business, often taking a number of years to complete.

Nevertheless, compensation is the fastest-growing form of countertrade in terms of dollar value. The Organization for Economic Cooperation and Development (OECD) has estimated that the value of compensation deals in East-West trade could have been as high as $30 to $35 billion for the years 1969-1979, with Soviet and Polish deals accounting for the greatest share. The use of compensation in major projects did not emerge until 1969 when it was employed by metallurgical firms of Austria and the Federal Republic of Germany to sell large-diameter steel pipes to the Soviet Union in exchange for subsequent deliveries of natural gas. It was not until 1974, however, that compensation began to flourish in East-West trade. In that year, according to the OECD, more compensation agreements were concluded by the Soviet Union and other CMEA nations than in all previous years combined.

These deals, referred to in Eastern Europe as "industrial cooperation," are particularly attractive to the USSR and other East European nations because they involve a long-term participation on the part of the Western company. Through this long-term relationship, the Eastern party can obtain the technology, training, and capital goods by which to achieve their highest priority industrial projects, and can finance these projects, often entirely, by guaranteed exports to the West.

China in its recent modernization drive, has begun to place great emphasis on compensation for the same reasons, and the rest of the developing world may be expected to increasingly seek these arrangements as they aspire to obtain technology for which they cannot afford to pay with hard currency.

Despite the complexity and risks, Western companies commit themselves to compensation agreements, particularly in times of slack industrial development in the West, as a way to secure major plant, equipment, or licensing sales. In some cases, compensation can also offer guaranteed long-term supplies of energy products, raw materials, or manufactured goods that may be difficult to obtain and essential to the company's operations. Manufactured goods may be less expensive in a compensation arrangement because of lower labor costs in developing or communist countries.

Additional profit may also accrue to the Western participant from sales that are not part of the compensation deal itself, but are closely related to it. It is common, for instance, for the purchaser in a compensation arrangement to satisfy its needs for the product that will finally be produced by a project from the Western participant until the project comes on-stream. Similarly, it sometimes occurs that domestic demand for the products of a compensation project is greater than the projected surplus production after meeting counterdelivery commitments. In these cases, it is natural that the Eastern participant obtain the needed products from the

Western party in the compensation deal under hard currency payment terms.

Compensation, however, can be a dangerous game to play with world markets. In the 1970's, only a quarter of compensation agreements concluded were in the manufacturing sector. The rest involved counter-deliveries of raw materials and energy products badly needed in the West. The trend in East-West compensation, however, is now moving decidedly away from raw material counterdeliveries toward the buyback of semimanufactured and manufactured goods. As this trend continues, the risk of market disruption increases by both the infusion of goods into an already saturated Western market, and the dumping of surplus goods in Western markets.

This sort of disruption has already occurred in the chemical markets of Western Europe. The petrochemical industries of West Germany, France, and Britain have been plagued in recent years by a flood of buyback imports and dumped products produced in excess of East European needs. This is particularly in bulk plastics. West European chemical equipment companies were happy to concede to compensation for major sales while their industry was facing hard times in the 1970's, but they are now subject to criticism from trade unions and chemical plant owners for their practices.

The danger of market hangovers from compensation deals has also been learned by certain companies on individual transactions. Fiat, for example, participated in the construction of the Togliatti auto plant in the Soviet Union with the assumption that models produced at the plant would be obsolete by the time the Comecon domestic markets absorbed production. Soon after the plant became operational, however, *Lada* models (Fiat analogues) began showing up on hard currency markets at what may be considered dumping prices.

Because of the problem of competition, Western companies sometimes consider a joint venture preferable to compensation. In a joint venture, the Western concern owns an equity interest in production facilities, and so has relatively greater control of the manufacture of products and market distribution. Unlike a compensation agreement, which has a fixed schedule for expiration, and guaranteed payment for technology and equipment, a joint venture requires long-term presence and a risk on investment. In addition, in those countries where direct foreign investments are allowed, joint venture laws are sometimes ambiguous in such crucial areas as taxation and repatriation of profits.

It may be useful here to make a distinction, as far as it can be made, between *cooperation* and *compensation*. East European trade organizations typically refer to any compensation agreement as "industrial cooperation." The reason for this is largely to place an attractive mantel on the transaction with the inference that both sides of the bargain benefit equally. The Western participant, however, often views the buy-back of resultant products as an unpleasant obligation that must be submitted to in order to make a sale, and so prefers to refer to the transaction as compensation. This, of course, is not always the case. An example of true cooperation would be the agreement between the Austrian firm, Stey-Daimler-Puch and Polish firms in which the Austrians provided assistance in the construction of a motor factory and a truck factory, and delivered a specified number of Austrian trucks. In return, the firm accepted counterdeliveries of truck components and heavy diesel engines from Poland. This deal is viewed by the Austrians as an important contribution to a desired specialization of production. Beyond this distinction of positive and negative connotation, the chief difference between the terms cooperation and compensation lies in their breadth of meaning.

The Economic Commission of Europe (ECE) defines industrial cooperation as follows:

> Industrial cooperation in an East-West context denotes the economic relationships and activities arising from (a) contracts extending over a number of years between partners belonging to different economic systems which go beyond the straight-forward sale or purchase of goods and services *to include a set of complementary or reciprocally matching operations* (in production, in development and transfer of technology, in marketing, etc.) and (b) contracts between such partners which have been identified

as industrial cooperation by government in bilateral or multilateral agreements.

The distinction of cooperation by mutual benefit is implied in the ECE definition in the line (italicized by this author) "to include a set of complementary or reciprocally matching operations." If a Western company's commitment to buyback must be disposed of through a trading house or marketed outside the company without an attractive profit margin, it may not fit within the scope of this definition. However, in a different sense, the ECE definition of cooperation is broader than that of compensation.

The following types of transactions are enumerated by the ECE as falling within the scope of cooperation activities:

(1) licensing with payment in resultant product
(2) supply of complete plants or production lines with payment in resultant products
(3) co-production and specialization
(4) subcontracting
(5) joint ventures
(6) joint tendering or joint construction or similar projects

The first two activities on this list are, by definition, compensation. The rest of the activities, however, may or may not involve counterdeliveries of resultant products. In conclusion, some cooperation agreements are compensation agreements, some are not; likewise, some compensation agreements are cooperation agreements, some are not.

Evidence Accounts

An evidence account is any arrangement between a company and a commercial organization of a country in which purchases are automatically credited against a company or country's sales. Arrangements of this sort between two national governments are commonly referred to as bilateral clearing agreements. In an evidence account, each side provides a list of what they offer for trade, and a ledger is kept (normally by the country's foreign trade bank) on which credits and debits are recorded in accounting units stated in terms of currency. For deals outside the CMEA, these accounting units are often stated in terms of hard currencies like the U.S. dollar or the Swiss franc. Within the CMEA, accounts are usually denominated in "transferable rubles." Time periods are set for the balancing of accounts and if a company or country is unable to find suitable goods to purchase to balance its accounts, it ends up with clearing credits. Although these are stated in terms of currency, they are not transferable into currency. The party with clearing credits must therefore resort to a complicated practice called *switch trading* which will be explained in the next section of this chapter.

Eastern bloc nations often find evidence accounts attractive because they fit well into their central economic planning systems, and allow a great deal of flexibility in buying Western goods with guaranteed, offsetting hard currency exports. Evidence accounts also hold certain advantages for Western firms. A broader range of goods is offered than in counterpurchase, protracted negotiations are not necessary on each transaction, there is no need for the approval of one trade organization for purchase from another. Sales can be conducted on purely commercial considerations, and Eastern goods are not inflated with the knowledge that they are taken as part of a countertrade arrangement.

In order to enter into such an agreement, however, a Western firm must gain the confidence of the other country's trade officials, and must convince them that the company's purchases will rise rather than decrease under the agreement. The Western party must also be certain that it can use products purchased under the account within its own operations, or can dispose of them profitably.

Switch Trading

Since credits in an evidence account or bilateral clearing agreement are not convertible into currency, the agreement often allows the country or company with a surplus credit to transfer all or part of its clearing account to a third party. This third party, often a switch trading house, uses the credits to purchase goods from the country in deficit and, through a complicated series of deals often involving barter, finally comes up with goods that can be sold for hard currency. The hard currency proceeds are then transferred to the party with the original account surplus, minus a considerable discount for the third party's troubles.

Chapter 3
NEGOTIATING COUNTERTRADE

Preparing for Negotiations That May Involve Countertrade

When a countertrade demand is introduced into a negotiation, the Western party finds itself negotiating a sale and a linked purchase simultaneously. The purchase commitment it is asked to make, moreover, is often so uncertain that it does not even know exactly what products it will be buying. The negotiation takes on added elements of risk and difficulty that may make the Western executive balk at its prospects, considering it better to return home without a sale than to take on the burden of unwanted goods that his company may not be able to unload at a profit. For reasons such as these, it is estimated that 90 percent of countertrade proposals fall through before a final agreement is reached.

Western companies that successfully conclude profitable countertrade deals are generally those with broad international trade experience, with the resources and commitment to pursue lengthy and thorough negotiations, and to anticipate possible problems and safeguard against them. The first step in a successful negotiation strategy is for the company to be prepared for countertrade demands by knowing its bargaining position. Negotiators in communist and lesser developed countries often do not introduce countertrade demands until late in the game, but it is important for the Western party to avoid being caught off-guard. Before entering negotiations that may involve countertrade, the Western company should have a clear idea of how large a countertrade commitment it is willing to accept as a percentage of its original sale, and it should have an idea of the types of products it is willing to accept in countertrade. A company may decide, for instance, that it will only accept goods that can be used in its own manufacturing operations or that can be marketed through its existing organization. On the other hand, it may decide that goods unrelated to its own operation will be acceptable. If the company decides it is not willing to accept goods for use in its own operation, it should determine whether to: (1) employ a trading house to dispose of the products, adding the trader's commission into the price of the original sale, (2) whether it will market the goods through an existing department of its company; or (3) whether it will set up a new department or subsidiary to handle the purchase and marketing of countertrade goods.

It is also of crucial importance for the Western company to know as much as possible about the country and the organization with which it will conduct negotiations. Research into the organizational structure of trade within a centrally planned economy may provide valuable insight into ways of obtaining desired goods for countertrade, and a study of the country's economic five-year plan may shed light on the priority of one's export product, and helping to clarify the company's bargaining position. Information concerning the reliability of a country or trade organization and the gambits and ploys it is likely to exercise in negotiating countertrade may be gleaned from discussions with other businessmen who concluded agreements in the area, or from government agencies such as the U.S. Department of Commerce.

Negotiating the Commitment

In negotiating a sale with a trade organization in a centrally planned economy, the Western negotiator should make every effort to ascertain as early in the talks as possible whether countertrade will enter into the terms of the agreement. In many cases, the foreign trade organization will attempt to negotiate the deal's price on a cash basis. Then, after receiving a final price quote from the Western company, it will present a demand for countertrade. Foreign trade organizations in Eastern Europe have been known to inform negotiators at the last minute that authorities at the ministry level have dictated that they must demand a countertrade commitment in order to make the purchase.

Another gambit that has been employed by East European trade organizations is sometimes referred to as the "double trap door." The foreign trade organization negotiates a purchase on cash terms, receives a final price quote, and then informs the Western company that it must demand countertrade for a percentage of the purchase. After the Western company has acceded to this demand, the trade organization informs the Western negotiators that the authorities have shifted their position and will allow the purchase to be made in hard currency after all. It then asks for a reduction of the previously quoted price, since the expenses associated with countertrade are no longer involved.

A Western negotiator must protect himself from these ploys by deferring a final price quote for a sale until an agreement has been reached on the terms and conditions of the sale. If terms are agreed upon early in the negotiation, the Western company may request a written protocol agreement, which is simply a commitment to agree on the already-discussed terms and to use them as the basis for a final contract. If the negotiators on the other side decline to be party to such a protocol, it is a good indication that countertrade will enter the negotiations further down the road, and that appropriate preparations should be made.

A company willing to accept countertrade obligations must estimate the cost of disposing of the goods, and include this cost in the final price quoted for its original sale. This may be the cost of a discount to a trading house for assuming the countertrade obligation, or it may be the aggregate cost of marketing the products—transportation, storage, insurance and price discount.

Trade organizations in centrally planned economies usually insist upon penalties for failure to fulfill countertrade obligations, usually ranging from about 5 to 15 percent. A Western company that does not wish to deal with countertrade goods may consider this penalty as an option. By simply padding the sales price to absorb the amount of the penalty, the Western party may make its profit from the sale, pay the penalty, and dispense with its obligation.

Exercising this option, however, may jeopardize a company's reputation in a market country, and its prospects for future sales. For example, if the foreign trade organization of a COMECON country demands countertrade partly as a means to fulfill export quotas, it may suffer serious reprisals from the ministry level if the countertrade exports do not occur. The trade organization would then, understandably, resent the defaulting Western party and avoid further dealings with the company. If future sales in that market are a concern, it is best to ascertain whether the buying out of an obligation is acceptable before opting for a penalty.

When negotiating the amount of the countertrade commitment, it is important to remember that trade organizations in centrally planned economies operate under secret government directives. Negotiators usually begin with a demand for 50 to 100 percent countertrade commitment, but this is normally only a starting point for bargaining. A skilled negotiator can often reduce the demand by one-half, and it is not unheard of for an initial demand of 100 percent countertrade to be whittled down to 20 or 30 percent. Actual demands for countertrade vary from country to country and from organization to organization. A chief determining factor is the priority given to the import in the original sale.

Imports necessary to the fulfillment of five-year plans may be purchased without countertrade commitments unless the cost exceeds allocations of hard currency, while consumer goods not included in the plan often require a 100 percent countertrade commitment. Planned imports of low priority technical products fall between these extremes, averaging between 40 and 70 percent, and planned imports of consumer goods carry relatively higher demands, averaging between 60 and 80 percent.

Selecting Countertrade Goods

Once a Western company has decided to accept countertrade as a condition on a transaction, it must take on the arduous task of finding goods that can be disposed of profitably. In counterpurchase arrangements, this task is becoming increasingly difficult. Only a few years ago, it was still possible to find raw material such as coal or metal ores to purchase in fulfillment of countertrade obligations. Today, these goods are reserved for hard currency sales, except in rare cases in which the imports from the West are of the highest priority. Since raw materials and commodities can be marketed through established channels at prices that are universally standardized by such indexes as the London or Chicago exchanges, they can be disposed of with a minimum effort and pose few problems in the areas of quality control, pricing and after-sale servicing. The cost of disposing of these goods through a trading house is therefore relatively inexpensive, often involving a discount of less than five percent.

The Western negotiator today, however, is more likely to find among its countertrade offerings manufactured products such as consumer goods, electrical and technical products or machinery. These products are made by a relatively inexperienced labor force, and often do not enjoy a good reputation in Western markets. Because of their low quality or lack of demand on world markets, they cannot be used to generate hard currency through direct sales and so are earmarked for countertrade. Trading house charge discounts that can range from 15 to 40 percent for disposing these goods.

Linkage

As a general rule, the Western negotiator in a countertrade transaction will want to press for the widest possible range of goods to choose from. Possible ranges of countertrade product offerings include:

1. Only products from the purchasing foreign trade organization in the original sale.
2. Only products from the industrial ministry that controls the purchasing foreign trade organization.
3. Any products offered in the purchasing country.
4. A certain proportion of the obligations fulfilled with purchases from the purchasing foreign trade organization, and the remainder fulfilled with purchases

from other foreign trade organizations under the same ministry.

5. A proportion of the obligation fulfilled with deliveries from the original buyer's foreign trade organization, the remainder with deliveries of the country's domestic products.

Because of the penchant for bilateralism on the part of East European as well as Chinese economic planners, a foreign trade organization will often press for a countertrade obligation that can only be fulfilled with reciprocal deliveries from the buyer in the original sale. Depending upon the relative priority of the goods offered by the Western company, among other factors, the range of countertrade offerings from which to choose can be expanded to include products from other foreign trade organizations as well. This sort of arrangement is referred to as countertrade linkage. Generally, the Western party will consider an obligation to purchase from among any products of the purchasing country to be the ideal condition, but the purchasing foreign trade organization portion of the counterpurchase be chosen from among its own product lines.

The Western negotiator may also press for a clause insuring that all purchases from trading entities designated in the obligation will qualify as countertrade. It has often occurred that a Western purchasing agent, after prolonged search, finds goods which his company can market to an identified customer only to be informed that the intended purchase could not be credited against the company's countertrade obligations because of the absence of a specific linkage clause in the contract.

Similarly, the Western party may want to negotiate for purchases exceeding its countertrade obligation to be credited as countertrade against future company sales. Some Eastern European trading entities have been known to allow purchasing credits to be transferred to third parties as well, but these are isolated cases which rarely allow for the transfer of the full value of sales. On a $100,000 sale, for instance, a foreign trade organization may allow a $50,000 countertrade credit transferred to a third party.

Lists

When negotiating the selection of countertrade goods in a CMEA country, a Western company is commonly supplied with a published countertrade list by a foreign trade organization. These lists are usually outdated, with many or most of the items no longer available. Upon request, trade organizations may provide a shorter, more accurate list of products. Even these items, however, are often not available when the Western firm tries to order them. Bids for hard currency sales will always supplant countertrade deliveries and goods offered as countertrade change according to market demand. A Western company that has regularly been buying certain textile articles in fulfillment of obligations, for instance, may suddenly find these unavailable if the products become competitive in hard currency markets. The best policy for the Western purchasing agents is to cultivate close relations, not only with the special foreign trade organization that handles countertrade, but with sales departments as well, with an eye to locating desired products through the year. Beyond these foreign trade organizations contacts, Western executives have found there to be no substitute for deep involvement with manufacturers in the Eastern country. As one American executive put it, "We were finding ourselves saddled with a million dollars worth of junk a year, until we started to go in there and show them how to make what we wanted."

Long-Term Arrangements

By committing itself to such a long-term agreement with the supplying foreign trade organizations, a Western company can increase its leverage in choosing products. In addition, long-term buying can facilitate arrangements for manufacturers to produce made to order goods as countertrade, or to expand their production of goods that they would otherwise not offer as countertrade in order to fill guaranteed orders. Long-term arrangements also serve to enhance the reputation of the Western company and increase its opportunities for future sales.

For example, Pepsico, which sold cola syrup to Hungary, could find nothing on that country's countertrade lists that could easily be marketed for hard currency. One of Pepsico's suppliers, Continental Can Corporation, however, use cans made in Eastern Europe if they were produced according to specifications. Pepsico's purchasing agent approached the appropriate industrial ministry and proposed to guarantee long-term orders in excess of its countertrade commitment if the manufacturer would, with technical assistance from Pepsico and Continental Can, expand its facilities to deliver the desired product according to specifications. This arrangement helped Hungary gain the benefits of generating hard currency through industrial expansion brought about with Western assistance; Pepsico no longer needed to dispose of unwanted goods, and Continental Can Corporation acquired a new, guaranteed source of cans.

In East European countries, long-term purchasing agreements are arranged with the ministry of foreign trade and with the industrial ministry responsible for the desired goods. Sometimes the Western purchasing agent will begin by finding a manufacturer that is willing to supply goods for countertrade, provided long-term orders are guaranteed. The manufacturer may then help the Western party to arrange with higher ministries for the purchases to be credited against future sales.

Choice of Products

A company's choice of countertrade products, will depend upon customers it has identified, the nature and scope of its operations, its marketing capacities and other factors. Generally speaking, the preferability of product types can be rated as follows:

1. *Raw Materials.*
   These can be marketed through established channels at standardized prices and pose relatively low risk.
2. *Products that can be used in the company's own operation.*
   Component parts, or simple tools that can be absorbed by the Western company into its operations, do not involve the cost of marketing the goods or the payment of a discount to a trading house.

3. *Goods related to the company's own product lines.*
Since these products can be disposed of through the existing marketing organization of the Western company or its suppliers, they do not require expenditures for trading house discounts or other costs associated with finding a third party buyer and transferring the goods.

4. *Manufactured products unrelated to a company's operation.*
These products are generally the least preferred because they must be either assigned to a trading house for disposal at a discount, or marketed to a third party with associated costs.

Among manufactured goods offered as countertrade, products that require no after-sales service or parts are generally preferred. Such products as ball bearings or simple electric hand tools are more easily sold on Western markets than are large machinery or engineering goods.

Chapter 4
CONTRACT
CONSIDERATIONS

In drafting countertrade contracts, the executive or legal professional must exercise both creativity and extreme care. Because of the unique variables and contingencies that arise in these transactions, he must be imaginative in drawing up provisions that will build a workable and secure legal framework for a particular deal. Experience has taught many businessmen that small legal points can be devastating if not negotiated to a satisfactory conclusion and drafted into the contract with clarity and precision.

Except in the case of pure barter, countertrade transactions commonly take the form of a "contractual triangle" composed of three separate but related legal instruments that, when taken together, establish the terms and conditions of the deal. The three points in this triangle are: (1) the original contract for a Western sale; (2) the countertrade contract which sets the terms and conditions of the original seller's obligation to purchase goods from the buyer in the first contract; and (3) the protocol that serves to link the two contracts.

The first contract in a countertrade agreement is a standard sales agreement not unlike a cash-for-goods instrument. In the case of compensation, this contract is far from simple or standard, but its complexity arises from the technology transfer factor and is not unique to countertrade.

The second, or "countertrade" contract also calls for payment in hard currency for deliveries. It is unique, however, in that it sets the terms for a purchase obligation that is directly related to a separate contract. Moreover, it is most commonly an agreement for the seller to purchase goods at a later date, or over a period of time, rather-than a simple agreement for the purchase of specified goods according to a definite schedule of delivery and payment.

The protocol, or as it is referred to in Britain, "Head of Agreement," is usually drafted last. This is an "agreement to agree" under which both parties commit themselves to enter into their respective contract to purchase the other party's goods. In addition to its primary function of insuring each party that one contract will not become valid without the other, the protocol also serves the critical function of insuring the seller in the first contract that his obligations under the second contract will terminate in the event of non-performance or cancellation of the original purchase.

With regard to the countertrade contract, it is of crucial importance that it be drafted clearly and unambiguously, and that nothing be left to common sense or to later interpretation. In transactions with communist countries, the Western firm will often be presented with a standard "frame contract," which the foreign negotiators will want to hold to rather closely. The Western negotiator, however, will often find it to his advantage to press for alterations in the provisions or for additional provisions.

Western parties often find it to their benefit to draft their own contract, rather than negotiating solely on the basis of the frame agreement. It can be helpful, in these cases, for provisions of the Western draft to be based on clauses from actual contracts that have been signed with the target country. These may be obtained through other Western businessmen, or from government officials in the Western party's home country.

In drafting the countertrade contract, there are several unique considerations that can be dealt with by various means, and by the use of different provisions and clauses. For this reason, rather than examine the contract as a list of possible provisions, the chief concerns unique to countertrade and its various contractual arrangements will be discussed.

Separation of Contracts

There are several reasons for the use of two separate contracts in countertrade transactions. One of the most crucial is the need for independent legal instruments in order to obtain financing and credit risk guarantees from commercial banks. Bankers are particularly reluctant to provide credit when the debtor's ability to repay the loan is contingent upon the contractual performance of a third (foreign) party. The use of two contracts also provides greater flexibility in performance of contract stipulations. Whereas one half of the countertrade transaction calls for delivery of goods within, say, two years, separate contracts allow the second half of the transaction to call for delivery within, for example, five or ten years.

A third reason for dual contracts is worthy of special attention. This is the need to keep payments for the original sale unencumbered by the conditions of the obligation to accept counterdeliveries. A Western company entering into a countertrade transaction under a single contract could place itself in the dangerous position of having to fulfill its countertrade obligation in order to receive payment for its export sale. In a worst case scenario, the foreign trade entity could deliberately make no products available for export to fulfill the obligation, and thus claim the right to withhold payment for goods received from the Western company under the contract.

Even with the use of two contracts, the Western party must be careful to protect its right to payment for its export, independent of its obligation to counterpurchase. To this end, it is advisable that the Western sale contract contain no reference to the countertrade contract. Also, any references to the Western export in the countertrade contract should be drafted in such a way that the two agreements do not merge into a single legal instrument.

A common method of ensuring the independence of the Western export is to include a special clause in the countertrade contract to that effect. This clause will usually appear as a provision that, in case of the Western party's non-fulfillment of its countertrade obligation, the payment of a penalty will release the Western party from any further obligation or responsibility.

In one sense, however, the Western party will want a degree of linkage between the agreement for the Western export and the agreement to counterpurchase. In the event that the Western sale is canceled or delayed, the Western party will usually want the option of being released from its obligation to purchase the other party's goods.

As has been noted above, this right of release is sometimes accomplished through the protocol, which may call for the cancellation of one contract, ipso facto, if the other contract is canceled or delayed. A connection between the Western sale and the countertrade obligation may also be made by a reference to the Western sale in the clause of the countertrade contract defining the Western party's obligation to purchase. This can be done either by explicit wording that states the obligation to be pursuant to the sale in the first contract, or it can be accomplished by stating the amount of the obligation as a percentage of the value of the Western sale.

If the latter procedure is followed, it is advisable to state the obligation as a percentage of the Western sales price F.O.B., so that the obligation will not be inflated as a proportion of the total import cost to the other party including shipping, insurance and duties.

Experienced traders often avoid reference to the first contract in the countertrade agreement, however, out of concern for the independence of the first sale contract. If such reference is made, it is crucial to include a clause in the countertrade contract to protect the Western sale from encumbrance.

Obligation to Purchase

The countertrade contract will commonly contain a provision defining the value of the reciprocal purchase to be made by the seller in the first contract, the time period during which the purchase must be made and, in transactions with communist countries, the trade organization from which the goods must be purchased.

In some cases, particularly in compensation deals, the products to be purchased as countertrade will be specified in the contract. If this is the case, the products should be described exhaustively and in minute detail with complete and unequivocal definitions of quality standards.

More often, however, the purchase obligation provision will call for goods to be selected from a certain range of products for later purchase. In these cases, it is generally advantageous for the Western party to have as broad as possible a range of products from which to choose. If the trading partner is a country with a centrally planned economy, the product range will usually be defined in terms of the government trade organizations from which the Western firm can purchase goods in fulfillment of its obligation.

The Western party, therefore, will want a linkage clause in the contract that will allow purchases from any organization in the target country to apply to its countertrade obligation. In Eastern Europe, however, negotiators will generally insist that a portion of the counter- trade obligation be satisfied with purchases from their own foreign trade organization, and are likely to be reluctant to allow purchases from outside its industrial ministry to apply as countertrade.

An alternative to linkage would be to select a list of goods offered by the purchaser of the Western export, and to specify these goods in the purchase obligation of the countertrade contract. If the goods to be counterpurchased are specified, it is essential that a clause be included in the contract releasing the Western party from its countertrade obligation if products ordered are not delivered according to schedule and quality specifications.

In Eastern Europe, negotiators are rarely willing to grant these guarantees of delivery. For this reason, experienced East-West traders counsel against narrowing countertrade options by specifying a product list. In the absence of firm guarantees, a specific purchase obligation may put the Western party into a position in which it must either accept the chosen goods (regardless of delivery delays or inferior quality) or pay a penalty for non-fulfillment of its obligation.

The Western party should press for as lengthy a period as possible within which to purchase countertrade goods. A longer obligation period allows the buyer time to find customers for the goods and reduces costs for storage of the products. The East European may ask for a time limit of six to 12 months for counterpurchase obligations, but this can usually be negotiated to a period of two to three years. In any case, the time limit for counterpurchase should extend beyond the period of financing for the original Western sale.

Penalties

When negotiating countertrade with a country using a centrally planned economy, one is usually faced with the insistence that a provision be included in the countertrade contract imposing a penalty on the Western party for nonfulfillment of its purchase obligation. This penalty is stated as a percentage of the unfulfilled portion of the obligation and typically ranges from 5 to 15 percent. In addition, the negotiator will require a guarantee for the total amount of possible penalties to be issued by a Western bank. Under this guarantee, the Western bank transfers the amount of the penalty to the state bank of the partner, unconditionally and without recourse, at the end of the Western company's countertrade obligation for the unfulfilled portion of the obligation.

It is essential for the Western party that a clause be included in the contract stipulating that payment of a penalty releases it from any further obligation to purchase, and from any other claims made by its customer. Foreign trade organizations in certain countries of Eastern Europe have been known to demand specific performance, even after a penalty has been paid.

Pricing

Since countertrade contracts usually involve either the purchase of unspecified goods, or the purchase of specified goods over a long term, pricing provisions normally contain pricing formulas rather than set prices.

In compensation agreements, the pricing formula often involves a review or renegotiation of the product value, typically at intervals of three to nine months. If the buyback product in such an arrangement is agricultural goods or raw materials, the price may be set as the value of the goods according to a mutually recognized index at the time of the order. An alternative in transactions of this sort is to set the price for deliveries in the contract draft with a formula that calls for a review of the price if the value of the goods rises above, or falls below, a certain value on the mutually recognized index for the goods.

If the buyback products are finished or semi-finished goods, the pricing formula may call for price readjustment periodically, depending on market conditions. The factors influencing the change in prices include a change in raw material prices, the demand for the production world markets, or in political conditions.

In transactions that involve a commitment to purchase unspecified products (most counterpurchase agreements), a clearly defined pricing formula should be employed. In the absence of such a formula, the Western party may be compelled to accept counterdeliveries at prices set by the foreign trade entity—often grossly inflated.

A common formula is to define the price of the goods as, "The acceptable international price at the time of purchase." The application for this kind of formula is a comparison of the price paid to the supplier by other customers in Western markets for the same product.

Another common formula may read, "Fair market value of goods in first party's country" (or a percentage above or below this value). This formula could be applied by a price comparison with similar goods of equal quality available to the Western party, under competitive terms of delivery and payment, from other foreign suppliers.

The method of applying a pricing formula, as well as the formula itself, should be clearly defined and as specific as possible. A provision should also be included that specifies that both parties shall submit to arbitration in the event that there is disagreement over the application of the formula.

Quality

Products taken in countertrade are notorious for being of inferior quality. It is, therefore, necessary for the Western party to be especially careful in drafting provisions for quality standards, penalties and the right to inspect.

In countertrade arrangements specifying counterdelivery products, quality standard provisions should be absolutely comprehensive and detailed, with all specifications attached to the contract as an addendum and referred to in the provision.

For many types of products (high-technology components, machinery or equipment parts), items that do not conform precisely to specifications are virtually worthless. For these products, the quality guarantee clause unequivocally state that deliveries will not be accepted. An alternative sometimes employed is a provision stating that nonconforming products will be returned to the supplier for retooling or repair (at the supplier's expense), or that the purchaser will remake the product to specification, and charge it to the supplier.

In another case, it may be appropriate to assign penalties, spelling out in detail which specifications have in fact not been met for varying degrees of nonconformance.

In countertrade contracts that do not specify products to be purchased the standard for deliveries is often expressed in such terms as "export quality." The application should be defined as clearly as possible. If the Western party's bargaining position is strong enough, it may also include provisions that would credit orders for products toward the fulfillment of its countertrade obligation if they are not accepted for delivery because of substandard quality.

The countertrade contract should provide the Western party with the right to inspect purchased goods before delivery. In some cases (usually in compensation arrangements) personnel of a Western company may inspect goods at the manufacturing site. If this is not allowed, a provision should at least allow the purchaser to inspect the goods before shipment.

Another provision that may be included in the countertrade contract would allow the Western party to choose a neutral surveyor to assess product quality.

Distribution

It sometimes occurs that a Western firm finds a customer for products it can purchase as countertrade, then discovers that the other party in the deal has granted an exclusive distributorship for the area of the planned resale. The Western firm must then either abandon the transaction, or pay a commission on the resale to the area distributor.

To avoid this problem, the Western party should include a provision in the countertrade contract that either allows the buyer to market countertrade goods in Western markets without interference from the foreign trade entity, or allows for exclusive distribution in certain markets.

Transferability of Countertrade Obligations

The countertrade contract should contain, either in the recitals or the provision stating the Western partner's purchase obligation, a clause allowing the purchaser to assign his countertrade obligation to a third party. This clause will sometimes indicate the party or parties to whom the obligation may be assigned, a trading house, for example. In other cases, the third party will not be designated.

Even if the Western firm plans to use the countertrade goods in its own operations, or market the goods without the aid of a trading house, this provision should still be drafted into the agreement. Transferability is an important option to preserve in case of unforseen contingencies.

Chapter 5

CASE STUDIES

Case Study No. 1:
The Subsidiary Trading Company

Combustion Engineering Corp.

Combustion Engineering Corp. (CEC) is a diversified, high-technology United States company with gross annual sales of more than $3 billion in 1983. The firm offers engineering services in steel refractory products, steam generation for electrical energy, and oil and gas drilling and exploration equipment.

In the late 1960's and early 1970's, CEC became involved in countertrade through its wholly-owned subsidiary, CE Lummus. During that period, Lummus entered into two large-scale chemical compensation deals involving design, construction, and downstream services for ethylene plants in Eastern Europe with partial payment in the resultant ethylene.

In the late 1970's, CE's participation in compensation arrangements increased to the point that management found it necessary to work with a mineral trading company to dispose of minerals taken as buyback. Finally, in early 1980, the corporation established CE Trading, a wholly-owned subsidiary, to conduct countertrade transactions.

CE Trading Company

CE Trading Company was established when corporate operating business encountered iron-clad demands for countertrade more frequently in negotiations in Eastern Europe and the People's Republic of China. Two principal reasons for forming the trading subsidiary were: (1) to avoid paying high discounts to outside trading houses; and (2) to bring the buying power of the entire corporation to bear in negotiations involving countertrade.

The trading company was set up as a support unit with the sole function of helping operating units to obtain orders that involve compensation. It is not a profit center, and it has no mandate to compel other subsidiaries to purchase or to dispose of countertrade goods. Under the unit's charter, CE Trading is directed to put forth every effort to negotiate a cash deal, and, if these efforts fail, to negotiate a minimum amount of countertrade and to accept only those goods that can be consumed or easily marketed by the corporation, or that can be marketed through recognized channels (i.e. raw materials).

In principal, CE Trading does not generate business or initiate negotiations. It is, instead, called in as a consultant when an operating division expects to encounter countertrade demands in the negotiation for a sale. If countertrade does become a component of the transaction, the trading company negotiates the counterpurchase without direct involvement in the sales negotiations.

CE Trading, in effect, acts as a trading house, contracting with operating units for its services, and charging a discount for the disposal of countertrade goods. Theoretically, the operating divisions are free to choose another trading house if they so desire.

When the trading company is "contracted" by another CE division, the operating unit must agree to the countertrade CE. If CE Trading is able to dispose of the countertrade goods at a discount number that is less than what it had charged, the difference is credited back to the operating unit. If it must discount the goods more than the amount charged to the operating unit, however, the trading company absorbs the loss. By this method of accounting, CE Trading's performance can be partially gauged by the discounts it charges, and by the sums credited back to the operating units against "losses" sustained when goods must be discounted further.

The chief method of accounting by which the performance of CE Trading is evaluated, however, is a consideration of the value of net sales (excluding pass-through number supplies and subcontracted services) that would not have been possible without the services of the trading company.

By this method of accounting, the countertrade unit was responsible for $600 million net sales in its first 3 years of operation, and by 1983 it had risen to $300 million.

Analysis

The organization and activities of CE Trading manifest a cautious and circumspect approach to countertrade. In considering the formation of a separate countertrade unit, the management of the corporation had three options:

(1) To let each operating division fend for itself in negotiating and conducting countertrade.
(2) To establish a trading subsidiary as a profit center.
(3) To form a trading subsidiary as a support unit for other operating divisions.

Option 1: Individual conduct of countertrade by operating units. This alternative was unacceptable to corporate management, largely because of the fragmentary structure of the corporation and because of the nature of its operations.

Since the products and services of Combustion Engineering involve a large percentage of pass-through in the form of supplies and subcontracting, the annual buying power of the corporation amounts to only about one-quarter of its gross sales—approximately $1 billion. If an operating unit acted independently in countertrade negotiations, it would not muster the clout of the corporation as a whole. Under these conditions, an operating unit would be more likely to accept goods that could not be used or marketed by the corporation, or disposed of through established channels, in order to make a sale. This would involve substantial risks and the added cost of discounts to trading companies. In addition, the separate divisions would be limited in experience and expertise to deal with the complexities of countertrade.

Option 2: Establishment of a trading subsidiary as a profit center. This option would hold many possible advantages. A profit center trading subsidiary number would be free to seek purchasing opportunities in market areas independent of other operating divisions. Profits could be made on the resale of goods while sales opportunities could be created by the accumulation of countertrade credits.

In order for a trading company to operate for profit, however, it must be free to deal in goods and markets outside the traditional scope of the parent corporation's operations, and it is often given the mandate to compel other divisions to purchase its goods.

CE's corporate management was unwilling to choose this option because of its possible threat to the independence of other divisions and, more importantly because of the added risks and complications that would result from allowing a subsidiary to operate outside the scope of the company's traditional operations.

Option 3: Establishment of a trading subsidiary as a support unit. CE's choice of this option arose from a perception of countertrade as an obligation. The corporation did not seek to expand into new forms of trading. Instead, it sought to deal effectively with countertrade demands without venturing away from the company's traditional products and services. A countertrade subsidiary was acceptable only if its function was clearly limited to supporting sales.

Since CE Trading is severely limited in its options for disposing of countertrade goods, the cooperation of top management is essential to its effectiveness. The trading company cannot compel other subsidiaries to purchase its goods, and so requires, at the very least, the power of persuasion. CE Trading is assured of management support in three ways:

(1) The president of the trading company is also vice president, international business development—a position in the top echelon of corporate management.
(2) CE Trading was chartered by the chief executive officer of Combustion Engineering.
(3) The board of directors number of CE Trading includes

executives from all disciplines within the corporation: chief financial officer, corporate legal counsel, vice president-international, and vice president of operations.

Case Study No. 2:
The Profit Center Subsidiary

Control Data Corporation

Control Data Corporation (CDC) is a major company in the computer and financial services business, with annual revenues of more than $3 billion and total assets over $6 billion. Based in Minneapolis, Minnesota, the firm sells goods, services and technology in 47 countries, in such fields as education, environment, energy, agriculture, research, manufacturing, petroleum and mining, health care, and electrical utilities.

Organization

After being active in Eastern Europe for some 15 years, in 1973 CDC became the first U.S. company to establish a countertrade subsidiary in a high-technology field. Commercial Trading International (CTI), with headquarters in Vienna, Austria, is still unique in being the only countertrade subsidiary of a major U.S. company based in Western Europe. In 1978, CDC took another unusual step by establishing a second countertrade subsidiary, Commercial Trading Imports (CT Imports), based in the U.S. The two units work together as a profit center to conduct countertrade and, increasingly, to generate profits by conducting trade not directly related to countertrade.

In the initial stages of its operations, CTI worked as a support unit for other CDC divisions that encountered countertrade demands in Eastern Europe. Since then it has taken an active role in initiating and negotiating countertrade transactions. It has also sourced and negotiated purchases from Eastern Europe not directly tied to countertrade obligation.

CT Imports Inc. was set up in the U.S. to distribute and market Eastern Eurpoean products purchased by CTI. In some instances, the U.S. subsidiary initiates transactions by locating a potential buyer of Eastern European goods, and directing the Vienna unit to purchase the goods according to specification. In CDC's recent activities in China, however, these roles are reversed: CT Imports makes purchases; CTI markets and distributes the products in Western Europe.

Both CTI and CT Imports are divisions of Control Data's *Technology Services* subsidiary, a holding of CDC's *Commercial Credit Company.* Two other divisions also operate under the control of Technology Services: *Control Data Technotec,* a subsidiary that provides technology search and clearing-house services, and *Control Data Worldtec,* which performs marketing and technology application in cooperation with Technotec.

Operations

As trading companies, in the full sense of the term, CTI and CT Imports are more concerned with buying goods at a favorable price and marketing them at a profit than with formal, contractual linkage between CDC purchases and CDC sales. Thus far, they have purchases almost exclusively from countries that are CDC customers and that impose countertrade demands as a matter of policy (i.e., Eastern European countries and the People's Republic of China). In doing so, they have operated under the philosophy that purchases from these countries will generate hard currency with which Control Data products can be bought.

By liberally following the practice of "buying forward" without specific linkage to future sales, the trading companies are free to buy goods of competitive price and quality whenever they are found. The vastly greater proportion of their operations, however, have been related to CDC countertrade requirements.

This is expected to change in the future. CTI and CT Imports have already begun to purchase from markets that are not CDC customers, and executives predict that trading unrelated to countertrade will form the major part of their operations in the future.

CTI prefers to purchase goods related to CDC product lines, but there are cases where unrelated products have been taken. Among the products CTI has traded are the following:

- electrical and electronic components
- machined aluminum die castings
- heavy foundry castings
- railroad freight cars and components
- light industrial products
- metals and minerals
- ships
- technology transfer
- art objects, reproductions, and hand-crafts
- furniture
- food and agricultural products
- jade and other precious stones
- art books and prints; children's books

In all of its transactions CTI exchanges cash for goods or goods for cash. It does not engage in barter. The trading company avoids acting as broker for other companies involved in countertrade, although it has engaged in such practices. More importantly, CTI does not carry inventories—it finds a buyer before accepting delivery of countertrade goods.

An example of CTI's creativity in orchestrating countertrade is the 1979 transaction that resulted in a two-year United States tour of masterpieces from the Hermitage Museum in Leningrad. The Soviet Ministry of Culture wanted a $3 million computer to catalogue the Hermitage Museum's collection. This was a low priority item, of course, and hard currency had not been allocated for the purchase. CDC finally closed the deal by agreeing to accept as payment the right to organize the tour of United States museums, along with exclusive sales rights for art books and reproductions at the exhibits.

Analysis

The principal reason for establishing CTI as a profit center was to have the marketing support of an aggressive countertrade unit without having to subsidize the unit out of the profit of other divisions. This is an aggressive approach to countertrade organization—one that allows the trading subsidiary to take advantage of any purchasing opportunities that arise, but one that allows the unit to venture into areas of high risk.

There is no question that, by aggressively purchasing in communist countries, CDC's trading subsidiaries improve the corporation's marketing position in those areas. The use of watchful purchasing agents close to Eastern European and Chinese markets allows Control Data to seize opportunities not open to a company concerned only with marketing its own goods and hoping to avoid countertrade. Moreover, by looking for the best available export goods in Eastern Europe and China at any time, rather than shopping only for goods that satisfy contractual obligations, CDC's trading companies can generate hard currency for CDC purchases without having to take the slim offerings available for countertrade during a given phase of a communist country's five-year or annual plan.

However, the countertrade units may make risky purchases that do not result in CDC sales. Additionally, since CTI must be concerned with its own bottom line, it is doubtful whether it can allow other divisions of the corporation the option of disposing of goods at a loss to secure a sale, and padding the sale price to make up the difference.

The test of this organizational strategy will be its results in the future, as CTI increasingly conducts trade independent of CDC's countertrade activities. To be successful, the subsidiaries must profit in the risky business of world trade while continuing to promote CDC sales through countertrade.

Case Study No. 3:
Cooperation in Eastern Europe—
No Special Countertrade Unit

Major U.S. Captial Goods Manufacturer

This is a company that manufactures a broad range of agricultural machinery and related equipment with yearly revenues of more than $3 billion. The company markets worldwide, and has engaged in countertrade.

Organization

This company has no special countertrade unit and does not employ trading houses. Instead, negotiations are executed by top corporate management and all goods taken as buy-back are used or marketed by the corporation.

Operations

The company's approach to countertrade is to enter long-term cooperation arrangements as a means to sell technology while setting up new sources of supply. Projects completed under these arrangements are considered by the U.S. corporation as complimentary production facilities. These have been completed by the company in two countries: Poland and Hungary.

The firm counts five sources of revenue accruing from its cooperation ventures:

(1) Fees for licensing and technology
(2) Sale of components needed to complete product
(3) Sale of parts and service
(4) Sale of whole manufactured products (the foreign partner sometimes continues to buy machinery in the extremes of the product range after their production goes on-stream)
(5) Purchase of components at favorable prices

Activities in Poland. In 1972, the firm entered into a long-term cooperation agreement with the Polish foreign trade organization, Bumar. Under that agreement, the United States company transferred technology to modernize Polish facilities for the manufacture of crawler tractors, and agreed to buy back resultant tractor components. Although the agreement did not specify the value of components to be purchased by the U.S. firm, the value of the purchases has been estimated to have reached nearly 100 percent of the value of the technology and parts purchased by the Polish organization.

Also, under the 1972 agreement, the United States firm cooperated with Bumar in the joint development of pipe layers in 1975. These were products not previously manufactured by the United States company, and the contract called for buyback of complete machinery units. So far, the pipe layers have been sold by the United States firm only in its home market, but the company is now considering marketing the equipment to Third World countries.

Activities in Hungary. Beginning with a contract signed in 1976, the United States firm has concluded six separate ten-year compensation agreements. Under all of these agreements, the United States company provided licensing technological assistance, design and components for the production of truck axles and agricultural machinery.

Prices for the buy-back of axles were based on a projection of prices 15-16 months forward of negotiations. Prices are adjusted annually according to United States Bureau of Census figures. Axles are produced according to the United States company's design and specifications. In case of substandard quality, the axles may be sent back to Hungary for retooling at the expense of the Hungarian foreign trade organizations, or they may be re-manufactured or repaired in the United States, with costs charged to the Hungarian partner.

Analysis

This corporation's conduct of countertrade is distinctive in that the technology it offers is of such high priority to the Eastern purchasers that it could probably be sold for cash. It is to the United States party's benefit, however, to consider the factories set up in Eastern Europe within its facilities planning for component production.

With this strong basis of mutual benefit and truly complimentary operations, it is logical that negotiations be conducted by top corporate management without the need for a special countertrade unit. In addition, the great benefit derived by the Eastern European organizations from the acquired technology and from the reciprocal sale of finished products induces the Eastern partner to be flexible and scrupulous on such points as pricing and quality control.

Chapter 6
FINANCING COUNTERTRADE

The phrase "financing countertrade" is somewhat of a contradiction, since countertrade represents a special financial arrangement for the exchange of goods and services. By assuring the buyer a full or partial return on the money spent for imports, cash-flow problems and hard-currency shortages became less of an impediment to the purchase of goods.

Traditional financing tools attain the same objective through different mechanisms. They allow the deferral of payment until a specific time in the future or for the spreading out of payment over a prearranged period. Strictly speaking, countertrade is not a financing instrument, not even for pure barter. For in barter, there is no exchange of money, thereby obviating the need for deferral or the spreading out of cash payment.

In most cases, credit is used in conjunction with countertrade to enhance, like countertrade itself does, the ability of the buyer to pay for the goods purchased. Credit arrangements are most necessary in compensation and production-sharing joint-venture deals, since not only do they involve very large sums of money, but the importer usually has to wait a number of years before the purchased equipment goes on stream and earns a cash return, or receive payment in a resultant product.

The export and import of goods undertaken in counterpurchase agreements, while not simultaneous, are usually much closer together than compensation deals and thus only require short-term financing. Since counterpurchase obligations frequently cover substantially less than 100 percent of the export contract, loans are also used to help the buyer cover the cost difference between the export and import contract.

In a sense, there is twice as much financial risk in countertrade because there are two components of risk instead of one. The first involves the foreign trade partner: Can it deliver the goods, or in compensation, can it produce and deliver? The second risk involves the Western trade partner: Can it pay for the deliveries? Banks, nonetheless, finance countertrade in much the same manner as other, more conventional forms of trade. In most cases—though this is beginning to change as banks venture into export trading—no conditions or requirements related to the counterpurchase are included in the credit arrangements of the export contract. Banks take the position that repayment of credit should not be formally made contingent upon counterdelivery sales to the West. Banks only consider the borrower's independent ability to repay the borrowed funds. In this way they provide the kind of credit typical for export contracts in general.

Western companies generally need less financing not because they are more solvent than their trade partner (though this sometimes is the case), but because of the different nature of the counterdelivery part of a compensation agreement. Western suppliers, before purchasing countertrade goods, usually find a buyer for those goods or commit them to a trading company. Thus, the Western firm is assured a relatively quick return on the goods. For companies that do not get rid of such products right away, banks will provide loans based on the creditworthiness of the supplier. Counterdeliveries thus exert a minimum strain on the cash-flow of a company. Similarly, if the goods are for in-house use, the company is relieved of making equivalent purchases elsewhere, so that a company's cash position remains unaffected by the counterpurchase. Western firms, if they do not want to commit their own working capital, thus require only short-term financing easily obtained from their own bank line of credit.

Financing countertrade involves such standard methods of financing as government-supported credit programs, bank-to-bank credit lines, and buyer and supplier credits. The particular method selected depends on the financial status and needs of the supplier and buyer, the duration of the countertrade contract, the cost of the countertrade contract, and the traditional credit preferences of the parties involved.

For the larger compensation deals, involving credit extensions of up to 20 years and credit exposures of $10 million and over, government-supported export credit facilities are usually used. Increasingly, government-export credits are also provided in association with private export credits. In such cases the financing covers a much shorter period—about five years, which is the typical duration for private supplier and buyer credits. Because mixed (government and private) and supplier credits are essentially short-term financing instruments, they are mostly offered for the smaller compensation deals and counterpurchase agreements. Buyer credits, on the other hand, are usually untied loans that may be used as the borrower sees fit.

Western banks involved in large compensation deals or production-sharing joint ventures tend to take a relatively assertive role in financing countertrade. In these cases, banks provide cash flow loans which may sometimes be secured by the resultant products. The banks actually hold title to the goods as collateral or through, for example, consignment of bill of lading. When they are sold, the banks receive the proceeds. Cash flow loans under these arrangements carry several advantages. If made to the joint venture, they do not show up on company accounts so a company's creditability is unaffected. These loans are also self-financing, and there is no debt or overhead to contend with. But for the banks, they entail considerable risks, especially when big projects are involved, and banks have been forced to reevaluate their lending policies. As a result, banks are now using assessing techniques, which they consider more accurately reflects the feasibility of a project, thus better protecting bank loans in such projects. Financing or loans incorporating these techniques are referred to as "project financing."

Guaranteeing Barter Transactions

While banks do not provide credit for barter deals (since no cash is exchanged), they do offer a reliable system of financial guarantees. This can be obtained even without the cash component of the transaction. It is done through the normal transfer of documents for each set of goods being bartered in conjunction with a set of non-cash or "standby" bank guarantees. Under such an arrangement, the Western party would request that the second party's bank issue a standby letter of credit. In case the second party failed to meet its obligation under the barter contract (i.e. failed to ship the designated goods to the Western party), the standby letter of credit would entitle the Western party to draw payment in hard currency for the goods. The first party would have the letter of credit issued by the second party's bank, confirmed by its own bank in its home country.

This arrangement provides protection to the first party only. If the second party seeks the same form of guarantee for its side of the transaction, it simply requests the same from the first party—a standby letter of credit issued in favor of the second party.

However, it is difficult to have the second party's letter of credit confirmed in some transactions, such as those with the People's Republic of China, whose state bank has not yet joined the standardized system of international banking. An alternative form of guarantee may then be used. The Western party requests that the second party's bank issue a performance bond, similar in substance to the standby letter of credit, which would subsequently be guaranteed by the first party's bank. Since U.S. banks are not permitted by law to issue "guarantees," a foreign branch of the U.S. bank can issue the guarantee required to secure the performance bond of the second party. The same form of protection could be established in favor of the second party by simply reversing the above process.

Supplier Credits

A supplier will often extend credit to a customer, allowing it to defer payment on the Western export contract for a certain length of time. Before extending credit, a company should secure a pro-forma agreement from its bank to provide the necessary refinancing. The bank's credit may be given on the basis of the supplier's or buyer's creditworthiness, depending on whether the credit is with or without recourse to the supplier. Usually, companies will supplement their credit applications to the Western bank by simultaneously arranging for the Western national export credit guarantee to reduce the bank's risk. One must keep in mind, though, that banks and insurance companies are more likely to provide financing and insurance coverage for countertrade transactions composed of separate contracts.

Supplier credits may be extended on a short, medium or long-term basis. Instead of going to a bank, firms may choose to carry the cost of short-term trade transactions on (sight) cash-against-documents basis (upon presentation of shipping documents by the seller, the buyer transmits cash for payment) or even on open account (current account) terms. The latter arrangement may run up to 360 days, but the loan is unsecured and therefore Western companies seldom agree to provide them.

A more popular short-term credit instrument is the letter of credit, which can be used in conjunction with bills of exchange or drafts. Most commonly, these types of credit are used in situations calling for short to medium-term maturity.

In cases where trading partners already have a well-established relationship, both sides tend to feel comfortable with payment against documents. The supplier, for example, feels confident enough to deliver the goods for shipment without any sort of security from the other side. The buyer, on the other hand, is equally confident that when he is presented with the bills of lading, though the goods themselves are still in transit, he can proceed with payment, knowing that his partner will have fulfilled all the terms of the contract.

Payment against documents requires the collection of the Western export proceeds in the purchasing country through the local bank. Most countries have a state central bank which handles collections. For "plain payment against documents," the exporter presents the shipping documents to his commercial bank with instructions to send them to his customer's state bank. The buyer, upon notification that the documents have arrived, may not claim the documents, and, thereby, title to its goods, unless it pays the full invoice value of the goods. For "paid against documents against bill of exchange," promissory notes or bills of exchange are accepted or issued by the buyer, with a guarantee from the foreign state bank after receiving and checking documents, and sent either to the exporter or to the exporter's bank. The bank may hold these commercial papers until maturity when payment is then made by the foreign state bank, or the bank may cash (discount) the paper and make the funds available to the supplier immediately.

For plain payment against documents in Eastern Europe and the Soviet Union, payment can take from a low of 30 days (Czechoslovakia) to up to 360 days (Romania). The rough average is between 45 and 65 days. Because of Poland's serious debt problems, it is advised that Western companies use payment against documents with the greatest caution.

Letters of Credit

Irrevocable letters of credit are the most important method of short-term (24 months) credit. They eliminate the buyer's risk by replacing it with that of the buyer's bank issuing the letter of credit. A letter of credit promises to pay the invoiced value of the negotiated contract price against receipt of the shipping documents (sight letter of credit) or against acceptance of bill of exchange made out by the Western exporter or promissory note issued and accepted by the buyer himself (letter of credit against bill of exchange). Both variants, which come with the foreign trade bank's guarantee, are negotiable. They call for payment on demand after proof of contract fulfillment, or they contain maturity dates corresponding to an agreed-upon payment schedule. For short-term they may run up to 725 days, for medium-term two to five years, and for long-term anything beyond five years. The documents required are specified in the letter of credit and may include detailed commercial and/or consular invoices (in several copies), original bill of lading or airway bill, export license (if required), freight insurance policy or certificate, and packing lists and/or packing inspection certificates.

Letters of credit against bills of exchange are more common in East European countries than in the Soviet Union for two simple reasons. First the USSR has always had a higher credit rating, making payment against documents the most prevalent form of payment; second, Soviet trade officials consider a request by a Western trade partner for a letter of credit an insult to their creditworthiness. The Chinese, who issue only unconfirmed and untransferable letters of credit through the Bank of China, simply aren't interested in discussing other forms of payment. Furthermore, letters of credit involving China trade often include a margin above the original price to cover excess delivery charges or additional insurance requirements.

Settlement periods for letters of credit are shorter than for payment against documents, averaging between 30–45 days. In Eastern Europe, they can be as short as 15 days (Hungary and the USSR) and as long as 75 days (Rumania).

One form of supplier credit in East-West trade is á forfait financing, this is used in instances where foreign receivables of a Western exporter are only partially, if at all, insured by a government export credit insurance system. Such a situation usually arises when the Western export contains a high proportion of foreign components which are ineligible for coverage. Since most companies feel uncomfortable carrying uninsured foreign receivables, usually in the form of medium-term promissory notes, on their books, they sell them to a commercial bank, preferably to one which specializes in East-West trade. The purchasing bank (forfaiter) thereupon absorbs the risk of collecting payment from the buyer without recourse to the Western exporter in case of default.

Before agreeing to purchase an exporter's receivables, a bank requires unconditional guarantees from either a major international bank or the foreign trade bank in the buyer's country. In order to provide such a guarantee, however, the state banks of Eastern Europe and the USSR usually demand that it be linked to contract performance.

A variation of á forfait is limited recourse financing. It is an agreement by a bank to purchase the exporter's receivables, with recourse only until the necessary guarantees have been obtained. In addition, should there be a commercial dispute and payment from the buyer is not forthcoming, the bank will be entitled to obtain payment from the supplier instead.

Limited recourse financing is a way for the Western bank and the exporter to share the risks, since both parties continue to be responsible until the customer abroad has made payment. In contrast, á forfait financing absolves the Western exporter as soon as the promissory notes are sold to the bank.

On the whole, the countries of Eastern Europe and the USSR do not encourage either á forfait or limited recourse financing. For reasons of prestige, trade officials in these countries hold the view that the buying and selling of their promissory notes on Western financial markets diminishes the symbolic value of their money. Moreover, since the banks receive a discount from the Western exporter when buying the notes, the customers in Eastern Europe and the USSR feel they never receive the best price for whatever goods they buy, and that both the exporter and the bank are making profits at their expense. In situations where Western firms are able to pursue á forfait or limited recourse financing, the state banks of Soviet bloc countries will demand the right to be the only customer for the notes, or to at least have the right of first refusal.

Buyer Credits

Supplier credits are supplemented by buyer credits which let the borrower use the funds to finance deals with any country. Both supplier and buyer credits are eligible for official support in varying degrees through refinancing facilities, subsidized interest, and insurance against political risks. When credits are guaranteed by governments, however, use of the funds is normally tied to purchases in the country providing the credit. The countries belonging to the Council for Mutual Economic Assistance as well as the People's Republic of China urge their commerical enterprises and foreign trade organizations to use buyer credits as much as possible.

Financing in China

After cautious use of supplier credits in the early 1970's, China entered into a new period of foreign financing policy. Since 1977, it has undertaken buyer's credit, direct foreign investment and intergovernmental aid. The Chinese government, however, has been slow to tap the $10 billion private credit extensions they have acquired. This is a reflection of China's fiscal conservatism as well as the high interest rates private foreign financial institutions offer compared to government loans.

Most of China's credit comes from official trade credits. It has concluded agreements worth close to $17 billion with 12 countries including the U.S., Australia, Britain, France, Italy, Japan, Canada, Argentina, and Sweden. But the Chinese have also been limiting their use of such credit to increasing their export capacity and modernizing old factories.

In terms of loans from foreign governments and international institutions, China has a total of over $2 billion in credit lines, obtaining over half from the International Monetary Fund. The remaining credit, worth over $1.5 billion, is in the form of direct investment. Compensation trade, an intangible form of direct investment, has accounted for $400–500 million tied up in over 1,000 compensation deals concluded since 1979.

With a growing foreign reserve debt (from $1.6 billion in 1979 to $4.5 billion in 1981), China is emphasizing low-cost, technology-enhancing governmental loans, loans from international monetary institutions, and private direct investment, including compensation deals. To finance trade, China often accepts combined financial assistance of, say, official credits (70–90 percent) and commercial credit.

The Chinese government, in addition, extends direct loans to Western companies involved in joint ventures. In February 1979, the Bank of China was granted authority to also guarantee foreign investment, including compensation arrangements. The bank extends letters of guarantee—based on its judgement of the creditworthiness of the transaction—which covers the Western bank loan for the export of machinery and equipment to China. This substantially lessens the financial risks inherent in loans to big projects. In certain cases, the Bank is prepared to guarantee the foreign contracting party against noncompliance by the Chinese side, if, for example, the Chinese manufacturer fails to deliver goods under a compensation agreement. In addition, the China Investment Bank, formed in 1981, provides investment loans to joint ventures between Chinese and foreign companies.

Chinese provinces and municipalities that earn foreign exchange are permitted to retain, for discretionary investment, a small percentage (10–30 percent) of the foreign exchange earned each year. These hard currency funds are held by the Bank of China, which must approve the use of the funds for any purchase or financing that a province sponsors, whether under countertrade arrangements or not.

Financing in CMEA Countries

The countries belonging to the Council for Mutual Economic Assistance (comprised of the USSR, all of Eastern Europe except Yugoslavia and Albania, Cuba, Mongolia, and Vietnam) facilitate the use of credit through guarantees extended by their foreign trade banks. Poland, Romania, Bulgaria and Czechoslovakia all demand guarantees from their state banks. Hungary pays dollar amounts from the funds of its important organizations and has to date been able to keep within its hard currency "avails."

East Germany won't give a guarantee to the importer. Rather, it follows a procedure called "book claim business," which is similar to facturing. When the importer receives an invoice, the Deutsche Aussenhandelsbank (DAB) writes a letter to the supplier saying that it will make foreign exchange available for the transaction. Though the letter is not a repayment guarantee, the supplier can take the letter, along with the purchase order and the invoice, and discount it at a local bank, normally for about 1 percent over the London Inter-Bank Offered Rate (LIBOR). This is a financing of trust since there is no attachment on assets as would be the case in the normal loan agreement.

In East European countries, long-term compensation agreements are financed generally by government-secured loans. In the USSR, for the shorter buyback deals, buyer or supplier credits may be used. The amount of the credit depends on the size of the deal. As a rule, the lower limit is 40 percent of the estimated cost of the buyback project. The Soviets prefer to commence repayment of credits in products from three to five years after signing the contract, with full repayment to stretch over 10 years or longer.

Project Financing

Project financing denotes more than just providing financial backing to a project. It is distinguished from previous methods of financing by the fact that lenders, be they commercial banks, insurance companies, or venture capitalists, look to the cash flows and earnings of a particular operation itself as the source of funds from which the loan will be repaid, and to the operation's assets as collateral for the loan. With the advent of project financing, banks have assumed a more active role in countertrade, particularly in compensation deals involving raw materials and minerals.

For example, in a country that has raw materials and requires the expansion of a mine, a joint venture may be established between a Western and local company. The Western firm receives compensation in the form of a resultant product, which is used to cover costs and pay off debts resulting from the expansion. In project financing, in general, a bank determines whether sales revenues are adequate to cover costs plus debt service. This leads directly to countertrade in many cases where loans made are actually repaid in product—directly from the sales revenues. Other necessary elements that define a feasible (mining) project under project financing are adequate measured reserves, demonstrated technology, and completion of mine development. Before granting loans, banks must perform such technical tasks as quantifying reserves, assessing the feasibility of the mining method, and evaluating the design of the wash plant. In other words, banks act as consulting engineers. To do this, banks either have in-house mining engineering expertise or use an independent engineering consulting firm.

Though project financing is very well suited for production-sharing joint ventures, the growth of countertrade in itself did not provide the impetus for the increasing use of project financing. (On the contrary project financing fosters the establishment of production-sharing joint ventures.) Rather, it was the inadequacy of normal financing—companies borrowing against their balance sheets on an unsecured basis—which prompted lenders and borrowers alike to seek financing alternatives. Cost escalation resulted in projects outgrowing the capital resources of their sponsors. Banks also found themselves backing projects that failed, were plagued with cost overruns, or required refinancing.

By basing loans on the quality of a company's (mining) operations, its reserves and its ability to sell the final product, the cost escalation problem is sidestepped. And in adopting new analytical approaches to the profitability of projects, banks have also protected themselves from many of the problems that have recently beset projects. Previously, project profitability was normally evaluated by discounted cash flow. Though this technique was particularly appropriate for oil projects, which have relatively short construction time and a quick repayment period, it tended to discriminate against projects with a long lead time, a long life, irregular prices for the output, and huge returns when mineral prices skyrocket. Particular problems are encountered when considering what price should be used to justify a mining project. To evaluate a mining project's cost feasibility, banks now look at the cost position relative to other producers of its major mineral. If it is favorable, then the project goes ahead regardless of the world price of that mineral at that moment. However, sometimes prices do not come near the level needed to justify a new project. In these cases, both analytical approaches should be used.

Other cautionary measures are being taken by banks. Completion agreements, considered too mild before, are receiving more scrutiny. A good completion agreement should cover all likely technical problems. Banks have also become more insistent on stronger sales (offtake) contracts. Under normal procedure, the market is guaranteed by offtake contracts against which the banks can lend for project construction or expansion. But contract negotiations have sometimes reduced the collateral value to banks of these purchase agreements. Banks are thus paying more attention to the credit strength of prospective buyers of the output as well as to conditions of supply and demand in the future market of the finished products.

To strengthen the chances that offtake contracts generate sufficient revenue to cover all financing, banks are now requiring floor prices and strong take-or-pay provisions, and that at least 80 percent of the output be covered by offtake contracts. This last stipulation encourages production-sharing joint ventures where financing and the terms of partner participation are linked in one comprehensive package deal that incorporates offtake commitments by the partners.

In the U.S., the money-center banks have cornered the market for financing projects. Most of the project financing is done by leading banks, such as Citibank, Morgan Guarantee, Chase Manhattan (all in New York) and Bank of America (San Francisco). Smaller banks cannot match the scope of services offered by these major banks, but they also finance projects and attract business by specializing in a particular industrial sector. For example, a Texas bank ($7 billion in assets) has developed a specialization in gas and oil, and has extended its expertise internationally through a presence in London and Singapore, and through a share in a consortium bank that specializes in energy projects.

U.S. bank involvement in project financing is bound to increase. Since U.S. banks cannot lend more than 10 percent of their capital and reserves to any single borrower, including foreign governments, project financing allows them to lend to separate borrowing entities (including projects) in a single country, thereby increasing the amount of money it can lend to a given government. Furthermore, the lending reserves of international agencies (such as the World Bank) are too limited to finance all the projects expected to come on stream during the next few years.

With the growing popularity of countertrade, a number of U.S. banks now offer facilities specifically for countertrade transactions. These include Chase Manhattan, Citibank, European-American Bank, Schroeder Bank, and Manufacturers Hanover Trust (all based in New York). While this represents a major step forward for U.S. banks, they still operate at a distinct advantage compared to their counterparts in Western Europe. Apart from loans to one borrower being restricted to 10 percent of bank net worth, West European banks (commercial and government export-import banks) generally offer more money at better terms, have lower credit standards, and provide government-guaranteed buyer credits.

Until recently American banks, unlike European banks, could not take a position in a product, now they can. They can finance and assist firms faced with countertrade obligations through standard banking practices and through arranging non-bank financing for a fee, syndicating privately-placed loans, offering financial advice, helping with mergers and acquisitions, underwriting international bond issues, and investing in the private sector. They can also finance trade transacted on their own account. Large U.S. commercial banks, limited in their operation by the Glass-Steagall Banking Reform of 1933, have nonetheless been increasing the merchant banking activities of their foreign branches and subsidiaries, and under the Export Trading Company Act of 1982, export bank holding companies have more latitude than previously. Moreover, foreign subsidiaries of U.S. companies can draw on West European government loans.

Chapter 7

GOVERNMENT ATTITUDES TOWARD COUNTERTRADE

Uncharted Waters

The great irony of countertrade is that, in the long run, it is probably more disadvantageous for those countries that push it than for those countries that accept countertrade demands. But, nobody knows exactly what impact countertrade has on individual countries or international trade in general. Lack of data is one major reason. Another is the enormous complexity of the countertrade issue itself. It does not represent a homogeneous form of trade containing well-defined rules and procedures to which countries must adhere. Quite the opposite; every country injects its own style and standards into countertrade practice.

Dispelling Myths

Though countertrade is practiced between East and West as well as North and South, it cannot be categorized as either an East versus West or North versus South issue where the East/South foists countertrade on the West/North. For one, Western countries also push countertrade, either among themselves or with developing nations. Japan, France, and West Germany are aggressive advocates of "development for import" trade. In addition, Canadian companies seek countertrade deals. For example, they have exacted countertrade agreements from such American companies as Brink's Inc. and McDonnell Douglas.

The view that the industrialized nations are being forced into countertrade disregards the lack of consensus on countertrade in the East and South. Though Eastern Europe as a whole favors countertrade, Hungary has publicly questioned the notion that it automatically brings big benefits and little or no harm to countries practicing it. Some Third World governments, in Indonesia, Mexico and Brazil, for example, believe countertrade to be an important if not the prime tool to improve trade balance. Other governments value countertrade but consider it only one of many ways to improve creditworthiness. In the West, few governments have officially staked out a clear position on countertrade. As a matter of fact, several governments, including the United States, tend to speak with many voices on the subject.

Most importantly, however, the view of countertrade as a practice into which the industrialized nations are coerced is belied by actual practice. On a case-to-case basis, there is neither perpetrator nor victim. Western companies enter into countertrade arrangements with the expectation of making money, and unlike conventional financial transactions, these companies have the opportunity to make money on both ends of the deal—the import and export contracts.

The other partner engages in countertrade with definite objectives in mind: to save on hard currency, increase exports, reach new markets, and gain access to Western technology. Of course, countertrade has claimed its share of victims. For example, several West German machine tool-makers have gone belly up in the past few years at least partially as a result of barter-type deals. This only means that countertrade, like all modes of commercial activity, contains elements of risk. At the microeconomic level, though, countertrade must be considered a mutually beneficial mode of trade.

Lack of Consensus Among Governments

What is at issue and at the center of a growing controversy is the cumulative impact of countertrade on international trade and, derivatively, on individual countries. West European governments are only now beginning to examine countertrade in this light, and only for East-West trade (ignoring North-South). The impact of chemicals from Eastern Europe and the Soviet Union flooding into a West European chemical market already plagued by overcapacity has resulted in a loss of export markets for Western chemical manufacturers. As a result, the governments of Western Europe are anxious to avoid a similar situation in other industries. The United States, on the other hand, faces a different set of concerns. Its industries have been little affected by the import of goods that were part of countertrade deals (witness the import of Yugoslav ham in exchange for McDonnell Douglas aircraft). In general, while recognizing that countertrade is necessary for developing countries, the United States government is more troubled by the overall distorting effects of countertrade on the flow of goods and services worldwide. Its basic attitude is that fiscal tools and incentives represent better ways to improve trade balance than production-sharing joint ventures and protectionist policies which countertrade engenders.

United States Concerns

Various United States government organizations are now involved in examining countertrade. The Office of the U.S. Trade Representative, in the executive branch, is looking at the "creeping bilateralism" brought about by countertrade. Specifically, as more countries turn to countertrade they look to bilateral trade agreements with their trade partners. This leads to fears that export markets for American companies will shrink. The Defense Department is reviewing policies on coproduction, industrial participation and offsets in light of the U.S. government's decision in 1978 not to participate in any of these agreements; each transaction involving military hardware production would be concluded directly between the manufacturer and the buyer. The Treasury Department, International Trade Commission and Government Accounting Office are all studying countertrade and its effects on the United States and world economies. The GAO, particularly, is concerned that this country's laws do not adequately prevent the potential dumping of foreign goods by American companies fulfilling their countertrade obligation.

Though there has been intergovernmental discussion of countertrade, it has not prevented a cacophony of government voices from expressing their opinion on the subject. The Treasury, a proponent of conventional financial transfers, opposes countertrade. The State Department, while opposing countertrade on the basis of its incompatibility with the General Agreement on Tariffs and Trade (GATT) and GATT's highly structured regulation of international trade, recognizes that United States companies must comply with countertrade provisions incorporated into a contract signed under the laws of another country. In sum, the above-mentioned agencies, while not actively interfering with countertrade, will not actively promote the concept.

The Commerce Department has evolved a policy that contradictorily synthesizes pro and con positions. While, on the one hand, countertrade has been described as "bad business" that "contravenes our commitment to an open international trade and monetary system" by Lionel Olmer, Undersecretary of Commerce for International Trade, on the other hand, Commerce assists exporters that face countertrade demands by providing advice on negotiating tactics, market information, and in selling the countertraded goods imported into this country.

The United States Trade Representative fears that countertrade is breaking down the multilateralism upon which world trade has flourished over the past 40 years. In light of the increase in bilateral trade agreements (between Brazil and Mexico, for example), countries outside the industrialized world believe that their interests are more fully achieved by a bilateral agreement than by the multilateral trade organizations. As a result, the Trade Representative sees grave implications for the flow of strategic materials. Focusing primarily on export performance requirements, the Trade Representative stated that countertrade agreements have the potential, if not actual effects, of distorting and fragmenting the world's interdependent trading system, including restructuring world trade in metals (a concern expressed by the Organization for Economic Cooperation and Development, as well). Countertrade, besides encouraging uneconomic investments and fostering uneconomic exchanges, takes away the incentive to respond quickly to changes in international market forces.

Development-for-import arrangements, whereby companies in industrialized countries develop long-range investments in joint venture projects, in order to secure dependable
sources of supply of a product (usually a raw material), have
already tied up substantial volumes of iron ore, manganese
ore, nickel ore, alumina and aluminum. By 1984, France, Germany and Japan will be receiving from develop-for-import
projects in Australia and Canada the following amounts:

- 69 million tons of iron ore and pellets
- 3 million tons of nickel ore
- 2.4 million tons of manganese ore
- 1.8 million tons of bauxite
- 1.8 million tons of alumina
- 0.9 million tons of aluminum
- lesser tonnages of copper, chromite and tungsten

Besides these figures, United States government agencies
have been hardput to document actual or possible negative
effects of countertrade on the national interest. Imports from
countertrade to the U.S. has been small because, for one,
American companies do not trade as much with Sino-Soviet
bloc countries as Japan and West European nations do. Countertrade only became an issue when the debt crisis in Latin
America developed. In addition, countertrade products tend
to be sold directly or indirectly to developing or West European countries, according to an International Trade Commission report. In fact, the report also states that United
States exports exceed imports received through countertrade
during any given period. This is because the value of goods
exported by American companies usually exceeds that of the
goods that make up the countertrade obligation.

The Case for Countertrade

East European governments are quick to point out the
benefits of countertrade. They claim that it opens up new
markets for Western companies and increases employment
in Western nations, which is particularly helpful in periods
of economic recession (a case can be made, of course, for the
idea that countertrade imports have a negative impact on

Western economies by displacing domestic production, hence, reducing employment).

The long-term benefits of countertrade agreements are also pointed out by East Europeans. They receive technology and equipment from the West to develop their key industries, while the West has access to a steady source of raw materials at a set price. Central planners point to the absence of destabilizing market forces as a key advantage to long-term countertrade agreements.

The Case Against Countertrade

The pros and cons of countertrade, as applied to the communist and developing countries, are also in dispute. One notable economist has described compensation and cooperation agreements as "an attempt to adapt foreign trade to the requirements of planning." Socialist economies are already suffering from an overdose of planning, and countertrade has tended to compound problems associated with planning. For example, the arbitrary setting of prices leads to distortions of supply and demand. In most cases, in socialist and developing countries, goods have to be sold at a loss (below cost price) in order to compensate the Western importers for the higher marketing costs and the risks of such transactions. These price discounts, whether openly recognized or hidden in the inflated price of the Western export, must eventually be paid out of state budgets that thus end up subsidizing export-for-a-loss practices of foreign trade organizations. It is, in fact, highly possible that the typically high cost of export subsidy and incentive programs practiced in developing and socialist countries outweigh the contribution to a nation's foreign reserve position through increasing exports. Furthermore, despite the increasing frequency of countertrade, indebtedness of many countries heavily engaged in countertrade is still growing.

Because countertrade eliminates the need for direct contact with Western markets, there is no transfer of marketing skill to the country receiving the Western export. Such countries have very little control over the pricing and distribution of their commodity exports and little chance of developing that expertise until (if it is a compensation deal) after the payback period. Measures that tend to encourage countertrade, such as import regulations, foreign exchange regulations and export subsidies, interfere with developing markets abroad and all lack one thing: the enhancement of competitiveness.

The Role of Western Governments in Countertrade

The debate about countertrade now taking place in government circles around the world has not yet been translated into active well-defined policies or regulations governing trade. Apart from the government-sponsored develop-for-import programs, few governments actively intervene in countertrade activity. The French government is one. If formed a group know as ACECO (Association pour la Compensation des Echanges Commerciaux), made up of bankers, industrialists and government officials, to advise French companies how to handle compensation deals. ACECO also tries to screen out deals that might be harmful to the French market.

Other governments in the West are beginning to consider a more assertive role in countertrade, particularly in defining the politico-economic framework in which countertrade must operate. Countertrade, currently so attractive because it is able to bypass the rules of the marketplace and government, may, in the future, be increasingly answerable to both. As the number of countertrade transactions increase, so will government attempts to regulate them. Several countries have already passed specific legislation requiring countertrade, and specifying how countertrade transactions are to be carried out. Three of the most notable examples are Indonesia, Brazil and Mexico, with other countries like Costa Rica and Argentina currently considering new laws.

Chapter 8

CREATING A COUNTERTRADE CAPABILITY

Making the Decision to Countertrade

Companies are never forced to countertrade. Instead, they face a choice: to bow out of contract negotiations, or as the case may be, a particular market altogether; to negotiate price discounts or other concessions in lieu of assuming countertrade obligations; or to agree to countertrade obligations. Countertrade is not for every company, but sometimes it is hard to resist. In times of economic recession, companies often agree to countertrade in order to close a big deal, though they often do so without considering all of the ramifications.

The acceptance of countertrade need not amount to a major corporate decision, especially in a one-shot deal. When a trading company is used, for one deal or even several deals, countertrade can be relatively painless way to increase business, provided that the cost of the export covers commissions to the trading company.

But for long-term market strategies in which countertrade-based business could be an important component, the decision to countertrade assumes more importance and several factors must be taken into consideration. Trading companies are still an option, but their services come high and after several countertrade deals, firms invariable reach a point at which forming their own countertrade unit can no longer be ignored.

Considering the Countertrade Option

A number of questions must be answered to determine if a company wishes to pursue countertrade. Does a company want a long term presence in a market, and at what cost?

How often will the export of a company's product require counterdeliveries? What percentage of sale should the downside risk of the countertrade product entail? Can a firm use or sell through normal company channels the products likely to be offered? Does the firm have the financial resources to support itself between the export of its product and the receipt of proceeds from counterdelivered goods?

If a firm wants to purchase countertrade goods for in-company use, it is a good idea to make an inventory of all purchase requirements throughout the company and then evaluate potential sourcing opportunities in countries where countertrade is expected to take place. If there are enough potential matches, a firm has an excellent basis on which to pursue countertrade. Very few matches mean that a company has to consider the counter-purchase of non-production goods and the hardship this entails.

Forming a Countertrade Unit

In establishing a countertrade unit, a set of policies describing the objectives, functions, and responsibilities of the unit should be formulated by top management with the aid of sales, purchasing, and international specialists or consultants. These policies should be set on a long-term basis to provide sufficient flexibility to company negotiators.

Countertrade units may pursue several objectives: to support product sales through one, several, or all forms of countertrade; to satisfy barter or offset requests; to minimize buyback through negotiation; and to negotiate bilateral trade agreements on favorable terms. These basic objectives can be modified to fit the specific needs of a company. Taking into consideration objectives and capabilities, firms must decide whether the countertrade unit is to deal in products and/or services; is to be concerned primarily with exports or imports; is to trade exclusively in company products or products outside the company; and if outside the company, is to deal in goods only related to company products or unrelated goods.

A company should also select the financial and legal status of the countertrade unit. Should it become a wholly owned subsidiary, or should it be merely a separate division of the international department? A prime consideration in setting up any kind of countertrade unit is to establish a sound business relationship with the parent company. Ideally, a countertrade unit should be kept relatively small but able to handle a heavy load of countertrade responsibilities. This can be achieved if the unit receives help from other company organizations and utilizes company resources as fully as possible.

There are several ways to foster cooperation between the parent company and the countertrade unit. In small, nondiversified manufacturing firms, the countertrade staff is usually placed in the purchasing department. Alternatively, autonomous trading companies can be under the vice president of sales or international operations, with good lines of communication to marketing and financial executives. Other corporations put countertrade subsidiaries under the senior vice president for corporation development, since he is responsible for expanding the company's business into new markets and developing strategic planning for sales and technology transfers to communist and lesser developed countries.

The composition of board of directors, under which a trading company subsidiary would operate, is also important in facilitating cooperation. It usually includes vice presidents from the purchasing, legal and finance departments. Sometimes, the vice president of the materials management department is also included (as in the Motors Trading Corporation of General Motors).

The Autonomous Profit-making Center

For companies that do a great deal of outside purchasing or that have countertrade demands made on them frequently by their customers, an affiliated though autonomous profit-making company with countertrade responsibilities might be established. Usually, only very large corporations such as Combustion Engineering, Control Data, Coca-Cola, Rockwell International, General Motors, IBM and General Electric have the resources to justify taking this step. Such profit-center trading companies usually require three to four years to absorb the multi-million dollar upfront investments in special talent, necessary research and development, and other start-up costs. In all, about a dozen U.S. companies have specialized wholly-owned subsidiaries that handle countertrade.

In the pursuit of profit, such a countertrade unit would aggressively seek promising countertrade (as well as non-countertrade) deals. But it might be reluctant to support countertrade arrangements by other divisions of the company if a reasonable profit was not assured. Furthermore, this unit would be operating in a high risk market (of buying, selling and brokering commodities).

These trading organizations are involved in all phases of countertrade operations. This includes planning a company's long-range marketing strategies—market research and development—in markets requiring or likely to require countertrade obligations. Ironically, it is up to these companies to limit countertrade as a tool of market penetration as much as possible, always giving priorities to straight export sales but also exploring other marketing techniques that might be profitable. Some countertrade units set specific guidelines and conditions for accepting countertrade deals. Others prefer a more flexible case-by-case approach.

Coordination is an important task for profit center trading companies, particularly those that have big parent companies. Countertrade obligations should be coordinated among product divisions. Evidence accounts should also be coordinated so that one division's imports can help out another division's counterpurchase obligations.

As a specialized trading organization, the trading company has access to market information otherwise not available to the parent company. All pertinent information should be made available to appropriate company personnel. It should keep product divisions particularly informed of countertrade operations and market intelligence in the respective product areas.

The most obvious task of a trading company is to negotiate and implement a countertrade deal. It would usually have prime responsibility to negotiate all agreements to countertrade, such as protocol agreements and evidence account agreements. For contract negotiations, a trading company would sometimes share this responsibility with the products division involved in the transaction.

For example, the countertrade subsidiary of General Motors, Motors Trading Corporation, has exclusive responsibility to negotiate only those contracts which fulfill countertrade agreements where the goods and services taken are not directly consumed by General Motors. If the goods are consumed by General Motors, MTC shares responsibility with the affected purchasing branch. Looking at the export side of countertrade, MTC shares responsibility with the GM subsidiary that manufactures the goods that will be sent abroad. In cases where a subsidiary exports its own product, MTC has no responsibility. Depending on the preferences of individual companies, a trading company may supervise, monitor, participate in negotiations alone or with other company divisions or subsidiaries, or may be shut out of the negotiations altogether.

In carrying out countertrade, the trading company also selects and disposes of goods. The purchasing department of the parent company would probably have input if the products are for in-house consumption. In such cases, it is not unusual for profit-center trading companies to specify to the manufacturing organization(s) of the country where countertrade obligations exist the type and design of products to be used in the manufacturing operation of the parent firm. Otherwise, the trading company is expected to locate outside buyers, and, in this capacity, it may likewise provide specifications of products to serve other markets. Though some countries do not allow it, trading companies will also try to credit routine purchases by the parent company from foreign countries against countertrade obligations.

Duties of the trading company also can include customs documentation, arranging credit, seeking outside assistance when needed, and periodically evaluating the overall costs and profits derived by the company from all countertrade transactions.

Taking advantage of their autonomous status, trading companies often arrange international trade deals independent of any countertrade obligations, receiving in return a negotiated fee or commission. These organizations also frequently facilitate trade among lesser developed countries and between lesser developed countries and East European countries. In addition to marrying buyers and sellers, they are also beginning to purchase goods on their own account for resale. That way, they control the price and terms of purchase more effectively than by selling on commission. Trading companies are also engaging in proactive buying—the policy of buy now, sell later. The idea behind proactive trading is that by initiating a purchase, the trading company opens the door for the parent company to sell its product at some later time.

The Direct Countertrade Organization

A countertrade unit subsidized by a company to support and give advice on countertrade transactions, sometimes called direct countertrade organization (DCO), is a safer alternative to the profit-center trading company. More cautious in its approach, its prime responsibility is to help the parent company satisfy countertrade obligations by finding buyers worldwide. Boosting sales and profits are not concerns. The expense of operating a DCO, usually made up of less than 10 people, is often built into the product prices charged to the foreign buyer.

The Indirect Countertrade Organization

A more limited role is played by an indirect countertrade organization (ICO). Eschewing direct involvement in the marketing or distribution of countertrade goods, the ICO primarily acts as an information broker to third parties consisting of agents, distributors, and buyers by supplying details on foreign products and services that are available in countries where countertrade obligations are owed. When a transaction results from the information provided by the ICO, the value of the transaction is credited to a countertrade commitment of the parent company. The ICO does not set specifications for the products tendered as profit-center trading companies or ICOs sometimes do. An ICO staff typically consists of less than five persons.

The Countertrade Purchasing Organization

The simplest, least disruptive organization a company can adopt is a countertrade purchasing organization (CPO). It does not have trading functions, since it is not allowed to resell goods. It acts strictly as a purchasing agent for the parent company, seeking countertrade products suitable for use by the various divisions and subsidiaries of the parent company. This arrangement is particularly well-suited for very large manufacturing companies, since they require large quantities of raw materials, intermediate and finished goods in their manufacturing process. The main problem facing the CPO (and other countertrade organizations buying production goods) is coordinating the purchase and delivery of counter-trade products to match production runs in the various corporate manufacturing facilities. CPO operations are usually handled by one to three persons.

The Countertrade Cooperative

Another kind of countertrade organization, better known in Western Europe than in the United States, is a counter-trade cooperative. It may be formed by a group of companies that join together to help one another absorb a wider range of countertrade purchases. This way, companies sidestep the problems of organizing a special countertrade unit. A coop-erative may arrange for combined disposal of products that would be difficult for individual members to dispose of in small quantities. In addition, by collecting data in one place, they eliminate duplication of data on sourcing and marketing. Three already exist in Germany and Austria, and one in France. One is now reportedly being formed in the United States by United Brands. Countries are beginning to see the value of having their own methods of assisting countertrade deals. The Swedish government has formed a trading organ-ization that handles Swedish companies countertrade deals. The Philippine government has formed, under the Ministry of Trade, a company that handles all countertrade with the Eastern bloc countries. Algeria has a state-owned firm which handles all countertrade, and the Koreans have just formed an advisory service to facilitate countertrade.

Multi-faceted Countertrade Programs

Multi-faceted countertrade programs designed to help customers pay for their products are presently limited to large corporations that sell aircraft, helicopters, and other defense-related products. For example, McDonnell Douglas has an offset program active in 24 countries. The program includes: arrangements for co-production, where a customer with aerospace capability manufactures a component or components for the product he will buy or participates in the development costs of the product; export development, where McDonnell Doublas identifies prospective trade partners, marries buyers and sellers, makes corporate purchases and arranges for supplier companies to make purchases; tourism, where McDonnell Douglas provides revenue to customer airlines through employee tour groups and trade mission; and ventures licensing and technology transfers, where external capital and technology are joined with plentiful labor and material sources in developing countries to be benefit of both McDonnell Douglas and the customer.

Other Organizational Alternatives for Countertrade

If a company is small and countertrade business is not expected to be large, countertrade functions may be performed simply by a bilateral trade coordinator without staff. He can work out of sales, purchasing or the corporate staff office. Another alternative is to designate a staff consultant who would advise all departments faced with countertrade or bilateral trade obligations. Such a person is often brought in from the outside and has extensive trade and marketing experience. A company may also choose to hire a consultant on a temporary or retainer basis. A consultant in this capacity could advise the company on countertrade policy and planning, help set up in-house countertrade organizations and provide assistance during negotiations.

Trading Houses

Many firms will encounter countertrade demands irregularly, some rarely. It is probably best for such firms, at least at first, to contact the services of a trading house. These houses offer services ranging from providing advice on countertrade practices in developing countries and assisting negotiations and assessing markets (of potential counterdelivered goods) to acting as brokers and, sometimes, acting as principals in countertrade transactions.

More than anything, trading companies are convenient. Firms, if they do not wish, do not have to be kept informed of the details of the transaction. They do not even have to know what products are being taken to fulfill the company's counterpurchase obligations.

Beyond convenience there are distinct advantages to using a trading company. A long-established and well-known trading house has contacts that a manufacturing firm is unlikely to possess. A trading house works daily with a variety of wholesalers, importers, and other trading companies, as well as with final buyers of countertrade goods. From continuous contacts with potential end users, they are in a position to make prompt cost estimates for the disposal of countertrade goods. And a seller that has linked up with a trading house and can thus quote its sales price earlier than competitors operating alone may often stand a better chance of winning the deal.

Using a trading house, in effect, reduces the risk of engaging in countertrade. A company no longer has to worry about the disposal of goods. If the trading company does not have a customer at the time of acquisition, it will stockpile the goods for future sale, a course manufacturers would be very reluctant to take. In addition, trading houses are useful for companies that do not want it known that they are reselling low-quality countertrade goods at subsidized prices for fear of damage to their reputation. When goods are sold through a trading house, the Western principal's name usually will not be connected to the transaction.

However, working through trading companies also has its drawbacks. The most obvious and, many times, the most painful, is cost. There is, furthermore, controversy as to what the actual profit margin of trade houses are in countertrade deals. They range from one to four percent in high-risk situations, if the trading houses themselves are to be believed. But these same houses are known to quote widely varying charges for the same deal. This can occur because traders with a wide range of known end users for countertrade goods of certain countries may be in a position to quote lower subsidies than other traders. Companies looking for assistance from trading houses should obtain quotations from more than one house.

The convenience of using trading companies has an additional negative side—dependence. A company does not learn how to countertrade on its own. This advantage is magnified when the same goods taken as payment are marketed by the trading company in a succession of countertrade transactions. The manufacturer is no closer to knowing how to market such goods in the last transaction as in the first. In addition, the seller's own negotiators are forced to rely on the somewhat one-sided advice given by trading houses and are in a weakened position to be flexible during negotiations.

Also, most foreign trade organization negotiators prefer dealing with the Western principal and consider trading house representatives as outsiders with no real vested interest in specific deals. Polish and Hungarian trade organizations are particularly inclined to this point of view. As a result, foreign trade organizations tend to be more flexible with the Western companies that identify the agent as much as possible with their own firm. A trade agent, for example, may be permitted to use the company's name on his calling card or write letters on company stationery.

The trading houses, aware of the many problems involved in countertrade, are sometimes less than enthusiastic over the prospect of representing a Western vendor in a countertrade transaction. Many will accept countertrade jobs only if it involves large sums of money. The ideal size of countertrade commitment, in the view of many traders, is between $250,000 and $750,000, depending on the product and its origin. Deals of less than $100,000 may require the same effort in finding a buyer as larger contracts. Therefore, the subsidy expressed as a percent of the obligation for a deal under $100,000 may be disproportionately higher than for, say, a $400,000 contract.

Most trading houses are two to five person organizations that specialize in a certain range of commodities or geographical area. There are also about thirty major trade houses in the world. Specialized trade houses will often decline to become involved in a countertrade deal where the type of goods to be brought falls outside their specialization. Sometimes, specialized trading houses, particularly in Britain and Germany, will handle a client's counterpurchase commitments only if they are allowed to take over its export business (to a certain geographical area) as well.

It is also unlikely that- a trade house would undertake a countertrade commitment for a Western firm contemplating a large buyback deal. As a rule, they are reluctant to accept countertrade that involves purchase commitments of products that will not become available for several years or that must be purchased on a continual basis for an extended period.

Chapter 9

COUNTERTRADE IN THE LESSER DEVELOPED COUNTRIES

The Growing Attraction of Countertrade

Countertrade in the lesser developed countries (LDC's) is as diverse as the countries that make up this large community of nations. Apart from being geographically dispersed, LDC's can have either market economies or centrally planned economies. Development strategies designed to meet the unique needs of individual economies also differ significantly from country to country. Moreover, some nations have strong economic relations with the West, while others have close economic ties with socialist countries in the East.

In reflecting these differences, countertrade assumes many various forms in the developing world. Though not all developing countries can be individually covered here, the significant types of countertrade practiced in these countries, and the important countertrade trends in these economies of the world will be closely examined, accompanied by examples from individual countries.

Many lesser developed countries have laws or trade policies that mandate countertrade. These mandates are now being either strengthened or implemented more actively to cope with such common economic problems in the Third World as negative balance of payments, lack of diversified export and strong capital bases, the ravages of inflation fed by spiralling oil prices, fluctuating currencies, and the urgent need for refinancing long- and medium-term debts.

Many lesser developed countries are dependent on one or two primary exports, and thus were hard hit in 1979-1980 when prices of primary commodities fell. This was a particularly crucial blow when coupled with rapid increases in the cost of key imports. The debt of lesser developed countries climbed to an estimated $820 billion in 1984, up from $142 billion in 1974. The economic and fiscal policies of Western governments exacerbated the developing countries' predicament. Recession reduced the availability of capital funds from public lending institutions and private banks. At the same time, Western nations adopted protectionist "import relief" measures while decreasing the real level of foreign aid to "hardship" countries.

As the 1980's got underway, lesser developed countries found themselves with increasingly less room to maneuver. As populations rose, average incomes increased (along with expectations) while real income decreased and governments continued their commitment to ambitious industrialization programs. The need for food, raw materials, and capital goods became more acute. Depleted hard-currency reserves, however, had to to first go toward the purchase of oil since oil-exporting nations were reluctant to accept payment in product (at least the products that developing countries have to offer). To salvage industrialization goals, economic planners turned to countertrade as a means of financing essential imports and increasing exports.

The stabilization of trade is the most important reason behind countertrade for most developing countries. By tying imports to exports and then ensuring a market for exports through countertrade, a country's foreign trade is shielded in part from the vagaries of the market. The hoped-for result is increased creditworthiness and a greater degree of planning. Countertrade is particularly crucial to countries that rely on export products with stagnating or decreasing demand on the world market; products such as rubber, tea and coconut oil. For example, Sudan, which relies heavily on the unstable cotton market for its export earnings, practices barter. Sri Lanka, Egypt, India are other countries that have turned to countertrade to balance the risky dependence on exports with low-demand elasticity.

In addition, major projects in the developing world are increasingly financed on the basis of countertrade—usually equity loans paid off in resultant product. These projects frequently involving mineral extraction can cost $1 billion or more. Most lesser developed countries lack the financial resources to finance such operations. These countries, even if they have hard-currency surpluses, turn to Western nations for money and, many times, for technical help in exploring, extracting and processing minerals. Western nations, for their part, are happy to offer financial and technological assistance in return for a guaranteed supply of a mineral in high world demand. Equity investments also protect Western investors' capital, and debts can be collected more easily if the venture is expropriated. For the non-oil producing developing countries, which have been generally unable to regulate a fluctuating demand for raw material exports (as opposed to the success of OPEC), these production-sharing joint ventures represent a means to stabilize the export of such raw materials as zinc, iron ore, bauxite, and copper. By requiring foreign owners to take a share of the venture's production to pay for their equity loans, host countries also exert a greater degree of control over the venture (and their natural resources). As the equity loan is paid off, equity reverts to the host country.

Neither have oil-producing countries been immune to the lure of countertrade. Nations with large populations and expensive development programs such as Nigeria, Algeria, Saudi Arabia, Iran, Iraq and Indonesia find countertrade particularly useful. They have proved willing to offer oil for needed imports and at advantageous terms, especially when the oil market is slack.

The Evolution of Countertrade

While present-day countertrade is becoming increasingly geared to the import of investment goods, technical know-how, and development assistance, in earlier years it was practiced with other objectives in mind. In the 1960's, countertrade spread primarily as a way to promote exports and to provide for essential imports of food products and raw materials. It also served as a convenient mode of trade. Surplus commodities, particularly unexpected agricultural surpluses, could be disposed of through barter. More importantly, barter-like trade allowed countries to diverisfy their economy and export products. These objectives, it should be said, remain valid for many lesser developed countries today.

To further encourage countertrade, barter regulations were adopted in the late 1960's in several developing countries, including India, Iraq, Pakistan, Colombia, Ecuador, Ghana, Sri Lanka, and Egypt. Soon after, Iran, Brazil and Algeria followed suit. In general these trade regulations, in addition to promoting countertrade, also defined the conditions under which countertrade was allowed to take place. India is a typical example of countries in the developing world that placed countertrade firmly under the wing of national interest. It had the following trade guidelines: 1) a minimum value of barter deals of $250,000; 2) only surplus products (manganese ore, ilmenite, chrome ore or vegetable oils) or non-traditional industrial exports for which an export market did not yet exist could be exported in a barter transaction 3) only essential raw materials or products essential for India's development or immediate food requirements could be imported under barter arrangements; and 4) the barter deals had to help save scarce foreign exchange.

Along with barter and counterpurchase, another form of countertrade was gradually gaining acceptance in developing countries: production-sharing joint ventures. The first was in 1957 and involved oil development in Indonesia. About a decade later, the first major production-sharing joint venture involving minerals took place in Ertzberg, New Guinea (now part of Indonesia). It was not until the 1970's, however, that production sharing joint ventures really caught on. By that time, a new kind of joint venture was gaining prominence whereby output was exchanged for service. First developed in Indonesia in the late 1960's (then called work contracts), these technical aid compensation arrangements are now most popular in the Middle East. OPEC oil is offered for management, production, exploration, or other technical services. They are also practiced elsewhere, such as New Caledonia where the French Mining Ministry is providing exploration services for nickel and matte development.

The Main Types of Countertrade

Countertrade may be mandated by government or undertaken on a strictly voluntary basis. It may be between private companies, between governments, or involve a mixture of private and public participation. Countertrade arrangements run the gamut from simple exchanges such as straight barter and bilateral clearing arrangements to complicated procedures and requirements that tend to characterize the kind of countertrade mandated by government trade regulations.

In some Third World countries all, or almost all, these forms of countertrade are practiced. Other lesser developed countries have been less flexible and allow or strongly favor one or two particular forms.

Bilateral Clearing Arrangements:

Most nations in the Third World have bilateral clearing arrangements. This kind of countertrade is usually practiced between the lesser developed countries themselves, but in some cases Eastern Bloc countries have these arrangements with developing nations. Among members of the Organization for Economic Cooperation and Development, France maintains special arrangements with its former colonies and Greece has a bilateral clearing agreement with Iraq.

Bilateral clearing accounts are established when two governments with foreign exchange controls and shortages of foreign currency enter into a bilateral agreement to exchange goods and/or services over a specified period of time (usually one year). The value of the goods is denominated in artificial accounting units (for example, clearing dollar, swiss franc or rupee). After specifying a certain level of trade and items to be exchanged, the two governments utilize their respective central banks to keep a balance sheet on the goods being sent between the countries and to pay the exporters in each country in domestic currencies. The agreement requires that all trade exchanges stop beyond a maximum specified trade imbalance or "swing" which is usually set at about 30 percent of annual volume. Such imbalances represent interest-free credit by the country with the trade surplus to the other country. At the end of the contracted agreement period, trade imbalances have to be settled in cash in the specified currency or converted to cash by "switching" the rights of the trade imbalance to interested third parties at discounted prices.

Agreements are typically made between countries of the same region. For example, Brazil and Mexico have such agreements with most Latin American nations, Iran has them with Turkey and Pakistan, and India with Sri Lanka and Burma.

Counterpurchase and Compensation

Apart from bilateral clearing agreements, counterpurchase agreements in lesser developed countries tend to dominate countertrade because such arrangements allow countries of the Third World to trade surplus commodities for needed supplies and manufactured goods. Agricultural products and staple manufactures are most frequently involved in counterpurchase transactions in these markets. Buyers in newly industrialized market economies favor compensation, in the form of buyback and production-sharing arrangements. A typical buyback deal, for example, was undertaken in Peru between Marubeni of Japan and the Peruvian company Mineroperu involving a copper project. The Japanese loan of $25 million is being paid back in resultant product. Beginning in 1979, Marubeni has been taking 70 percent of output. In a typical production-sharing joint venture, equity loans for a bauxite project in Australia were provided by the U.S. firm Reynolds (40 percent), the British firm Billiton (30 percent), the Australian company BHP (20 percent) and the Kobe Aluminum Association (10 percent), made up of three Japanese firms. Output, begun in 1983, was to be distributed according to the equity shares.

Development for Import

Buybacks and production-sharing joint ventures are, many times, more sought after by the Westerner than lesser developed countries, especially where the production of minerals is involved. In order to insure a guaranteed supply of a certain raw material or strategic mineral, a Western government will offer low cost loans to finance the countertrade deal. Such arrangements are called develop-for-import or resource diplomacy. In this kind of countertrade, Third World acceptance of Western participation in a mineral project depends on the subsidy element in the loan or credit arrangements. The actual economics of the project is regulated to secondary importance.

Japan, France and Germany are the leading practitioners of develop-for-import deals. Japan is the most successful. Its International Cooperative Agency (ICA) gives grants for offshore processing facilities in which the host government is the participant. When the Japanese government declares a project to be a "national project," it becomes eligible for subsidized loans from the Overseas Economic Development Fund (OEDF). Japan at present has four national projects: petrochemical complexes in Iran and Singapore; the bauxite-aluminum complex at Asahan, Indonesia; and the bauxite-aluminum complex at Belem, Brazil.

Through subsidized loans and credits France has also concluded several buyback agreements. It extends mixed export credits to develop-for-import projects in non-Francophone countries on the condition that part of the resultant production from the purchased French machines is committed to France. In a typical buyback arrangement, France loaned India $425 million in subsidized mixed credits to enable India buy French machinery and equipment. In return, India has committed to France 400,000 tons a year of aluminum plus any aluminum in excess of India's domestic needs.

Japan, France and Germany will subsidize exploration costs by private firms if the resource-rich country agrees to commit part of any discovered resources to them. France will subsidize exploration costs of French firms if they are exploring in New Caledonia or Guyana. Japan will subsidize two-thirds of exploration costs anywhere. Germany will subsidize 50–75 percent of a German firm's exploration costs in any foreign country. Through such programs, Germany has developed ten develop-for-import projects. The largest is the Ok Tedi gold/copper complex in Papau, New Guinea, scheduled to come on stream in the late 1980's. Three projects already delivering output to Germany are a nickel mine in Brazil, a tungsten and titanium processing project in South Africa, and a tungsten mine in Austria.

Construction expertise and production management are other types of technical assistance for which subsidized loans will be made if payment is in resultant product. Japan has made several arrangements of this kind. For managing Zaire's Kinsenda copper mine, for example, Japan receives 80,000 tons per year. And for providing construction expertise to an aluminum refinery in Dubai, Japan receives 8,100 tons of aluminum annually.

How Lesser Developed Countries Encourage Countertrade

If countertrade is defined according to the particular conditions that give rise to it, there emerge three basic kinds of countertrade in the third World. The first is countertrade which is negotiated either between private firms or between a private company and a state company free of government inducements. A Western company enters into these agreements either as a concession to close a deal, as a means to purchase desired products at favorable prices, or to solidify its presence in a lucrative market.

The other kinds of countertrade result from the active role the governments of lesser developed countries take in foreign trade. The latest variant of government-initiated countertrade is "economic cooperative agreements," undertaken on a bilateral basis between governments for a period of roughly 10–15 years. For example, the Canadian government has agreed to provide Mexico with technology for processing petrochemicals, wood products and byproducts, food, coal mining, and oilfield development, as well as equipment for electric power generation and transmission, transportation, telecommunications, and petroleum and gas. In return, the Mexican government will supply oil. Mexico has similar agreements with Spain and Japan. Its economic cooperation agreement with Brazil is a little different, calling for mutual exchange of minerals (oil is not included) and technical aid.

The third kind of countertrade is that which is mandated by foreign exchange regulations and policies. Many lesser developed countries have an import licensing regime that promotes exports through countertrade arrangements. This may involve export and/or investment performance requirements. In these countries, imports that are not considered essential often require special licenses. These licenses may be granted if the importing party generates hard currency earnings covering whole or part of the cost of the imported item. Import and export licensing regimes may be aimed at a particular industry or may be industry-wide (such as Brazil). Several countries like Australia, Korea and Mexico, in order to prevent serious balance of trade and payments problems resulting from increasing domestic demand for passenger automobiles, require that the import of autos and/or auto parts must equal the export of same product. In this manner, they are able to protect their own fledgling auto industries from stiff foreign competition. In Argentina, auto parts exports must be three times the value of auto parts imports, and in Uruguay auto exports must exceed imports by 5 percent. A different approach was taken by Ecuador, which prevented a flood of imported alcoholic beverages and raised the exports of its chief foreign exchange earner by requiring the export of bananas equal in value to the alcohol being imported.

Another way to mandate export performance is to stipulate that an imported machine or assembly line must cover part or all of its costs by selling its output on the export market. This is done, for example, in Turkey. A third way to mandate export performance is to require the export of a portion of production resulting from foreign investment. This is done in almost all lesser developed countries.

Lesser developed countries also try to rectify trade imbalances by attacking the import side of foreign trade. Instead of promoting exports, they reduce imports. In import entitlement regimes, this is achieved by licensing manufacturers in production-for-export sectors to import a specified portion of the value they export. Bangladesh, India and New Zealand all have import entitlement regimes for all or at least some of their manufacturing-for-export sectors.

Countertrade mandates can originate from a variety of

government-related sources in the Third World: trade regulations, banks, investment boards, tax regulations, tax review boards, ministries of finance, ministries of trade, state-owned corporations and state trading firms. Though practices vary from country to country, all lesser developed countries have investment screening boards which frequently mandate countertrade.

These boards often do not explicitly impose export performance criteria on investment proposals. But almost always, in the absence of such explicit criteria, export performance requirements are informally imposed. In a typical scenario, the state bank would approve the investment upon the condition that a certain portion of the output, say, 80 percent, has guaranteed sales. Then a government authority would either informally or formally (the ratio of goods for export to goods sold on the domestic market is usually set between 60:40 and 40:60) require that a certain portion of the guaranteed sales, say, half, be designated for exports. If a company is dealing with a state corporation either to export goods or establish a joint venture, the pressure to countertrade is more likely to be of an informal nature. But that's not always the case. The Pakistani State Trading Firm, for example, handles specified products (20 were listed in 1981) only on a counterpurchase or barter basis.

It makes little difference whether pressure on companies to countertrade is of an informal or formal nature. Depending on a country's economic position, the nature of the products involved in possible countertrade transactions, informal pressure can be more effective than official countertrade mandates. For example, many foreign suppliers selling to the Israeli government comply with that government's requests to buy Israeli products equal to the value they export, in order to maintain their own markets. On the other hand, the Mexican government has had difficulty enforcing its official countertrade quotas.

Some of the more advanced lesser developed countries such as Australia and the industrially advanced Scandinavian countries, have special organizations to administer countertrade. Some governments of developing countries will provide lists of products to satisfy licensing requirements. However, because some of the lists are narrowly proscribed, the prospect of countertrading loses some of its appeal. Companies should inquire whether lists exist and obtain copies before making any commitments to countertrade.

Most lesser developed countries go about formulating specific countertrade obligations and priorities in roughly the same manner as East European countries. Typically, an executive committee from or affiliated with the Ministry of Finance will review the balance of payments and make forecasts for the upcoming year. Targets for exports and imports will be made and priorities assigned to specific imports. These imports will carry different countertrade requirements according to their level of priority. Countertrade requirements will then be transmitted to government bodies and state corporations that supervise or in some capacity are involved in foreign commercial activity.

Policies limiting imports or promoting exports do not necessarily encourage countertrade. For these policies to engender countertrade, it is necessary to link the level of imports with that of exports in order to enhance the state's overall control of the economy. Promoting exports will not prevent a flood of imports and the resulting drain on foreign reserves, for example.

Countertrade Practices in Individual Countries

To give a better idea of the different ways in which specific countries go about formulating countertrade mandates and how these mandates are combined and implemented to obtain the desired mix of countertrade in a country's overall foreign trade, the remainder of the chapter will examine in greater detail countertrade as it is practiced in individual countries. The countries selected provide a look at the wide range of countertrade practices in the Third World.

Nigeria

Nigeria, whose foreign exchange reserves plummeted from $8 billion in July 1981 to $2.7 billion in March 1982, uses all the basic types of countertrade mandates. The government requires that all foreign loans be paid with goods whenever possible, and administers import regulations prohibiting luxury items (alcohol, cigarettes), requiring special licenses or having to meet specific conditions. The authorities may grant special licenses only upon the condition that the importing party produce orders for a proportion of the import value in goods from the industrial sector of the Nigerian purchasing organization, or in other domestic goods. Reciprocal orders may also serve as compliance with special conditions governing the import of certain items. It is also possible, but less likely, that import prohibition may be waived on a particular item if it can be demonstrated that the import will "pay for itself" with countertrade.

Nigerian export subsidies also encourage production sharing. In particular, full reimbursement of import duties is granted for the import of components that are used to produce exports. This provides an added incentive for the creation of production-sharing joint ventures where operating costs would be cut by the foreign partner being compensated with domestic products. The products could then be marketed outside Nigeria for hard currency.

The most direct form of mandating countertrade in Nigeria came in 1978 when the federal government instituted a requirement under which a compulsory "advance deposit" for non-essential imports was established amounting to the value of the import. An exporter to Nigeria would be required to deposit in Nigeria an amount of hard currency equal to that which he expected to receive in payment for his sale. This deposit could only be used to pay for orders of domestic products. Such a regulation constitutes a 100 percent countertrade requirement. This regulation was abolished in 1980, however, when it was decided that other existing fiscal measures were adequate to control imports.

Another important way in which Nigeria's foreign exchange regulations may pressure foreign companies to engage in countertrade is through limits on the repatriation of profits from joint ventures. If a foreign company wishes to invest in a Nigerian joint venture but cannot repatriate all of the return on its equity, the company may choose to take the return in the form of resultant product. Thus, the transaction becomes a production-sharing joint venture.

Apart from the need to limit imports and encourage exports, the need to market oil below OPEC prices may also give rise to barter transactions. Oil barter is often employed by OPEC nations to market oil with high sulfur content or to dispose of oil during times of surplus production. By artificially raising the valuation of the goods it barters for oil, a foreign company may obtain oil at rates more favorable than OPEC standard prices, while obscuring the discrepancy from other cartel nations.

Indonesia

In January 1982, the government of Indonesia announced a policy of linking government procurement of foreign goods to the export of Indonesian products, excluding oil and natural gas. The policy goes far beyond the typical countertrade mandates of other Third World countries, and in terms of its potential to restructure Indonesia's foreign trade, it is also far more ambitious than the countertrade policies pursued in China and the CMEA countries.

Unlike other countertrade mandates, Indonesia aims to affect almost all of its government imports. Exempt are foreign investment in joint ventures with private or state-owned companies and projects or parts of projects and product orders financed by bilateral and multilateral concessional loans. The policy applies to all government construction projects and major government orders for equipment and products.

Under these new arrangements, if a company's bid on a government tender is successful, it must purchase goods with one or more Indonesian exporters to satisfy its export obligations under a Letter of Understanding. The Department of Trade and Cooperatives will periodically draw up a list of export commodities that are eligible for meeting linkage requirements for various countries or group of countries. These lists include the names of the exporters and commodity associations. Firms will be able to select agricultural goods (including rubber, coffee, white pepper, tobacco and manioc) or industrial goods (including cement, timber, plywood, processed woods, and textiles).

Companies are allowed to deduct the cost of goods and services spent in Indonesia in fulfilling a government contract from the amount of Indonesian goods it is under obligation to purchase. Apart from this minor concession, Western suppliers must conduct their countertrade under a number of restrictive guidelines. The following are the most important:

- Goods must be used or resold in the company's country of nationality unless authorization is obtained to sell these goods in a third country. In such a case, the third country must constitute a new market for the export commodity concerned.
- To avoid the purchase of export goods at the very end of the project, companies must take title to imports periodically over the life of a contract, and must complete their obligation prior to the termination date of the procurement contract.
- Although a company may arrange for purchase of goods by another firm, it will have the primary obligation to purchase or arrange for the purchase of such goods.
- Purchase commitments already in effect cannot be credited against counterpurchase obligations. In addition, any future exports to traditional customers of Indonesian products at levels usually attained in the past cannot be counted in fulfillment of counterpurchase obligations.
- If a supplier has not fulfilled his export undertaking upon completion of the procurement contract, it is liable to a penalty of 50 percent of the value of the remaining counterpurchase obligation.

Despite widespread opposition to this policy from hopeful exporters in Indonesia, the government's first attempt in mid-1982 to issue tenders based on countertrade was successful. The resulting $127 million contract to supply fertilizers went to the International Commodities Export Company, the trade brokerage division of ACLI International, Inc., a unit of Donaldson, Lufkin & Jenrette, Inc. Of course, the glut in the world fertilizer market almost certainly rendered foreign suppliers more pliable to Indonesian demands than they probably would have been otherwise, and it remains to be seen whether Indonesia can effectively implement this countertrade policy over the long term.

In recent years, Indonesia has averaged about $4.5 billion annually on imports of construction equipment and other large product orders by the government. According to the Ministry of Trade and Cooperatives, growing protectionism in industrialized countries and the recent decline along with falling prices in non-oil and gas exports, especially agricultural commodities and minerals, necessitated such countertrade measures.

Brazil

Brazil's countertrade policies, though not as potentially far-reaching as Indonesia's, are on the whole much more intricate. In this respect, Brazil serves as a good example of the ways in which Third World countries can disguise countertrade, to the point where in many cases the distinctions between policies that encourage countertrade and policies that promote different but related trade phenomena becomes very blurred indeed.

Brazil is rich in resources but poor in foreign exchange reserves. Its large capital growth requirements have resulted in a soaring foreign debt which reached $80 billion in 1982, second in size only to Mexico among developing countries. Debt service, a major part of Brazil's balance of payments deficit, exceeded $12 billion in 1980.

To combat its fiscal problems, the Brazilian government enacted trade legislation in 1973, and revised it in 1980, which, in effect, engendered the practice of countertrade. An export promotion program, along with provisions offering financial incentives to foreign-owned subsidiaries and joint ventures, was launched in order to alleviate trade deficits and their resultant foreign exchange depletion. The government also passed trade regulations linking its approval for investment proposals to commitments by foreign investors to export, providing it with an opportunity to demand certain performance standards on limiting imports and promoting exports.

The government's BEFIEX (Comissao para Concessao do Beneficios Fiscais a Programas Especiais de Exportasao, Commission on Fiscal Incentives for Special Export Programs) program leads to countertrade, though it is not specifically mentioned in any of the program's provisions. Established in 1972, BEFIEX requires companies that participate in its projects to export $3 worth of goods for every dollar that is imported. Export levels may be averaged over a 3-year period to achieve the 3:1 ratio.

The BEFIEX program, administered by the Industrial Development Council has so far approved 147 projects for a total export commitment of $50.4 billion. The latest agreements, arrived at in April 1982, were for $17 billion. The automobile industry, led by Ford do Brasil, accounted for $10 billion of the sum, upping auto manufacturers' total export commitment to $21 billion. These projects generally cover 10-year periods. There are also 26 additional proposed projects currently under review by BEFIEX.

The BEFIEX program is strictly voluntary. Companies join because of the benefits they receive. Under BEFIEX, they qualify for 70–90 percent reduction of import duties and the Tax on Industrial Products. This is substantially better than the export incentives that operate outside BEFIEX. It is also possible to obtain 100 percent exemption, but this requires presidential action which takes additional time for approval.

Another mechanism the Brazilian government uses to encourage countertrade is the Foreign Trade Department (CACEX) of the Banco do Brasil, which has established ceilings for purchases made by private and public companies. To obtain import licenses, companies in Brazil cannot exceed the value of their previous year's imports, which, when adjusted for inflation, means a lower quantity of imports. In addition, an export contract must accompany each import license application, and the export must equal or exceed the value of the import.

Finally, Brazil offers partial or total reductions of import duties and other taxes on commodities which are processed in Brazil and re-exported (the "drawback" system), and up to 90 percent reduction on import duties and taxes for the import of equipment not made in Brazil and intended for the expansion or reequipment of firms with significant export plans. In enforcing this program, it is possible that the Ministry of Industry and Commerce, like CACEX, exerts pressure on firms to balance imports with exports.

The Brazilian government expected products exported under export incentive programs to account for 12 percent of total 1981 exports and 24 percent of 1981 exports of manufactured goods. However, Brazilian products often do not meet Western standards of quality. While this hurts Brazil's export trade, it has also induced firms from the West to introduce new technology under compensation agreements into Brazil so that resultant products will meet Western specifications.

Since no real reduction in Brazil's foreign debt is expected to occur soon, the government will have to continue to increase exports while keeping imports in check. This means more pressure to countertrade in the foreseeable future, since debt arising from compensation arrangements does not appear in international payment accounts.

Mexico

Mexico's countertrade policies offer some interesting parallels and contrasts to Brazil's. Both countries' motivation to countertrade stems from foreign debt of roughly equal size: $80 billion. Furthermore, both use export incentives and investment performance requirements as part of their countertrade mandates. Unlike Brazil, however, Mexico uses oil to obtain needed technology and development assistance; it has focused much of its countertrade policy on the automobile (or "terminal") industry, and it places no restrictions on imports.

Mexico has also instituted export performance requirements for the electronics and pharmaceuticals industry. For the electronics industry, requirements include increased Mexican content for selected electronic components produced in or imported to Mexico, and higher tariffs for imports of electronic components. For those foreign companies wishing to

acquire equity ownership of enterprises manufacturing selected components, compensation requirements must be met.
They have to buy back or export at least 75 percent of the
output from the facilities in which they have equity.

The experience of foreign-owned automotive companies
in Mexico may serve as a primer to those firms interested in
investing in a country where the pressure to countertrade
looms significant. The Mexican authorities, like many Third
World governments, welcome foreign investment while at the
same time manipulating the business environment, including
the laws governing commercial activity, so that private sector
activity may promote (or at least not come into conflict with)
the national interest. Mandating countertrade is one of several means to accomplish this. Companies in the automotive
sector in Mexico have had to learn the fine art of accomodating government demands while minimizing any damage
to the commercial viability of the firm.

The government first focused its attention on the automobile industry in 1962, when it decreed that by 1964 vehicles
made in Mexico must have 60 percent local content. Production quotas were given to individual manufacturers. They
could be raised by exporting locally-produced parts and finished vehicles.

Since these export incentives were not tied to imports,
they did not strictly constitute countertrade. However, these
automobile companies traditionally imported most of their
equipment and component needs (in 1960, passenger cars had
less than 15 percent local content and trucks 20 percent), so
the implicit intent was to help exports catch up to imports.
It was only a matter of time that the link between imports
and exports would become more apparent in Mexico's trade
policies.

As it happened, it took another decade for Mexico's export
promotion regulations to evolve into an explicit countertrade
mandate. In 1972, the second automotive decree was published. It called for more stringent policies for not meeting
local content requirements and provided fiscal incentives for
exports. By phasing out production quotas at an annual fixed
rate so that by 1979, all production parts imports would have

to be fully compensated by exports, the government introduced countertrade into the automotive industry.

The 1972 decree, however, proved ineffective in light of the deep recession which overtook the industry world-wide in 1974 and 1975. Nonetheless, the Mexican auto industry sidestepped the effects of this recession and thrived during these years. The result was rapid increases of component parts imports while exports, due to the drop in world-wide demand, did not keep pace. A further deterioration of the trade deficit of Mexico's automotive sector thus took place.

The Mexican government was in a bind. Its trade deficit was becoming increasingly intolerable but so was unemployment. Cracking down too hard on imports would shut down vehicle manufacturers and most parts suppliers, while severely curtailing dealership operations. With the auto industry employing more than 130,000 people, the government was thus prevented from taking strong remedial action. Yet it faced a problem that was unlikely to go away without some kind of government intervention.

The Mexican government made its move in 1977 with a new automotive decree. To better regulate foreign exchanges, an exchange quota was authorized for the automobile industry. Export quotas for individual companies would be determined by:

- historical foreign exchange position
- degree of Mexican ownership
- local content

The decree set a timetable for the automobile industry—except the parts industry—to compensate all its exchange requirements, for example, imports, interests, and royalties. By 1982, companies would have to adhere to an annual foreign exchange budget in which imports of materials as well as other payments made abroad would be balanced by exports. If the export commitment is not reached, the firm would be penalized by having to "pay back" a multiple of the shortfall. The decree also includes local content requirements calling for 75 percent local content by 1981 for passenger cars and even higher for trucks. If local manufacturers cannot meet these levels, they must compensate the shortfall by exporting more than the equivalent value of their imports.

To prevent the automotive industry from generating heavy deficits similar to those of 1974-1975, the Mexican government now exercises substantial control over the industry. Through implementation of its auto decree, it has final say on three vital industry operations: 1) the number of units produced (with separate figures for trucks and cars); 2) the foreign exchange that each firm may spend; and 3) the minimum export receipts that must be generated. It also approves investment proposals on the basis of the company's export plans. For example, Ford, GM, and Chrysler are building plants to make more than 1 million auto engines annually in order to be allowed to expand their Mexican assembly plants. Much of the plants' output will be exported to the United States.

Additional regulations to the auto decree, announced in July 1982, have tightened the government's grip on the terminal industry. This latest development grew out of the government's realization that the 1977 decree was not progressing according to schedule. The government calculated that balanced trade in auto components would not be reached before 1985 or 1986, rather than by the projected year of 1982.

The government thus made known its intentions in 1982 that the 1977 decree would from then on be implemented without the flexibility that had made the decree tolerable— even profitable—for the auto firms. For example, the government decided to no longer allow credit toward foreign exchange objectives before they came on stream. Since July 1982, however, the government has taken a somewhat more accommodating position, especially toward its quotas on the mix of cars and trucks to be produced in 1982. But profits are still likely to suffer, and the Mexican auto industry seems headed for troubled times.

The Mexican experience of increasing government intervention to enforce countertrade policies is not necessarily typical for the Third World as a whole, but it is a pattern that is bound to be repeated in an increasing number of developing countries.

Given the slow development of Mexico's indigenous autoparts industry, it was difficult for the large auto manufacturers to avoid large imports. This made the goal of matching exports with imports very difficult to attain. Now a less secure future awaits Mexico's auto industry, and the government, in trying to balance the need to accommodate foreign investors with the objective of balancing its budget, is facing a dilemma where the government stands to lose no matter which way it leans.

Special Countertrade Arrangements

In many instances unique approaches to countertrade have been developed. Service and production-sharing contracts first gained prominence in oil-producing countries. They were developed as in alternative to concessionary contracts as the governments of lesser developed countries rebelled against what they considered inequitable terms reflecting the old colonial order. Host governments were excluded from participating in the ownership, control, and operation of the undertaking. The transnational corporation was usually given exclusive, extensive, and plenary rights to exploit the particular natural resource and was, in effect, assured ownership of that resource at the point of extraction.

There was also no royalty in the modern sense—a fixed percentage of gross proceeds. What passed for royalty was payment for a small percentage of the declared profits of the companies. Nor were there provisions for renegotiating the concessions.

France undertook two early service contracts with Iran (1966) and Iraq (1968). These agreements called for the foreign firm to bear the entire risk capital for exploration and also for production if petroleum was discovered. If commercially exploitable were found, exploration costs would be repaid in crude oil over a 15-year period without interest. Development costs would be repaid with interest over a shorter period.

Operation or risk contracts in Latin America substantially followed the basic structure of Middle Eastern service contracts. For example, in a 1971 deal between Occidental and the Peruvian State Oil Agency, Occidental was responsible for all the risk capital and technical services, in return for which it received 44–50, percent of the hydrocarbons extracted, net of taxes paid to the Peruvian government.

Production-sharing contracts are essentially a variant of service contracts, except that output is shared according to a more complex formula. There are two main models in the Third World (excluding the new China model, discussed in another chapter), and they are briefly described as follows:

Indonesian model. Indonesia's petroleum industry is managed by the national Pertamina. Under "contract of work" agreements, the oil company as operator puts up capital, technology, managerial and marketing expertise. Pertamina receives 25 percent production off the top at cost plus a negotiated amount per barrel, plus 20 percent of the crude at 'export prices,' and 69 percent of the profit.

Indonesia also engages in production-sharing arrangements, which allow Pertamina management control while the companies shoulder exploration and development risks. These costs can be recovered up to 40 percent per year if a commercial discovery is made. After taxes, crude oil rather than profits is split, with Pertamina's share amounting to 85 percent. In addition, equipment becomes Pertamina's property and the companies must lease it.

Algerian model. The government, through the Societe National pour le Transport et la Commercialization des Hydrocarbones (SONATRACH), is the manager of Algeria's oil industry. Foreign companies participate in Algerian oil ventures as "active" or "passive" participants. An active participant owns 49 percent of a joint venture with SONATRACH, which owns the remainder. Algeria's production-sharing contracts allow companies to claim in crude the net from their gross 49 percent of production before taxes, royalties and duties.

In contrast to other developing countries (except for development-for-import arrangements), the initiative for countertrade in oil-producing countries often comes from the country supplying the investment goods. Countertrade is an effective means for such Western countries to acquire oil.

Oil-producing nations such as Iran, Iraq, and Algeria frequently enter barter-like arrangements with a wide variety of countries: the nations of the Organization for Economic Cooperation and Development, the Sino-Soviet Bloc, and lesser developed countries such as India, Brazil and South Korea, in order to pay for development assistance and imports of capital goods and know-how with oil. By one estimate, 75 percent of OPEC enters into countertrade transactions of this kind.

Countertrade with OPEC nations began in 1975/1976 when the Shah of Iran used oil barter, over other OPEC members' objections, to finance development schemes and purchases of military hardware. In general, Western suppliers at the time agreed to take oil as payment in order to win the supply contract.

One of the biggest agreements occurred in 1976 in a triangular arrangement whereby British Aircraft Corporation (BAC) agreed to take up to 20 million barrels of crude per day for eight years. BAC then sold the crude to Shell Petroleum Co. which received two discounts on the deal: one was from the National Iranian Oil Company (NIOC) and the other from BAC in the form of a "management fee." The effective reduction came to about 30 percent per million barrels.

A less visible form of countertrade grew popular in the late 1970's as Iran tried to avoid alienating other OPEC members. This kind of countertrade involved "parallel" deals in which a supplier of equipment gets paid in cash generated by a parallel sale of crude to an oil company, generally of NIOC's choice. The oil is discounted through raising the price of the equipment delivered to Iran.

Today, however, oil is seen as more valuable than supply contracts in Western eyes. Thus oil-producing countries are enticing otherwise reluctant Western companies into big industrial projects by offering oil in parallel deals. This is sometimes called reverse countertrade, and refers to deals in which an OPEC nation imposes a requirement on the foreign party purchasing the oil to sell another scarce commodity unavailable to the OPEC country or to undertake a financial investment in the country.

A recent example of reverse countertrade occurred in Saudi Arabia where several U.S. oil companies invested in refining and related petrochemical plants in exchange for the right to receive additional quantities of crude oil on a long-term contract basis.

Another strong proponent of reverse countertrade is Venezuela. Preference is given to countries which, in addition to paying the dollar price for the oil, agree to supply food (such basics as sugar, beef, milk, grain), goods, and technology "at favorable market prices." Buyers can also enter bilateral arrangements on development of agriculture, housing, urban transport and technology in Venezuela. They may even be asked to find markets for Venezuelan industrial products. In a recent example of reverse countertrade, the French firm Elf-Aquitaine, in return for the oil it imports, signed a contract to build a refinery to process Venezuelan crude. Italian and Japanese firms have entered into similar agreements with Venezuela, providing industrial equipment for crude oil.

In the slack world oil market of 1982, reverse countertrade is once again giving way to regular counterpurchase deals as oil-producing countries seek to increase crude sales without appearing to undercut the OPEC cartel's official prices. Libya and Algeria have been offering to swap discounted oil for European machinery and Japanese trucks. Iran is selling oil in exchange for steel from Japan, and receives ships and services from Greece and Yugoslavia for oil. In addition, Iraq has a German trade company coordinating its purchases from Germany and encouraging German companies to buy more farm products and minerals, as well as oil, from Iraq.

In a somewhat unusual move, Iraq offered oil in a buyback deal which, instead of enhancing its industrialization, contributed to the industrial infrastructure of another country, Greece. The compensation agreement creates a joint venture that establishes an alumina-aluminum smelter utilizing indigenous bauxite, operating on Iraqi fuel oil, and exporting its output of finished aluminum to Iraq.

Turkey

Turkey's experience demonstrates the flexibility of countertrade and the ingenious forms it can take. When Turkey was suffering from a hard-currency famine, countertrade helped it to pay many of its outstanding bills. Though circumstances were special, it proved the usefulness of countertrade as a tool for balance-of-payments crisis management.

At first, the Turkish government frowned upon the possibility of bartering goods, since its trade laws expressly forbade barter by private firms (though bilateral clearing agreements were allowed and practiced in Turkey). Turkey's balance of payments position became so untenable, however, that the government reversed its position and permitted countertrade.

Into the breach stepped two U.S. firms, the American Bureau of Collections (ABC) and the U.S. National Association of Credit Management. They launched the Turam Corporation, which by arrangement with the Turkish government, was supplied with Turkish products to be sold abroad for foreign exchange. Creditors could collect 65–75 percent of the selling price against their claim and the local manufacturer could receive up to 25 percent of the selling price in hard currency and the rest in local currency, if the item was easily marketed. Otherwise, the Turkish firm was completely paid in Turkish Lira.

Turam was supplied with listed items drawn up by the government. Most of the list comprised "non-traditional" Turkish products—products with no established foreign markets—like handicrafts, souvenirs and native artwork, but also included a wide variety of other items such as textiles, synthetic fibers, chemicals, antibiotics, air conditioners, and black-and-white television sets. The Turkish government had the final say on both the types and selling prices of goods exported. Before Turam obtained a product from the list a supplier was already pegged, thus ensuring that Turam would not be stuck with a backlog of unwanted products.

Although the Turkish government didn't recognize it as

such, Turkey had already practiced countertrade before the Turam scheme was implemented. Like most lesser developed countries, it has export performance requirements. Certain machines can only be imported if export orders for 30 percent of their output is already committed.

Export performance criteria may become more stringent as Turkey continues to grapple with severe payments problems that are sure to hinder imports and prolong the recovery of Turkey's troubled economy.

As the general economic difficulties of the lesser developed countries continue to plague the international financial system, it is a certainty that more countries will turn to countertrade for help. Whether it be in the form of export incentives or specific legislation demanding a matching of import and export levels, each nation will determine that method of countertrade which it believes best fits the needs of its economy. And in order to remain competitive in the international market place, companies in the industrialized world will have to be flexible to adequately respond to the divergent needs and demands of their client countries.

Chapter 10
COUNTERTRADE IN EASTERN EUROPE

The nations of Eastern Europe rank as some of the most experienced practitioners of countertrade in the world. As far back as the mid-1960's, they (excluding Albania) used countertrade techniques to finance technology imports. From this early sporadic use, countertrade increased to account for 38 percent of East European trade in 1981, and this figure is sure to climb in the remainder of the decade.[1]

Because compensation offers numerous advantages for the East Europeans, it is the largest and fastest growing form of East-West countertrade. Compensation deals assure East European countries of a steady, relatively long-term market for the goods involved. Because compensation agreements involve the importation of Western technology and the application of Western quality control standards, they also tend to upgrade East European manufacturing standards. In addition, buyback deals are usually self-liquidating. Compensation agreements and other cooperation deals with elements of compensation are tailor-made to cure such East European ills as low product quality and stagnant export trade.

Buyback deals, including joint equity ventures and nonequity joint ventures, now comprise upwards of 50 percent of Eastern Europe's countertrade business and around 7 percent of that region's total exports to OECD members (counterpurchase account for a stable 40 percent of countertrade business).[2] Poland and Romania allow both direct foreign ownership and contractual rights to equity through licensing and technical service agreements. Bulgaria and Hungary permit only contractual rights to equity. From 1969 to 1977 the total value of Eastern Europe's compensation deals was approximately $5.6 billion;[3] the Soviet Union's was $22.4 billion. By

1980, 220 buyback contracts—including 102 in manufacturing, 65 in chemicals, 27 in agricultural products and semifinished products, and 11 in raw materials—generated $3 billion in exports annually. Compensation projects are expected to produce exports of approximately $5 billion by 1985.[4]

Compensation deals have already transformed the chemical trade between Eastern Europe and the West. Western exports of chemical facilities under compensation contracts, particularly for anhydrous ammonia and potash, are the single greatest contributors to Eastern Europe's large compensation business. By the mid-1980's, these plants should generate a net chemical trade surplus with the West, easing Eastern Europe's trade deficits.

Negotiations

Negotiating countertrade contracts with East European Foreign Trade Organizations is often a grueling, protracted affair that can take as long as four years from the initial inquiry to the signing of the contract. Delays in negotiations are, many times, unavoidable because Foreign Trade Organizations, as organs of a vast, centralized government, must receive instructions not only from their own Ministry of Foreign Trade but also from other ministries and government agencies. However, in many cases, negotiations will be deliberately drawn out in order to wear down Western negotiators and exact more favorable terms.

Firms should enter negotiations fully prepared to respond to countertrade demands. East European bargainers sometimes secure hefty countertrade commitments from weaker, more accommodating competitors in order to extract larger countertrade from other companies vying for the same contract. Firms should also be prepared to explain the technical advantages of their product over a competitor's. (For this reason, it is often a good idea to place a technician on the negotiating team.) Western companies can also soften East European countertrade demands with concessions such as 1) extending the East European payment schedule, 2) extending performance guarantees, 3) expanding intra-East European training programs, 4) expanding post-sale support services, 5) guaranteeing fixed prices for spare parts, and 6) providing for delivery of spare parts in the contract.

A Foreign Trade Organization's preference to adhere to a form contract may add to negotiation difficulties. Member countries of the Council for Mutual Economic Assistance (CMEA) all agree to base their contracts on a set of laws called the CMEA General Conditions. These laws govern international trade; negotiators will be reluctant to agree to contracts that deviate from standard General Conditions form.

Import Priorities

It is virtually impossible for a Western firm to determine exactly where a product offered for export falls in the hierachy of East European imports—such information is a key bargaining tool and thus closely guarded by the Foreign Trade Organizations. Nevertheless, an educated guess can be made through familiarity with the role imports play in a planned economy as well as through market information available in the West. To get some idea of specific import priorities and likely hard-currency allocations, Western vendors should carefully scrutinize the FYP, or annual import plan, of the Eastern European country. Imports that lead directly to an improved hard-currency position will usually have the highest purchase priority and the lowest countertrade requirement. These imports usually include plants, equipment and know-how producing either goods previously imported for hard-currency or goods that can be readily exported for hard-currency. In addition, annual import plans indicate with varying degrees of accuracy what goods are associated with those already slated for import and which imports will require subdelivery of Western goods. Upon further investigation, firms may hear of plants that are nearing completion and have been selected to receive Western machinery or technology. These products will probably have low countertrade requirements. Another import generally enjoying high priority is machinery designed to rationalize and modernize production in existing factories. Table 1 summarizes the amount of countertrade initially de-

TABLE 1

Average Countertrade Demands for Products and Deal Types in Eastern Europe *(as of end-1980)*

product and deal classifications	*countertrade percentage*
Compensation deals; non-planned imports; non-essential goods	100–130
Planned imports for domestic sale	75–100
Planned, low priority technical goods	60–80
Equipment producing goods previously imported	30–60
Planned imports; high priority equipment	10–30
Emergency imports; consumer goods for sale in hard-currency shops	0

Source: Business with Eastern Europe

manded for Western exports. The actual percentage of countertrade agreed to may fluctuate greatly from deal to deal, however.

A rising trend in countertrade in Eastern Europe, and particularly in Poland, is to pressure Western suppliers to ship their exports via a third country. This practice grows out of Eastern Europe's preference to balance Western trade on a bilateral basis. If an East European country has incurred a large deficit with a Western nation in a particular year, that CMEA nation will attempt to switch the billing away from the Western country from which it is importing to a third country with which it has fewer debts. East European authorities may insist on procuring a certificate of origin from the billing third nation. This shuffle may be waived if the import is of high priority.[5]

Selecting and Obtaining Countertrade Goods

East European foreign trade organizations usually offer finished industrial goods as counterdelivery. They are apt to resist offering semi-manufactured products, or, even more so, raw materials. Some East European nations such as Czechoslovakia, Poland, Hungary, and the GDR, however, allow firms to purchase such services as transportation as part of countertrade fulfillment.[6] According to Table 2 a capital good is the most likely product to be offered for countertrade. Fuels such as oil, coal, and natural gas, formerly frequent countertrade goods, are now rarely offered because of rising fuel prices and dwindling East European energy supplies.

Regardless of the type of countertrade good it seeks, a Western firm often encounters numerous obstacles including product storages, shipping delays and red tape in obtaining counterpurchase products. East European negotiators place many constraints on the variety of goods available for coun-

---

TABLE 2

Products Offered for Countertrade in Eastern Europe *(as of end-1980)*

product	percentage total countertrade
Engineered capital goods	49
Fuel, oil, natural gas	23
Chemicals	14
Consumer goods	11
Food	3

Source: Business with Eastern Europe

---

terdelivery. One constraint stems from their distaste for linkage. Foreign Trade Organizations officials prefer to export goods from the industrial sector of the primary import or the same Foreign Trade Organization. Western firms should, nevertheless, attempt to secure linkage by obtaining a protocol agreements, Western firms agree to select goods from a list or range of goods from the linked Foreign Trade Organizations.

At the negotiating table, companies may narrow the product choice to as specific a description as possible in order to place a stronger obligation on the East European organization responsible for the availability of the product. Or, the firm may opt for as wide a selection as possible in the hope that this will increase chances of finding a suitable product. Either alternative has its own drawbacks and advantages. However, using a general list does have the distinct, overall advantage of flexibility. If a firm's original countertrade goods prove unacceptable, under a general list the firm has a better opportunity to search for substitute products.

Product lists offered by East European negotiators are neither binding on the East European partner nor very often accurate. In choosing a product heading to define selection, the Western company must be sure it knows which goods the East European country places under a certain heading. For example "general goods" usually includes consumer products, chemicals, and textiles; while "industrial goods" includes finished products from the metal-working sector. Bulgaria, Czechoslavakia, and Poland all use the terms "industrial" and "general goods." The GDR uses the term "metallurgical products," while Romania simply refers to "goods from the machine building sector."

After the contract is signed the Western trader will not always be able to obtain suitable countertrade goods. A product selected by a company with a buyer already set up may mysteriously drop from availability. In another instance the Western partner may have negotiated a contract with a particular product in mind, only to discover that what is actually offered bears little resemblence to the product the partner envisioned. Furthermore, if a Foreign Trade Organization discovers the buyer to whom a Western firm plans to sell countertrade goods, it may remove these goods from availability and sell them to the buyer itself. The ideal solution would be a contractual guarantee requiring the East European nation to make available the goods it promised. Cancellation clauses in such instances of nonavailability are rare, but the Western partner should at the very least obtain specific quantities of shipment and delivery dates.

A popular myth among Western traders has been that in the fourth quarter of the year, East European countries will make available for counterdelivery high quality goods previously reserved for hard-currency export. At one time East European nations did pursue the practice of allowing goods earmarked for cash export to be offered for countertrade if they had not been sold by the last quarter of the year. In this way relatively marketable goods might appear as countertrade offerings in November and December. However, CMEA countries have most recently begun disregarding the calendar year and adopting their export plans to coincide with Western purchasing cycles. East European countries have also been placing more emphasis on meeting FYP's as opposed to annual export plans. By this method export quality goods may be available at the end of an FYP but not a single year. Because of these new developments, predicting when a CMEA country might release unexported goods for countertrade has become little more than guesswork. The fourth quarter is no longer a time of windfall high quality goods.

Product Quality

A firm may locate the kind of product it thinks it can market, only to discover that the quality of the product is far below Western standards. Though some East European countries produce better products than others, all these countries manufacture goods that, with few exceptions, are inferior to their Western counterpart, not only in performance levels, but also with regard to safety standards, appearance, and packaging. In countertrade the problem of product quality is exacerbated since an East European nation's best products are usually not available for countertrade. Such products can be sold for hard-currency by the East European country itself.

Quality varies greatly among the five main product categories offerred for countertrade: mechanically engineered equipment, electronics, chemicals, consumer goods, and raw materials. Chemicals are one of the few commodities manufactured on a standard comparable with Western goods. On the other hand the typically poor quality of consumer goods make them very difficult to sell in the West. Even products manufactured under Western licensing and with Western equipment sometimes fail to measure up to standards because of poorly skilled work forces and different quality control procedures.

Regardless of a product's quality, it may suffer from unfavorable market prejudice simply because it is an East European good. The Western company may prefer to minimize a product's association with Eastern Europe both to avoid customer aversion to purchase and to lessen the East European's position as a potential competing supplier. By the same token, East European suppliers may feel they have much to gain from product identification and may bargain hard for public recognition.

Western traders can try to avoid quality problems by stipulating in the contract that goods must be of a certain standard and/or by securing the right to inspect goods before taking title to them. East European negotiators will generally advocate using the intra-CMEA standards, written in 1969, to govern the quality of countertrade goods. However, these guidelines are not as rigorous as Western standards and tend to cover product features rather than performance. If a product is not covered under these rules, it would then normally fall under the firm's individual standards. Because some East European countries are members of the International Commission on the Rules for Approval of Electrical Equipment, the quality of electrical products is more likely to be on par with those manufactured in the West.

Firms may gain access to more marketable countertrade goods with the emergence of a new trading trend within CMEA. The members of CMEA trade according to rigid, bilateral clearing arrangements. Lately, some East European nations with currency deficits to other CMEA countries have been sending high quality goods to these creditor countries in lieu of cash to pay for imports. Sometimes these goods are pure surplus for the importing Eastern European nation, and in such cases, they are often offered for countertrade.

Pricing

Long negotiations, agency firm commissions, import duties, transaction taxes, audit costs, transportation, and warehousing all add to total final costs. Pricing an East European good is especially difficult because domestic prices in centrally planned economies are arbitrarily fixed by administrative fiat. Even enterprise officials often do not know their real production costs. It is essential that negotiators formulate a precise definition of "net world market price" and state specifically whether transportation and insurance costs are included.

How the countertrade obligation is stated in the contract also affects costs. If the countertrade commitment is calculated as a percentage of the Western export, as opposed to a monetary figure, the Foreign Trade Organization can then compute the price of the Western export by cost-insurance-freight (c.i.f.) East European destination rather than ex-factory (exclusively production costs). This increases the amount of countertrade products a Western firm is obligated to buy because a c.i.f. calculation is usually 2-3 percent higher than the actual value of the Western goods.

Even with the pricing formula set, the actual price of the goods should not be quoted until the last possible moment. This will undermine a favorite East European negotiating tactic; asking for small but accumulating and increasingly costly concessions, often as negotiations are winding down, after securing a price. Since attempting to raise an already agreed upon price will damage a company's reputation in the eyes of the FTO, even prices quoted late in the negotiations should be high enough to absorb further modifications of terms.

Since compensation deals span several years, a price-escalating device must be included in the contract. Ideally, the Western partner would have prices keyed to East European wages or raw material indices. East European governments keep these artificially low. CMEA negotiators are more likely to peg prices to Western indices. Western negotiators may want to stipulate that East European prices cannot exceed, some acceptable percentage of the Western partner's ex-factory costs. If this path is followed, the Western firm must reveal its production costs, which are invariable much higher than East European costs. A more acceptable solution to Western suppliers, though less so to East European countries, is to tie prices to the amount the firm charges to its distributors. One very simple method of computing price is to keep the price a given percentage below what the Western firm's strongest competitors are charging its customers.

Like any kind of commercial transaction, countertrade deals sometimes go unfulfilled after a contract has been signed. In countertrade, penalty clauses covering non-performance very rarely apply to the East European partner. Instead, almost all penalties pertain to a Western firm's nonfulfillment of its countertrade obligations. Foreign Trade Organizations will generally try to impose penalties of around 5-15 percent of the deal's worth, but some have gone as high as 100 percent. When a penalty is not too prohibitive, a Western firm is often tempted to ignore the countertrade agreement and pay the penalty. While this ploy may save the company some money, the damage it inflicts upon the reputation of the firm will affect any future dealings with that East European country.

On occasion, a firm may be able to fulfill only part of its countertrade commitment. To provide for such a development, firms should stipulate that the penalty will be reconciled to the amount of obligation already met. Most East European countries will demand penalty payment immediately; however, companies should secure at least a thirty day grace period and the right of release upon presentation of papers issued by East European officials documenting damage, defects, or unavailability.

The complexities of countertrade arrangements lend themselves to misunderstandings and disputes. Should a disagreement arise that cannot be solved by mutual discussion, the countertrade contract should provide for third party arbitration. East European Foreign Trade Organizations prefer Switzerland, Sweden, or Austria as an arbitrating country. They are neutrals with a written arbitration code.

Negative Files

"Negative files" (documents describing the unsuccessful efforts of a Western company to obtain countertrade goods) may sway an East European Foreign Trade Organization into granting an extension of the countertrade fulfillment schedule. Requests for such extensions should be made no later than eight weeks before the date the counterpurchases are due to be completed. Companies should find most Foreign Trade Organizations sympathetic provided they are convinced of an earnest attempt by the Western partner to locate countertrade goods.

Letter of Release

After all countertrade obligations are fulfilled, a countertrade contract is still not complete until the Western interests obtain a letter of release—the East European acknowledgment of Western fulfillment of the countertrade agreement. The East European Foreign Trade Organization may be reluctant to turn over this proof. Rather than rely on requests at this time to receive the document, Westerners should state in the contract that the letter of release must be presented against release of their letter of credit payment for the countertrade goods.

Future-Buying

A firm may use countertrade to gain a foothold in an East European market by future-buying. This involves purchasing counterdelivered goods before exporting products to Eastern Europe. Firms that have a stake in long term relations with Eastern Europe are most attracted to this approach.

Future-buying is most feasible when the Western firm secures linkage with all Foreign Trade Organizations in the country. The East European partner will probably agree to linkage with the proviso that products already marketed in the West cannot serve as counter-delivered goods. If a firm can find suitable countertrade goods and profitably dispose of them, then it can develop a long term relationship more conducive to a stable supply of high quality products.

Bulgaria

Though Bulgaria has severe hard-currency problems, it is the least active countertrader in Eastern Europe. It is also one of the most difficult countries with which to conduct countertrade.

Bulgaria boasts a total trade surplus despite its predominantly agricultural economy. According to Table 3, in 1982 the Bulgarian total trade surplus was $630 million. But Bulgaria's thirst for modern, high quality industrial equipment to mechanize its economy produced a trade deficit with the West amounting to $763 million in 1980. Its total net hard currency debt in 1980 was approximately $2.7 billion and in 1981, approximately $2.1 billion (see Table 4).[7]

TABLE 3

Bulgaria: Trade With the West and Lesser Developed Countries[1]

(in millions of dollars)

	1975	1978	1979	1980	1981	1982
Imports	937	1548	2335	3021	3198	2570
Exports	1498	1400	1621	2035	2547	3200
Balance	+561	−148	−714	−986	−651	+630

[1]Export and import data are F.O.B. Data do not include intra-CMEA hard currency.

Source: U.S. Government

TABLE 4

Bulgaria: Gross and Net Hard-currency Debt
(millions of dollars)

	1975	1976	1977	1978	1979	1980	1981	1982
Gross	2640	3198	3707	4263	4415	3510	2795	2850
Net	2257	2756	3169	3710	3700	2730	2135	1980

Source: U.S. Government

The Bulgarians are tenacious negotiators. They routinely make demands for 100 percent countertrade while offering countertrade goods with low marketability. They are not totally uncomprising, however. Sometimes they permit transportation costs to be counted as part of the countertrade fulfillment. Tables 5 and 6 show that Bulgaria has demanded and received high countertrade obligations. The average countertrade obligation for low priority imports grew from 40-50 percent in 1976 to 50-70 percent in 1979.[8] These years saw a relatively small number of countertrades, however. As Bulgaria increases its countertrade and carries out its plans to

TABLE 5

Countertrade Demands for Selected Products in Bulgaria (1980)

products	demands, percent
Machinery and vehicles	50–70
Chemicals	25–40
Consumer goods	60–80

Source: Business with Eastern Europe

TABLE 6

Countertrade Required by Selected Foreign Trade Organizations and Products in Bulgaria (1979)

FTO or product	requirement (percent)
Neftochim and Industrial Import (general goods)	10–30
Machinoexport and Technoimport (industrial goods)	20–40
Consumer goods	80–100

Source: OECD

concentrate on buy-back deals, statistics will be more indicative of developing trends. While the rest of Eastern Europe plans to concentrate hard-currency on equipment to modernize and sustain existing industrial installations, Bulgaria is still in a stage of economic expansion. Worldwide high energy prices will certainly cut into Bulgaria's plans for growth. Nevertheless, the 1981-1985 Five Year Plan should see substantial hard-currency investment in high-technology electronics equipment and know-how for the chemical and food packaging industries. Other high priority items should be coal and copper mining machinery and petrochemical and plastics technology and equipment.

Because suitable goods are so difficult to find in Bulgaria, countertrade deals may last two to three years. Delays are sometimes aggravated by Bulgaria's method of scheduling counterdeliveries. To ease the burden of a large countertrade deal on its industry, Bulgaria prefers to have purchases fulfilled in percentage increments over a period of time. Because Bulgarian goods are generally of low quality and sell badly in the West, Western partners have had to use high discounts, as shown in Table 7.

As of 1980, Bulgaria managed to press Western firms into pledging 15-25 percent of import value in machinery and ve-

TABLE 7

Discounts by Selected Products in Bulgaria (1980)

product	discount (percent)
Machinery	35
Chemical products	20
Consumer goods	15
Electrical goods and electronic equipment	30

Source: Business with Eastern Europe

hicle deals. Like Romania, Bulgaria demands unconditional penalty guarantees from foreign banks payable on first request. It will not accept a parent company's guarantee for one of its subsidiaries.

Bulgaria has no one Foreign Trade Organization specializing in countertrade with the West. Each organization conducts countertrade under the supervision of its parent ministry. The Ministry of Foreign Trade approves all import and countertrade contracts and issues subsequent import and export licenses. However, the Ministry of Foreign Trade has a special division called the Department for Cooperation. This office should be approached for discussion of long-term cooperation or buy-back deals.

Bulgaria passed Decree 535 in March 1980 to push cooperation agreements. Because of its favorable stance toward profit repatriation and equity ownership, it is one of the most liberal in Eastern Europe. This law includes time limits on titles to machinery and stipulates Bulgarian personnel quotas, but it also allows profit repatriation after taxes, joint equity ownership in Bulgaria for the first time, and Bulgarian-Western cooperation in third countries. Few firms have so far taken advantage of this new opportunity. However, Decree

TABLE 8

Products Offered for Countertrade in Bulgaria (1980)

product	proportion of total countertrade[1] (percent)
Machinery and vehicles	50–70
Chemicals	25–40
Consumer goods	60–80

[1]No import over $1 million regardless of its priority is immune to countertrade demands.

Source: Business with Eastern Europe

535 is typical of recent East European legislation designed to legally facilitate a region-wide push for cooperation deals.

Czechoslovakia

Czechoslovakia ranks with Hungary and the German Democratic Republic as one of Eastern Europe's most successful exporters. With its industry running mostly on imported fuel, however, Czechoslovakia is vulnerable to future deficit problems. To protect its favorable hard currency position against possible instability in the world-wide energy market, Czechoslovakia is demanding countertrade on all items except hard-currency producing imports and energy technology imports.

In 1980, Czechoslovakia achieved a $24 million trade surplus with the West. Table 9 shows that Czechoslovakia, after incurring trade deficits with the West and lesser developed countries during the years 1975-1979, was able to rectify its trade balance in 1980 and 1981. Among East European states, it had the third highest trade surplus in 1981, after Bulgaria and Romania. However, Czechoslovakia's hard currency debt has grown steadily from 1975 to 1981, and, according to Table 10, reached approximately $3.8 billion by 1981. This is still the lowest debt in Eastern Europe after Bulgaria.[9]

TABLE 9

Czechoslovakia: Trade with the West and LDC's[1]
(millions of dollars)

	1975	1978	1979	1980	1981	1982
Exports	2,379	3,122	3,734	4,544	4,708	4,090
Imports	2,745	3,503	4,117	4,520	4,361	3,610
Balance	−366	−381	−383	+24	+347	+480

[1]Export and import data are F.O.B. Data do not include intra-CMEA hard-currency.

Source: U.S. Government

Because there is more hard currency available to Foreign Trade Organizations in Czechslovakia, its countertrade demands, except for consumer goods, are usually the lowest in Eastern Europe. Nevertheless, as in all of these countries, demands in Czechoslovakia have grown since 1976 when they averaged 30-40 percent. Table 11 show that countertrade requests are only above 50 percent for consumer goods, and Table 12 shows that final agreed-upon percentages range from 10-50 percent. Foreign Trade Organization officials will press hard for countertrade on most deals, occasionally allowing Western firms to establish evidence accounts.

TABLE 10

Czechoslovakia: Gross and Net Hard-currency Debt
(millions of dollars)

	1975	1976	1977	1978	1979	1980	1981	1982
Gross	1,132	1,862	2,616	3,206	4,099	4,890	4,620	3,970
Net	827	1,434	2,121	2,513	3,070	3,640	3,755	3,200

Source: U.S. Government

TABLE 11

Countertrade Demands for Selected Products in Czechoslovakia (1980)

products	demands, percent
Machinery and vehicles	25–45
Chemicals	20–40
Consumer goods	70–100

Source: Business with Eastern Europe

Czechoslovak planners consider modernization essential because insufficient innovation and slow response to Western market conditions threaten to undermine their valued export program. Western traders can expect Czechoslovakia's 1981-1985 Five-Year Plan to give the highest capital investment and thus lowest countertrade requirements to those imports

TABLE 12

Countertrade Required by Selected Foreign Trade Organizations and Products in Czechoslovakia (1979)

Foreign Trade Organization or product	requirement, percent
General average for engineered goods	30–40
Kovo (precision engineered products)	10–25
Strojexport (all types of machinery)	10–20
Strojimport (tools)	20–30
Prajoinvest (engines, compressors, heavy machinery)	50

Source: OECD

that will help its energy situation or help modernize and complete various industrial installations. These imports include high technology energy equipment, mining equipment, and machinery for food packaging.[10]

Thus far, the lack of modernized industrial facilities that seems particularly to worry Czechoslovak planners has not yet seriously impaired Czechslovakia's reputation for producing high quality countertrade export goods. Czechslovakia produces some of the best machinery and heavy equipment, chemicals, food products, and technical components in Eastern Europe. According to Table 13, Czechslovak Foreign Trade Organizations prefer to offer machinery and other products makes it easier to obtain suitable countertrade goods than in all other East European countries except East Germany.

Czechoslovakia's discount rates, the lowest in Eastern Europe, attest to the quality of the goods. Only technical components require substantial subsidy, according to Table 14. Discount rates are in danger of rising, however, if Czechoslovakia does not maintain product quality with more research and development.

Czechoslovak negotiators demand low penalty pledges. The two most important groups of countertrade goods, ma-

---

TABLE 13

Products Offered for Countertrade in Czechoslovakia (1980)

product	proportion of total countertrade percent
Machinery and vehicles	50
Chemical products	20
Consumer goods	20
Electronic and electrical equipment	10

Source: Business with Eastern Europe

TABLE 14

Discounts by Selected Products in
Czechoslovakia (1980)

product	discount, percent
General goods	8–12
Technical equipment and components (from Strojimport)	11–30
Machinery (from Strojexport)	7–11

Source: Business with Eastern Europe

---

chinery and vehicles, and chemicals, require 6-12 percent of the import's total worth as penalty. Foreign Trade Organizaitons will usually allow a deal to be extended by two years, but will impose penalties if a firm needs more time to fulfill its part of the deal.[11] Given the marketability of Czechslovak goods, this should not be considered a serious disadvantage.

There are two special organizations in Czechoslovakia which facilitate linkage and carry out countertrade. Transacta is one. It is not involved in purchase and sales, nor does it have its own trade budget, but it does put Western countertraders in contact with sellers usually inaccessible to foreign traders. Transacta essentially offers goods from Czechoslovak firms or cooperatives not licensed to do foreign trade. It also has access to goods Czechoslovakia obtains through bilateral clearing arrangements. Western firms that have difficulty locating suitable goods within the importing Foreign Trade Organization may turn to Transacta for help. The second organization, Fincom, is in charge of joint venture operations which ensure necessary imports of raw materials and open new markets. These joint ventures may or may not include countertrade. Fincom, in addition, handles the import of all foreign technology that involves countertrade, including turnkey projects licensing and know-how.

German Democratic Republic

Though the German Democratic Republic is considered to have one of the more efficient and sophisticated economies in Eastern Europe, it still suffers from the same balance of trade problems that characterize East-West trade in general.

As the most industrialized and technologically-advanced nation in Eastern Europe, the German Democratic Republic has developed expensive needs for highly technical equipment that only the West can provide. From its trade with the West, which is 30 percent of its total foreign trade,[12] East Germany accumulated a debt of $529 million in 1980.[13] According to Table 15, the German Democratic Republic's total non-CMEA trade deficit in 1981 was $1.4 billion. Such annual trade deficits added up to a hard-currency debt of $15.3 billion by 1981, as shown in Table 16. Like other East European countries, East Germany is expected to place increasing emphasis on countertrade to ease its chronic trade problem.

To cope with its hard-currency debt (the third highest in East Europe, after Poland and Yugoslavia), the German Democratic Republic makes some of the highest initial countertrade demands in Eastern Europe. East German Foreign

---

TABLE 15

German Democratic Republic: Trade with the West and LDC's[1]

(millions of dollars)

	1975	1978	1979	1980	1981	1982
Exports	3,062	4,158	4,541	5,898	6,100	7,870
Imports	4,189	5,295	6,566	7,620	7,500	6,370
Balance	−1,125	−1,137	−2,025	−1,722	−1,400	+1,500

[1]Export and import data are F.O.B. Data do not include intra-CMEA hard-currency.

Source: U.S. Government

TABLE 16

German Democratic Republic: Gross and Net Hard-currency Debt

(millions of dollars)

	1975	*1976*	*1977*	*1978*	*1979*	*1980*	*1981*	*1982*
Gross	5,188	5,856	7,145	8,894	10,912	14,410	15,300	13,400
Net	3,548	5,047	6,159	7,548	8,950	11,750	12,640	11,430

Source: U.S. Government

Trade Organizations tend to be unyielding in negotiations and will resist lowering the initial countertrade percentage while accepting few modifications to their semi-standard contract. The German Democratic Republic has indeed been successful in attaining high countertrade commitments, according to Table 17. Though the general average commitment in 1979, between 20 and 50 percent, which was only a bit higher than

TABLE 17

Countertrade Required by Selected Foreign Trade Organizations and Products in German Democratic Republic (1979)

FTO or product	*requirement percent*
General average	20–50
Unscheduled imports	80–100
Industreanlagen-Import (main buyback organ)	100–130
Unitechna, Technocommerz W.M.W. export-import (metal and industrial products)	50

Source: OECD

TABLE 18

Countertrade Demands for
Selected Products in German
Democratic Republic (1980)

products	demands, percent
Machinery and vehicles	80–100
Chemicals	20–40
Consumer goods	80–100

Source: Business with Eastern Europe

the 1976 average of 20-40 percent, Table 18 shows East German countertrade demands are on the rise.[14] Since 1977 East Germany has been exerting more pressure for compensation agreements than counterpurchases, and compensation deals traditionally receive a higher countertrade obligation than other forms of countertrade.

Western suppliers can expect the highest priority hard-currency allocations to go to high technology imports and hardware that will contribute to industrialization. These imports include machinery and transportation equipment, with particular emphasis on automation equipment, computers, and industrial robots. The German Democratic Republic also plans to step up its purchases of turnkey plants bought under compensation arrangements, regarding such transactions as an effective way both to import Western products and technology and increase hard-currency revenues.

The usually high quality of German Democratic Republic goods removes one of the typical drawbacks of East European countertrade. Ironically, however, the efficiency with which East Germany operates its industry has made availability of countertrade products a difficult problem. The various industrial sectors operate under strict quotas and targets that limit production to the amount needed for domestic consumption and export to the rest of CMEA. There is thus little surplus from which Western traders can select goods to fulfill counterpurchase obligations. Western partners may find goods available only at certain times of the year or sometimes after a delay of several years. Furthermore, East Germany prefers to ship goods in scheduled increments, thereby gaining more time to meet its counterdeliveries. East Germany's best countertrade products came from the metal-working, chemical, machine, heavy equipment, electronic, and consumer sectors. Table 19 shows how frequently the German Democratic Republic offers various products for countertrade.

Low discount rates are required for East German goods, as shown in Table 20. Unlike other East European countries, consumer products from the German Democratic Republic are considered high quality merchandise and do not merit large discounts.

Given the high quality of German goods, Westerners have rarely withdrawn from countertrade obligations because of reluctance to buy German Democratic Republic goods. Therefore, penalties are not as important an issue in East Germany as in other East European countries. The German Democratic

---

TABLE 19

Products Offered for Countertrade in German Democratic Republic (1980)

products	proportion of total countertrade percent
Machinery and vehicles	35
Chemical products	25
Consumer goods	15
Chemicals and electronic equipment	25

Source: Business with Eastern Europe

TABLE 20

Discounts by Selected Products in German Democratic Republic (1980)

product	discount percent
General goods (textiles and goods)	8–14
Industrial, engineered goods	12–16
Industrial, metal-working sector	7–10

Source: Business with Eastern Europe

Republic extracts rather low penalty pledges, usually between 7 and 10 percent the import's value in deals involving both machinery and vehicles and chemicals. Like Bulgaria and Romania, the German Democratic Republic demands unconditional penalty guarantees payable on first request.

An organizational shakeup of the German Democratic Republic's economic system has made 90 percent of FTE's (Foreign Trade Enterprises) into divisions of the industrial sectors they serve. One objective was to allow Foreign Trade Enterprises to work more closely with the actual production facilities in order to facilitate foreign trade and countertrade. As a result of this reorganization, German Foreign Trade Enterprises have been relatively cooperative in countertrade, especially in offering products and product linkage.

Many Foreign Trade Enterprises now trade on their own account. These divisions, less bound to rigid export/import quotas, enjoy greater flexibility in making trade decisions. They still must keep their hard-currency in line with national targets, however, and, above all, show a profit for any independent trading. Linkage is a relatively simple matter among Foreign Trade Enterprises, but should be agreed upon outside the written contract. Mentioning it in the contract may call it to the attention of higher authorities and thus jeopardize it.

Three East German Foreign Trade Enterprises may help Western firms carry out countertrade. Industreanlagen-Import arranges joint cooperation projects, particularly those involving the building of turnkey plants. It usually requires 100-130 percent compensation. Zentral Kommerz Gmbh is a trading house that imports on behalf of itself and other German Democratic Republic enterprises. Zentral Kommerz can also help foreign firms locate suitable goods throughout the country. Another trading company, Intrac, specializes in the trade of non-ferrous metals and acts as a profit center for barter-switch operations.

Romania

While countertrade has been a *de facto* requirement in East European trade for over a decade, Romania's recent legislation illustrates the evolution of countertrade toward an institutionalized form of commerce. By passing Law Number 12 in 1980, Romania became the first East European nation to make countertrade a lawful requirement of trade. Law Number 12 states that countertrade must be used to reach a favorable balance in international trade. This is accomplished by tying individual Foreign Trade Organizations' countertrade requirements to its import level and currency availability.

Romania is now trying to revitalize its hard currency earning power to reduce its trade deficit with the West. In the past, Romania relied heavily on Western exports. In 1980 alone Romania was $500 million in the red to the West.[15] Although Romania's aggregate trade balance with the West and LDC's during 1975-1981 (Table 21) shows the vast improvement Romania made in 1981, it is still deeply in debt to the West. Table 22 shows that Romania's net hard-currency debt more than doubled during 1978-1981 and now stands at approximately $10.4 billion. This increase has prompted Romania to institute an austere Five Year Plan for 1980-1985. Romanian planners are counting on the Five Year Plan to develop more competitive exports and reduce imports such as raw materials and energy.

TABLE 21

Romania: Trade with the West and LDC's[1]
(millions of dollars)

	1975	1978	1979	1980	1981	1982
Exports	2,884	4,094	5,522	6,413	7,724	6,240
Imports	3,017	5,020	6,623	7,914	7,173	4,710
Balance	−133	−926	−1,101	−1,501	+551	+1,530

[1]Export and import data are F.O.B. Data do not include intra-CMEA hard-currency.

Source: U.S. Government

The Romanians, along with the Bulgarians, have earned a reputation as the most hardnosed and shrewdest bargainers with the West in countertrade negotiations. Starting with a mandatory 100 percent countertrade demand, Romanian Foreign Trade Organizations will not bargain down as low as most other East European nations. A favorite ploy of Romanian negotiators is to make countertrade demands as the Westerner, having already quoted a price too low to absorb countertrade costs. Tables 23 and 24 indicate the amount of countertrade demanded and required for selected groups of imported goods. Requirements noticeably increased from 30-40 percent general average in 1976 to 50-70 percent in 1979.[16]

TABLE 22

Romania: Gross and Net Hard-currency Debt
(millions of dollars)

	1975	1976	1977	1978	1979	1980	1981	1982
Gross	2,924	2,903	3,605	5,221	7,009	9,500	10,700	9,770
Net	2,449	2,528	3,388	4,992	6,700	9,180	10,350	9,460

Source: U.S. Government

TABLE 23

Countertrade Demands for Selected Products in Romania (1980)

products	demands percent[1]
Machinery and vehicles	70–100
Chemicals	40–70
Consumer goods	60–80

[1]Compensation deals may require 10–20 percent less countertrade because of special inter-bank financing.

Source: Business with Eastern Europe

TABLE 24

Countertrade Required by Selected Foreign Trade Organizations and Products in Romania (1979)

Foreign Trade Organizations or product	requirement percent
General average	50–70
Machinoexport and Electronum (engineered goods)	50
Chemical producing machinery	35–50
Chemicals	25–40
Light industrial goods	30–50

Source: OECD

The 1981-1985 Five Year Plan places highest import priority on the machine building sector, energy, chemicals, and metallurgical processing. Such high priority usually means that hard-currency has been allocated to these sectors to purchase needed equipment and technology. For those products most in demand, countertrade may not even be necessary, and in those cases where it is, there's a good chance that countertrade demands will be lower than those listed in Table 25.

Romania's reputation as a difficult countertrader does not rest only on its high countertrade requirements. Its products are generally of poor quality and are over-priced; spare parts are not readily available for technical products on even the better lists often they are not available; and negotiated prices do not include after-sales service.

Delays caused by problems of availability and delivery can wreak havoc with a company's operational and marketing timetable. They stretch out even simple counterpurchase agreements to over 2-3 years. Furthermore, Romania insists on having the Western partner fulfill its obligation in scheduled percentage increments.

High Western sales discounts of countertrade goods may undermine the profitability of Romanian countertrade unless

---

TABLE 25

Products Offered for Countertrade (1980)

product	proportion of total countertrade percent
Machinery and vehicles	15
Chemical products	15
Consumer goods	15
Electronic and electrical equipment	15

Source: Business with Eastern Europe

a firm absorbs such discounts by raising the price of its exports. Table 26 shows the high subsidies required in 1978 and 1980.

If a Western firm has difficulty fulfilling its countertrade commitment, it will not find its Romanian partner very sympathetic. For example, the Ministry of Chemical Industry will grant a contract extension only if part of the agreement has already been met. The Foreign Trade Organization Masinimportexport will demand higher countertrade or other concessions before granting an extension. If extensions fail to provide Western companies with enough time to fulfill their obligations, the Romanians will demand an unconditional penalty guarantee issued by a foreign trade bank and payable on first request. In deals involving machinery and vehicles, the Romanians have demanded penalties of 20-30 percent of the imported product's worth. In deals involving chemicals, Romania has demanded 10-15 percent penalties.

TABLE 26

Discounts by Selected Products in Romania (1980)

product	discount percent[1]
Machinery	18–26
Electrical equipment	14–20
Furniture and wood products	12–22
Consumer goods	15–22
Chemicals	10–14
Electrical and engineered products	16–19

[1]Goods from the Ministry of Machine Building usually require very high discounts. (Wolff addendum A)

Source: Business with Eastern Europe (Wolff addendum B)

Several Romanian government agencies actively work with Western firms in implementing countertrade. The Planning Department, a special section of the Ministry of Foreign Trade and International Cooperation, has a separate office to coordinate counterpurchases by linking various Foreign Trade Organizations throughout the country. Tera is a government-run trading house. Its functions include: importing goods for sale to third countries with only discretionary countertrade demands; locating, for a commission, suitable countertrade goods; and working with Western trading houses on switch operations.

Delta is another government trading house whose duties parallel those of Tera and additionally include the export of licenses and knowhow plus engineer consulting.

Mercur, a Foreign Trade Organization under the Ministry of the Interior, barters Romanian consumer goods for foreign consumer goods. It also imports goods with low countertrade requirements for domestic consumption or sale in hard-currency shops.

Another Foreign Trade Organization, Ileseim, acts as a clearing house for countertrade goods from light industrial sectors such as consumer goods, furniture, ceramics, glass, clothing, and small tools.

Should a Western firm reject the services of Romanian countertrade organizations and dispose of countertrade goods on its own, the Romanian will attempt to impose certain restrictions. They will most likely try to protect their own markets by placing limitations on where goods are to be sold. They might also insist that any third parties be located in the seller's nation or at least in the West.

Hungary

Hungary's brand of countertrade is very different from that of other East European countries. One unique practice is its clear-cut distinction between planned and non-planned imports: The National Bank of Hungary gives hard-currency funding to planned imports, and these goods require no countertrade. Unplanned imports, however, are supposed to be self-financing. Since 1979 these products have been subject to stiff 100 percent or more countertrade demands.

This apparent inflexibility does not, however, create the hardship it may appear to. For 15 years, the Hungarians have been reorganizing the decentralizing of their economy. The latest phase, instituted in 1978, is not unlike the recent G.D.R. shakeup. It is further divided up the huge industrial ministries into smaller sectors. In lessening the power of the Foreign Trade Organizations, it has given more trade authority to the producing enterprises themselves. These enterprises, because they are closer to actual production, are able to lobby with the central government to obtain more hard-currency funding and less countertrade requirement for imports they deem essential but are non-planned. They also have hard-currency funds to trade on their own account. This means that if a firm can convince the Foreign Trade Organizations or enterprise negotiators that an unplanned import is essential to current production or future plans or that an unplanned import can help earn hard-currency, the Western company can sidestep or mitigate Hungary's 100 per cent countertrade demands.

Another unique feature of Hungarian countertrade is Hungary's responsiveness to Western firms' countertrade problems. In 1977 Hungary's Department for Exchange, Financial and Price Matters issued a five-point policy to govern Hungary-West countertrade. It resolved to give Western firms only goods they can use or dispose, reaffirmed Hungary's preference for compensation deals, and urged Western firms to lodge countertrade complaints with the Ministry of Foreign Trade. While the five points constitute national policy for all foreign traders, in practice they serve only as a framework for goodwill and have yielded limited tangible results.

If Hungary's commitment to 100 percent or more countertrade agreements decreases the number of firms willing to engage in countertrade, it will be in line with Hungary's recent economic policy of slowdown and entrenchment. Excessive and misguided expenditure, particularly in 1978, together with the worldwide energy problem, has prompted a switch of emphasis from sheer economic growth to modernizing in-

TABLE 27

Hungary: Gross and Net Hard-currency Debt
(million of dollars)

	1975	1976	1977	1978	1979	1980	1981	1982
Gross	3,135	4,049	5,655	7,473	8,529	8,810	8,800	7,800
Net	2,195	2,852	4,491	6,532	7,300	7,510	7,900	7,050

Source: U.S. Government

dustry, improving hard-currency status, and reconciling domestic needs to national capacity.

Hungary's agricultural economy, energy dependency, and raw material poverty added up to large import bills in past years. In 1980 Hungary's trade with the West resulted in a deficit of $475 million.[17] According to Table 27, Hungary's hard-currency debt is relatively small (third smallest after Bulgaria and Czechoslovakia in Eastern Europe), but Table 28 shows Hungary to have a large overall trade deficit. It is second after Yugoslavia. Tables 27 and 28 do indicate, how-

TABLE 28

Hungary: Trade with the West and LDC's[1]
(millions of dollars)

	1975	1978	1979	1980	1981	1982
Exports	1,691	2,535	3,359	3,888	3,650	3,750
Imports	2,464	3,920	4,012	4,567	4,439	4,100
Balance	−773	−1,385	−653	−679	−789	−350

[1]Export and import data are F.O.B. Data do not include intra-CMEA hard-currency.

Source: U.S. Government

ever, Hungary's success in the last three years in slowing imports and debt growth.

Before Hungary embarked on its "planned/not planned" system, its countertrade rates were generally the lowest in Eastern Europe (see Tables 29 and 30). As Hungary's push for 100 percent or more countertrade with additional compensation arrangements gains impetus, countertrade should correspondingly rise. In Hungary's favor, though, is its inclusion of road transportation costs in countertrade fulfillment and an occasional willingness to accept evidence accounts.

As with all the East European nations, Hungary is expected to place high priority and no countertrade requirements on imports that contribute to economic problem solving and profitability. About five percent of the 1981-1985 FYP investment will go toward energy development, the acquisition of energy efficient machinery and processes, and toward mining and oil-to-coal conversion equipment. Items that facilitate industrial modernization such as tools and machine parts should also merit low countertrade. Since processed food is one of Hungary's large scale hard-currency exports, mechanized food packaging equipment will undoubtedly be placed high on the priority list.

TABLE 29

Countertrade Demands for Selected Products in Hungary (1980)

products	demands percent
Machinery and vehicles	10–30
Chemicals	10–30
Consumer goods	25–50

Source: Business with Eastern Europe

TABLE 30

Countertrade Required by Selected Foreign Trade Organizations and Products in Hungary (1979)

Foreign Trade Organization or product	requirement percent
Nikex, Techoimpex, Transelektra (industrial products)	15–30
Ferunion (general goods)	15–30
Low priority	60
Unscheduled	100

Source: OECD

TABLE 31

Products Offered for Countertrade in Hungary (1980)

product	proportion of total countertrade percent
Machinery and vehicles	45
Consumer products	25
Chemical products	15
Electrical and electronic equipment	15

Source: Business with Eastern Europe

Among countertrade products, heavy equipment, electronics, and chemicals are Hungary's highest quality offerings. According to Table 31, these goods make up 75 percent of the products Hungary has historically offered for countertrade.[18]

Hungary prefers to carry out counterpurchase deals within a six-to-twelve month period unless Western deliveries are on an extended schedule. Like Poland, it often allows preshipment quality inspection.

Sometimes Western traders may find high quality and very marketable goods from other CMEA countries offered as countertrade within Hungary. This is because Hungary's sales to CMEA partners have exceeded purchases in the past. Consequently, CMEA countries are pressuring Hungary to purchase such goods as raw material, metals, fuels, food and high-quality machinery in order to help ease their own trade deficits with Hungary. These goods, often exceeding Hungary's domestic needs, are thus offered to Western sellers as countertrade.

Though trading house rebates are increasing for Hun-

TABLE 32

Discounts by Selected Products in Hungary (1980)

product	discount percent
Non-engineered products	11–13
Technical products	7–10
Containers	10+2
Engineered products from Nikex, Techoimpex, Transelektra, Vidiotron	10–21

Source: Business with Eastern Europe (Wolff, addendum B)

---

garian goods, new product offerings in chemical, electronic, and machine sectors hold promise. Table 32 shows that discounts on Hungarian countertrade goods have been quite low.

Hungarian negotiators usually ask for low penalty promises. About 10 percent of the Western export's value is the average.[19]

Unlike other East European countries, Hungary has no special Foreign Trade Organization devoted to countertrade operations. Each Foreign Trade Organization and some independent enterprises can engage in countertrade with the West. Each industrial ministry has a special operations department which sells goods obtained through bilaterial clearing arrangements or locates, for a commission, goods in other East European countries.

One Foreign Trade Organization, Interag, that specializes in foreign representation and cooperation agreements, has combined the Hungarian sympathy for Western countertrade problems with Hungary's desire for large countertrade commitments to devise a scheme that may be beneficial to both Hungarian and Western interests. If a Western firm agrees to a large countertrade contract prior to its initial sales bid, Interag will ensure that the firm's eventual sales offerings to Hungary will be treated with priority and the Western firm will have access to a large selection of countertrade goods, including items usually reserved for case export. By this plan, Hungary is assured of a large countertrade commitment, and the Western firm is virtually certain to find marketable goods.

Poland

Until a few years ago Poland ranked second to the Soviet Union in volume of countertrade, but has had to endure worsening hard-currency and trade problems worsened in the past three years by labor and consumer unrest and debilitating energy shortages. Poland has responded to current problems by switching emphasis from raw material buyback deals to fewer and more currency-conservative turnkey compensation and cooperation agreements.

Countertrade with the West may be heading for trouble,

however, as Foreign Trade Organizations increasingly feel compelled to make unusually high and inflexible countertrade demands during a period when trade between the West and Poland is already shaky. Disappointing coal production, due to inadequate investment and labor unrest, has dealt a crippling blow to economic recovery hopes. The coal shortage has diminished a precious hard-currency earning source and has forced Poland to spend larger sums of hard-currency on foreign oil and gas. While labor problems have hurt industrial sectors, consumer dissatisfaction is being appeased by greater hard-currency expenditures on chronically short consumer items.

Though Poland is Eastern Europe's largest and most resource-rich nation, a series of badly timed and poorly administered investment moves in the 1970's have saddled Poland with a consistently high trade deficit and a hard-currency debt—at $26 billion—surpassed only by Yugoslavia in Eastern Europe. In 1980, Poland's trade deficit to the West, $793 million, was the highest in Eastern Europe.[20] Though Table 33 indicates the considerable recovery Poland has made in its trade balance with non-CMEA countries, it was accomplished at the expense of reducing total foreign trade by 28 percent from 1980 to 1981. According to Table 34, however, Poland has not been able to reverse its worsening hard-currency debt.

TABLE 33

Poland: Trade with the West and LDC's
(millions of dollars)

	1975	1978	1979	1980	1981	1982
Exports	4,477	5,498	6,350	7,306	5,448	4,840
Imports	7,104	7,392	8,038	8,488	5,422	3,690
Balance	− 2,627	− 1,94	− 1,688	− 1,182	+ 26	+ 1,150

[1]Export and import data are F.O.B. Data do not include intra-CMEA hard-currency.

Source: U.S. Government

TABLE 34

Poland: Gross and Net Hard-currency Debt
(millions of dollars)

	1975	1976	1977	1978	1979	1980	1981	1982
Gross	8,014	11,483	13,967	17,844	22,669	25,120	25,000	24,800
Net	7,381	10,680	13,532	16,972	21,500	24,500	24,250	23,800

Source: U.S. Government

To stop its slide into possible bankruptcy, Poland has cut imports to the bone while reserving precious hard-currency for a handful of high priority imports and demanding high countertrade commitments on all others. Table 35 shows Poland's high countertrade demands. From 1976 to 1979 the general average of countertrade demands grew from 20-30 percent to 20-40 percent.[21] The countertrade requirements of 1979, shown in Table 36, compared to the high demands of 1980, indicate Poland's determination to raise countertrade commitments. Demand for compensation deals should also grow, nurtured by Poland's need for Western products and technology. Compensation deals with their built-in buybacks

TABLE 35

Countertrade Demands for Selected Products in Poland (1980)

products	demands percent
Machinery and vehicles	50–70
Chemicals	40–60
Consumer goods	75–100

Source: Business with Eastern Europe

TABLE 36

Countertrade Required by Selected Foreign
Trade Organizations and Products in
Poland (1979)

Foreign Trade Organization and product	requirement percent
General average	20–40
Polimex-Cekop, Varimex, Elektrim Rafamet (industrial goods)	20–30
Metalexport (machine tools)	40–50
Ciech (chemical products, intermediate goods)	30–50
Chemicals and petrochemicals	50

Source: OECD

---

are practically the only means through which Poland can afford to import.

Poland will concentrate its limited financial resources in three areas: agriculture, energy, and equipment that contributes to the completion or updating of industrial installations. In the agricultural sector, Western firms can expect lower countertrade demands on such high priority goods as farm commodities, farm chemical and farm equipment. In energy the acquisition of coal extraction machinery and oil and gas exploration tools is considered most important. Other goods with expected low countertrade requirements include industrial machinery spare parts.

Western firms involved in countertrade in Poland will encounter the familiar East European problems with product quality, availability, and delivery. Westerners should have the least trouble in selecting goods in the machine and chemical sectors, as these sectors offer the most marketable products.

TABLE 37

Products Offered for Countertrade in Poland (1980)

product	proportion of total countertrade percent
Machinery and vehicles	45
Chemical products	25
Consumer goods	10
Electrical and electronic equipment	20

Source: Business with Eastern Europe

Fortunately for the West, Poland has historically favored machines as a countertrade good, as shown in Table 37. However, negotiators from all industrial sectors offer outdated, useless product lists. Once a product is finally selected, companies often have to wait a long time before it is available and delivery can be made. Poland's general inefficiency combined with its preference to ship counterdeliveries in scheduled increments transforms relatively simple deals into long ordeals of three years or more.

The Polish government has pursued two practices that mitigate some of these countertrade hardships. In pre-martial law Poland, Western firms were allowed to engage in evidence accounts. In addition, Polish officials have proven unusually accomodating in permitting inspection of countertrade goods prior to shipping from Poland.

Table 38 shows that Poland's discount rates are rather standard for Eastern Europe. Some deterioration of the rates has occurred, however. Subsidy rates for machinery used to be lower before lagging research and development stymied progress in quality improvement.

TABLE 38

Discounts by Selected Products in Poland

product	discount percent
Engineered products	16–19
Chemicals	10–14
Non-machinery	12–16
Machinery	20–25

Source: Business with Eastern Europe
(Wolff addendum B)

For penalties Poland has required moderate percentages of an import's value. The rate for machinery and vehicles has been 20-30 percent and for chemical, 10-15 percent. Polish Foreign Trade Organizations demand unconditional penalty guarantees payable on first request.

Poland has the oldest and best organized countertrade enterprise in Eastern Europe. Established in 1937 as a private, international trading firm, DAL became nationalized in 1959 and was reorganized into three branches. These three subsidiaries are in charge of DAL's planning, countertrade, and joint venture operations (30 percent of DAL's total business). DAL is an anomaly in Eastern Europe because it acts as an independent trade house and operates with its own capital on the basis of profit, not quota. Though almost all Polish Foreign Trade Organizations are licensed to countertrade, linkage among them requires special, infrequently granted permission from the Ministry of Foreign Trade and Maritime Economy. When linkage is given, firms must then work through DAL.

DAL performs three major services for Western companies besides coordinating linkage. During product selection it will put the Western partner in touch with various sectoral trading organizations. Once the goods are purchased, DAL will take title to them if the Western firm chooses not to or cannot market these products. A Western company can unload its entire countertrade obligation on to DAL at one time and, with necessity made into virtue, let a Polish company earn hard-currency, thereby enhancing the Western firm's image. If the deal was arranged on a "package" basis (e.g. 60 percent from a Foreign Trade Organization in one sector, 40 percent from another sector), then DAL will charge a lower commission than for goods from a single Foreign Trade Organization. It can also put Western firms in contact with buyers on the world market without actually taking title to the goods.

DAL's versatility goes as far as arranging for a Polish manufacturer to modify a good to Western specifications. Once DAL has taken over a countertrade commitment, it can persuade a Polish manufacturer to alter its product with far greater ease than a Western firm.

DAL may sometimes be a little more expensive than a Western trade house for services rendered, but it is considered to have generally greater skill at disposing of Polish goods.

The U.S.S.R.

Though the Soviet Union is not in the dire financial straits, particularly in regard to hard-currency shortages that have prompted Eastern European countries to pursue countertrade, it conducts in terms of value the highest amount of countertrade business of any country and more than all other East European countries combined. The U.S.S.R.'s volume of countertrade results from the enormous size of Soviet countertrade projects, particularly those involving raw materials. Given the scale of the Soviet economy, which reached $1.8 trillion GNP in 1980, the government has traditionally been inclined toward large industrial ventures. As these projects grow larger and more complex, Western technology, management, and financial support have increasingly been sought after. Countertrade, mostly through compensation deals, has enabled the Soviets to expand certain industrial sectors with

Western assistance while minimizing the drain on Soviet resources.

The Soviet Union has had clearing arrangements, now numbering 30—mostly with developing countries—long before countertrade became an important factor in East-West trade. The distinctive brand of countertrade that the U.S.S.R. practices today with Western countries, however, had its beginnings in the mid-1970's. In 1974, a special countertrade department was created in the Ministry of Foreign Trade. Two years later Leonid Brezhnev himself indicated growing Soviet interest in countertrade. In his 1976 report to the Twenty-fifth Party Congress of the CPSU, he called agreements on a compensation basis a new promising form of economic relations with the West. It was left to Sushkov, the Soviet deputy minister of foreign trade, to further define "cooperation on a compensation basis" as embracing "the construction of major industrial projects and complexes through the use of foreign credits, which will be paid back with products from these new plants as well as those already existing".[22]

As the Soviets have primarily been interested in buying turnkey plants from the West, the emphasis has been more on buyback deals than counterpurchase agreements. By 1980, over 70 separate compensation agreements with the West had been signed, and in the past several years several more countertrade agreements have been reached. The most important countertrade deals have been for Soviet imports of gas piping and drilling equipment, coal mining equipment, fertilizer plants, chemical and petrochemical plants, aluminum refineries, and forestry equipment and cellulose plants.

For raw materials such as gas and coal, Western firms have been more than happy to accept buyback obligations of over 100 percent. Though there has also been about 100 percent product repayment for chemicals and semi-processed goods, these arrangements have aroused a good deal of concern among Western traders. Some 30 chemical plants worth $3.5 billion were ordered from Western companies in the past several years through buyback deals.[23] Now, as a direct result of these contracts, the Soviets are exporting growing amounts of ammonia, methanol, polyethylene, polystyrene, and several other chemicals. Ammonia and methanol are expected to cause the biggest problems. Soviet sales of ammonia resulting from buyback agreements as well as separate exchange agreements with Occidental Petroleum Co. could average 3.15 million tons annually during 1978-1987 if agreements are implemented. The buyback deal for the methanol project involves the purchase of 300,000 tons per year of Soviet methanol. Western markets are expected to have great difficulty absorbing such large additions of chemicals without seriously depressing chemical industries in the West.

The Soviet penchant for large-scale compensation ventures is not likely to abate. The U.S.S.R. engages in countertrade for different reasons than East European countries. The latter are attracted to countertrade primarily because it eases balance of payments difficulties. In general, they rely on a large part of their export earnings to cover debts to the West and carefully regulate imports according to how much hard currency exports generate.

For the Soviets, a short-term expansion of exports and payment relief problems are not major concerns in pursuing large-scale compensation ventures. Though their financial position has worsened somewhat in the last year or two, they are still considered a top credit risk by Western bankers. The U.S.S.R.'s $20 billion debt to the West is small compared to the size of its enormous economy. Its debt service is only about 12 percent of its annual trade in hard currency, a lower ratio than, for example, Canada. Furthermore, Moscow has well over $30 billion in gold reserves and hard-currency deposits in the West, and annual Soviet gold production is estimated at 300 tons worth $3-3.5 billion. Its excellent credit rating and Western Europe's dependence on East-West trade allows the Soviet Union to acquire substantial Western credit without great difficulty. In early 1982, for example, it obtained credits totaling $900 million from France, Austria, and Sweden on top of credits worth $6 billion from West German banks for the controversial Yamal pipeline that is to bring Soviet natural gas to Western Europe.[24]

The Soviets seem to engage in large-scale compensation transactions with long-term pay-offs in mind. Compensation deals would soften the impact of any serious deterioration of credit rating that could occur down the road. The Soviets also establish long-term delivery relationships and concomitant long-term sales guarantees with Western purchasers. This facilitates planning while placing Soviet trade with the West on a more stable foundation.

Pressure on Western firms to engage in countertrade is growing, but it varies greatly according to the products involved and the level of sales a firm has with the Soviet Union. Soviet officials see potential for new buyback agreements involving the production of road machines with high unit capacities, plants for production of automobile engines, diesel engines, and forklift trucks, farming tractors and harvesting combines, industrial steel pipe fittings, large-diameter valves with precision bearings, and chemical fibers, dyestuffs, pesticides, rubber, caprolactum, butadiene and vinyl acetate. Oddly enough, companies with large, regular sales to the U.S.S.R. are prime countertrade targets. The Soviets view countertrade and compensation agreements as a form of 'industrial cooperation' that is most appropriate for firms which have an established long-term stake in the Soviet market, as opposed to firms interested only in a one-shot deal.

Beyond this general attitude, the Soviet approach to countertrade is very haphazard. This is in part due to the lack of coordination and cooperation between ministries and Foreign Trade Organizations within the foreign trade system. And, unlike other East European countries, the U.S.S.R. does not have a Foreign Trade Organization specializing in counterpurchase transactions.

The U.S.S.R. should be increasing its reliance on compensation arrangements, in light of growing demand for Western machinery, equipment, and materials combined with slight slippages in its hard currency position. If exports do not involve the sale of turnkey plants, the Soviets have not, as a rule made regular counterpurchase demands on the Western seller. However, pressure on Western exporters to counterpurchase is increasing and companies which accept counterpurchase may gain an important competitive advantage over other firms vying for the same contract.

Priority sectors that are expected to import equipment

and technology from the West under the Eleventh Five Year Plan (1981-1985) include the lumber, pulp and paper, natural gas, mineral fertilizers, rolled steel, computers, and agricultural machinery industries. Though high-priority sectors usually seek low countertrade demands because they receive generous allocations of hard currency to import equipment, there are many exceptions to the rule in the U.S.S.R. In the past, for example, gas and fertilizer deals have commanded at least 100 percent countertrade obligations, even though they have been high-priority sectors. The Soviet record indicates that no matter what the priority, compensation deals involving raw materials, chemicals, and semi-processed products require at least 100 percent or more buyback commitments. Only for compensation deals involving manufactured goods is the countertrade obligation less, usually well below 100 percent.

Countertrade demands for counterpurchase deals are much lower except for imports of consumer items, light industrial goods, and other low-priority products. These have encountered 100 percent countertrade requirements in the past. This pattern is not expected to change even though light industry is projected to grow faster than heavy industry under the Eleventh FYP—a reversal of the traditional growth relationship between heavy and light industry. Planned imports of "industrial goods," such as heavy machinery from Machinoexport, electronic and printing equipment from Techmashexport, and machine tools from Stankoimport, normally require a 20-30 percent counterpurchase obligation. Counterpurchase demands would be lowest for exports of equipment used in the iron and steel and electronics industry. Imports of industrial goods which are not planned may be expected to have a higher counterpurchase requirement.

Countertrade obligations in compensation deals whereby Western companies get paid in resultant product, be it oil, gas, coal, chemicals, copper, or other raw materials, are usually fulfilled with a minimum of difficulty. After all, selling fuel and raw materials is no great challenge in today's market. There are obstacles, however, in concluding compensation deals involving plant imports. The biggest is the issue of quality control. The Soviets are very reluctant to allow on-site quality control, though their brand of quality control does not measure up to Western standards. Since the Soviets intend to increase compensation deals involving finished products this problem promises not to go away. Chemicals may also cause problems. Not only are many Western markets for chemicals saturated or near-saturated, the Soviets have experienced problems packing bulk chemical goods. Western companies are increasingly insisting on mix-package deals for countertrade involving chemicals. Such deals comprise 30-50 percent counterpurchase of other Soviet products. This result is often difficult to achieve, however, since mix-package deals may involve more than one industrial ministry and coordination among Soviet ministries is sorely lacking.

Compared to East European countries, the U.S.S.R. offers the widest, but, unfortunately, not the most attractive range of products for countertrade. The Soviets will usually offer "general goods" for counterpurchase. This means that about one-third of the 62 Soviet Foreign Trade Organizations must be queried for available goods. Such searches are complicated by the unwillingness of one Soviet ministry to provide products for export so that another ministry may import plant and equipment. Nor is there a Soviet organization responsible for facilitating linkage for counterpurchase trade.

In addition to waiting at least six months for delivery of goods after they've been selected, the Soviets drive a hard bargain on how the goods are to be marketed. They typically request marketing rights for the entire CMEA region and other selected countries. More restrictive is their insistence that countertrade products can only be marketed in the same country from which the Western delivery came. With some hard negotiating, the Soviets can sometimes be persuaded to withdraw this condition. Moreover, the transfer of compensation commitments to a trading firm is often not permitted.

Despite all the constraints and inflexibility built into countertrade deals, sometimes the unexpected happens and the arrangement may rebound to the benefit of the Western company. On several occasions in the past, for example, Western sellers who have agreed to take products from delivered equipment succeed in changing their commitment to unrelated products. This occurs when the Soviets conclude that they will need all the output for domestic consumption and the Western company prefers to take unrelated products rather than plant output.

Normal procedure is followed for calculating the price of the return product, based on some mutually agreed-upon index of representative prices, with the likelihood of a discount. Western suppliers should expect subsidies of about 25 percent to dispose of "industrial goods." If products are delivered with instructions for use in Cyrillic and tied to Soviet after-sales service, subsidies may run as high as 45 percent.

It will be almost impossible for Western sellers to avoid a maze of bureaucratic stumbling blocks in arranging a countertrade deal. It is worse for counterpurchase agreements than for compensation ventures. For compensation, an organization called the Main Administration for Compensation Arrangements with the West (MACAW) was set up under the Ministry of Foreign Trade in 1974. It is responsible for coordinating compensation arrangements among different industrial ministries, but it does not get involved with problems of counterpurchase. Recently, however, a division of the MFT, the Office of Technical, Scientific and Economic Cooperation, has been assigned parttime responsibility for promoting counterpurchase deals. Like the MACAW, it will not help a firm locate the products it wants, but it will assist in bringing together the relevant industrial ministries and Foreign Trade Organizations involved in a particular counterpurchase transaction.

Soviet Foreign Trade Organizations have recently been reorganized in an effort to orient domestic production to the needs of the export market. Now Foreign Trade Organizations operate on a profit and loss basis, and they have new departments handling two-way trade in certain product lines. Moreover, incentives have been introduced, consisting of material funds and benefits, to encourage profitable export trade. These changes should encourage greater countertrade and may eventually ease the problem of product selection.

FOOTNOTES

1. Business International Institute, "Composition of Countertrade," *The Future of Countertrade*, Seminar on New Developments on Doing Business with Eastern Europe (October 1981).
2. Organization for Economic Cooperation and Development, *East-West Trade: Recent Developments in Countertrade*, Conference Transcript, Paris, p. 32.
3. Miriam Karr and Jerzy Zachariasz, *Countertrade Arrangements*, (New York: Chase World Information Corp), p. 138.
4. D. Barclay, USSR: "The Role of Compensation Arrangement in Trade with the West," in *Soviet Economy in a Time of Change: A Compendium of Papers Submitted to the Joint Economic Committee, Congress of the United States* (1979).
5. Business International Institute, "The Outlook for Countertrade," *The Future of Countertrade*.
6. Organization for Economic Cooperation and Development, *Recent Developments in Countertrade*, p. 45.
7. *Business America* (October 5, 1981), p. 15.
8. OECD, *Recent Developments in Countertrade*, p. 73.
9. *Business America* (October 5, 1981), p. 11.
10. OECD, *Recent Developments in Countertrade*, p. 74.
11. Business International Institute, "Penalty Provisions," *The Future of Countertrade*.
12. United States Department of Commerce, *Foreign Economic Trends: G.D.R.*, (February 1982), p. 8.
13. *Business America* (October 5, 1981), p. 9.
14. OECD, *Recent Developments in Countertrade*, p. 74.
15. *Business America* (October 5, 1981), pp. 7-9.
16. OECD, *Recent Developments in Countertrade*, p. 74.
17. *Business America* (October 5, 1981), p. 13.
18. Business International Institute, "Changing Classification of Countertrade Goods," *The Future of Countertrade*.
19. Ibid., "Penalty Provisions."

20. *Business America* (October 5, 1981), p. 6.
21. OECD, *Recent Developments in Countertrade,* p. 78.
22. W. Sushkov, "Long-term Cooperation of the U.S.S.R. with the Capitalist Countries in Trade and Economy on a Compensation Basis," *Vneshnaya Torgovlia,* no. 5 (1977).
23. "Growing Soviet Trade in Buy-Back Chemicals," *Business Eastern Europe* (September 19, 1980), pp. 299-300.
24. Hedrick Smith, "Money Problems Plaguing Soviets, Figures Indicate," *New York Times* (March 14, 1982), p. 1.

Chapter 11
COUNTERTRADE IN CHINA

The Role of Countertrade in China

Countertrade comprises a very small percentage of China's overall trade. However, the People's Republic of China will continue to engage in countertrade, (1) as an alternative to its cautious debt acquisition policy; (2) to help ease the burden of obtaining foreign technology and equipment; (3) to offset its trade imbalance with Japan and the U.S.; and (4) to boost hard currency earnings. The Compensation Trade Bureau of the State Import and Export Commission (SIEC) has stated that countertrade is "indispensable" to China as a tool of economic planning.[1] Priority areas for countertrade are, in order of their importance: (1) energy; (2) textile and light industries, food, and the electronic industry; (3) building materials, machine building, iron and steel and chemical industries; and (4) agriculture.

China's emphasis on promoting exports, reflected in its countertrade policy, has brought welcome results. China recently recorded its first world trade surplus and its 1982 foreign trade surplus stood at $4.6 billion. Total exports have risen at an annual rate of 29 percent and exports to the U.S. have risen at almost twice that rate. Beijing's foreign currency reserves in 1982 were more than $13 billion. Trade with the U.S., once imbalanced with too many imports and not enough exports, has turned around: Chinese imports form the U.S. leveled off in 1981 and declined 19 percent in 1982, while exports grew by leaps and bounds. The result was a mere $689 million U.S. trade surplus in 1982. A balance of payments between the U.S. and China can be expected to occur in 1984. Some experts feel that if invisible earning—from tourism, freight charges, insurance costs, etc.—are included in the assessment, the U.S.-China trade is already balanced.

The bottom line is that China's caution in its borrowing policy is not shared by international bankers who view China as one of the few good remaining credit risks.

Because Beijing looks favorably upon business transactions offering countertrade as a form of payment, countertrade is often used by foreign firms to gain entry into the China market. The majority of countertrade in China is in the form of compensation via joint venture or processing arrangements.

The Chinese prefer to keep countertrade transactions simple. Because of a rigid, unwieldy bureaucracy and the absence of clear directives from central authorities, countertrade almost never involves linkage of goods outside the negotiating party's jurisdiction. Counterpurchase agreements, therefore, have been few and far between. Chinese negotiators will usually indicate during the early stages of negotiations whether countertrade is required.

Almost all countertrade agreements are unique, constructed to meet the peculiar needs of each situation. The paramount consideration in approving processing and compensation arrangements is the impact of a project on the local economy. Will the proposed projected deprive other enterprise of needed fuel? Will it produce goods leading to oversupply? How will a particular agreement fit in with national economic priorities?

Nonetheless, Chinese compensation agreements share certain basic characteristics. A major tenet in China's economic development calls for refurbishing of over 400,000 plants with new technology and equipment rather than the importation of turnkey plants. For deals involving high technology, the Chinese favor phased assembly agreements. In the initial period, the foreign company usually supplies all but the very simple equipment components and is compensated with resultant components or finished products. The Chinese gradually assume responsibility for the more difficult and technical parts of the manufacturing process until, after a number of years, they are producing the item without any outside assistance.

The Chinese also favor companies training Chinese technicians on imported equipment. In some cases companies may market their technology simply by signing non-binding agreements for long-term technical cooperation with Chinese organizations. If the first stages of industrial cooperation are successful, the Chinese are often willing to move on to more complex forms of industrial cooperation that may involve countertrade arrangements.

The Chinese seek countertrade that combines technology transfer with the buyback of made-to-order goods, and, if possible, also includes complete financing on the Western end. Deals must usually satisfy very strict requirements. Compensation agreements, for example, require the manufacture of exportable products, limited credit, and low interest rates.

Barter

Although compensation is the favored form of countertrade in China, barter is also paracticed. China has concluded barter trade deals with many neighboring countries, including Sri Lanka, India, and Bangladesh. Under a five-year agreement with Bangladesh, for example, the two countries are to exchange goods worth $250 million from each side.

Evidence Accounts

Evidence accounts are also used in the Peolpe's Republic of China. For example, MACHIMPEX officials are particularly enthusiastic about evidence account trading and stress its suitability to present economic conditions in China. MACHIMPEX signed an evidence account protocol with the Motors Trading Corporation, a subsidiary of General Motors Corporation. This protocol provides that each will purchase the other's products in cash transactions, and that the Bank of China (BOC) will charge every transaction to the evidence accounts of both sides. The accounts will be reviewed annually so as to ensure a rough balance of trade between the two corporations during the period of the protocol. MACHIMPEX has already agreed to import approximately $800,000 worth of diesel engines from General Motors which, in turn, indicated interest in buying auto parts, cutters, and other products from China.[2]

Processing Arrangements

In August 1978, the State Council approved a 22-point resolution setting down broad, fairly simple guidelines concerning processing and compensation trade. In the case of processing, the foreign customer supplies raw or intermediate materials to be processed, assembled, or manufactured in China. The Chinese partner receives a contracting fee for its services, after which the processed material is accepted at a discount and resold abroad by the foreign firm. Most of the growth in processing and compensation trade has taken place in south China. About 70 percent of all such deals are between Hong Kong companies and enterprises in Guangdong Province.[3] Hong Kong deals with the bulk of the business because members of both sides, P.R.C. officials and expatriot Chinese business executives, are more willing to conclude deals with relatives or friends. A majority of compensation trade arrangements involve long-term Hong Kong customers who understand the Chinese manufacturer's situation and needs.

Arrangements involving processing and assembly with supplied materials have earned China $328 million in processing fees since 1979.[4] The majority of processing deals have been limited to textiles and other light industrial products, including footwear, beer, asparagus, peanuts, fish, electrical equipment, chemical manufactures, kitchen implements, handicrafts, radios and tape players.

Unlike compensation trade, processing has increased in volume between the second half of 1979 and 1981. During this period, roughly $6 million was invested in 3,000 projects, averaging $2,000 per project. In 1981, $35 million was invested in 8,896 projects, increasing the average investment per project to $3,900.[5]

Compensation

The 1981 investment in compensation, however, dropped dramatically to about $79 million, compared to $381 million invested in 1979–1980. There was also a drop in the number of projects, from 417 in 1979–1980 to 173 in 1981, and in average foreign investment, from $914,000 per project in 1980 to $457,000 in 1981.[6]

However, China has embarked on a fund-raising drive to attract investment of approximately $5.3 billion in 1,001 local and 121 national projects.[7] They are being sponsored by 23 provinces, municipalities and autonomous regions with the assistance of the Ministry of Foreign Economic Relations and Trade (MOFERT) and the United Nations International Development Organization (UNIDO). Although the specific form of overseas investment will be highly flexible, the majority of projects which generated letters of intent were reported to be for compensation trade deals.

Joint Ventures

Almost all joint ventures in China constitute production-sharing countertrade arrangements, since any other kind of arrangement would be far less attractive, under most circumstances, to both the Chinese and Western sides. The main alternative to countertrade arrangements would be for the Chinese to take title of the entire output of a venture and pay the Western side a share of the profits. Given the exchange rate structure of Chinese and foreign currencies, however, the Chinese would not come close to paying their Western partners in Renminbi what they invested in hard-currency.

Although Beijing officials consider joint ventures the best way to maximize the import of high technology and Western management know-how, they are not yet very common. Some 48 joint ventures were approved through the end of 1982, 20 in 1981 and 20 in 1980, worth $189 million (of which $8 million was contributed by foreign parties). Only eight were formed in 1982. The foreign contribution to 1981's 20 ventures was only $20 million, compared to $60 million the year before. According to Ji Chong, a senior official at the Ministry of Foreign Economic Relations and Trade, some 13 joint ventures are now operational.[8]

Chinese attitudes toward joint ventures are undergoing yet another transition. In 1979, when China adopted the Joint Venture Law, the Chinese negotiated major projects involving large investments. Most of these grandiose projects proved too ambitious and fell through—either before or after contracts were signed. The Chinese interest in joint ventures was then redirected toward smaller projects, instead. Thus, the average joint venture decreased in value from about $3 million in 1980 to just $1 million in 1981.

Now the Chinese are again interested in big projects. Evidently, they have concluded that small joint ventures were too bothersome considering the relatively small contributions they made to economic development. Priority will be given in the future to joint ventures involving industrial projects such as development of energy resources, as opposed to the building and running of hotels or the setting up of photography studios.

China's renewed enthusiasm over foreign participation in major infrastructure and energy development projects is expected to boost 1983 investment over last year's. Discussions on a number of joint venture projects are already at an advanced stage.

Joint Ventures and Resource Development

If China is to keep pace with its overall modernization effort, the development of its indigenous energy resources is of paramount importance. This fact is reflected in China's ambitious plans to double its coals output to 1.2 billion tons by the end of the century, and the stepped-up development of its offshore oil reserves through joint venture schemes.

Coal

To attract foreign investment capital for coal development, China is using a compensation trade approach. In return for technical and financial assistance, companies will receive coal at some future date. Several firms have already begun such ventures, getting a head start on a possible Chinese coal rush.

The Ministry of Coal's new development plan places more emphasis than in the past on the development of infrastructure, particularly rail lines and port facilities, necessary to accommodate an increased flow of coal to the market. An example of the new approach is a recent five-year accord signed between Italy's Technotrade, a Rome-based consortium which includes Slaini Costrurrorri, Astgaldo Costruzione and DeBagtolis SpA, and the China Southwest Energy Resources United Development Corp (CSERUDC) for a $500 million coal field development project. The Italians are to provide detailed coal-mine engineering and technical assistance as well as design and supervision of construction work for a 250 kilometer coal transportation rail line. Technotrade will be compensated with 8-10 million metric tons of Chinese steam coal per annum.

The opportunity to engage in China's coal development in a compensation arrangement is available on both the national and provincial level. For instance, Shangdong Province is ready to cooperate with overseas firms through compensatory trade to open a new coal mine, the Zhe Zhen. The most lucrative contracts for investment lie in design engineering and consulting services, extraction equipment and technology, and thermal generating technology and equipment.

Oil

Offshore oil production is the biggest, most lucrative area for joint ventures. China plans to develop fields in the South China Sea, Yellow Sea, Tonkin Gulf, and, eventually, East China Sea. China's lack of experience and low technical level in offshore oil production has allowed a major Western role in China's offshore development. If the geological situation is favorable, anywhere between 5-10 million barrels per day of oil could be gushing by 2000.

The China National Offshore Oil Corp. (CNOOC) recently released its model contract, which contains compensation provisions, to help speed up the development of its 150,000 sq. kilometers (58,000 sq. miles) off China's coast. China's six large offshore basins may contain as much as 50 billion to 70 billion barrels of recoverable reserves, of which the South China Sea may account for as much as 15 to 30 billion barrels.

The model contract provides that successful bidders will bear all exploration costs until an exploitable oil or gas field is discovered. After a find of commercial potential is made, CNOOC will invest 51 percent of development costs, with the foreign partner providing the remaining 49 percent investment. If the Chinese side chooses to invest less than 51 percent, the Western party could then exceed its 49 percent share by offering to cover some of CNOOC's share of development investment.

Once commerical production begins, 50 percent of the oil obtained will be used to recover exploration, development, and operating outlays. The remaining 50 percent will be divided as follows: 12.5 percent for royalty tax, 5 percent for sales tax, and 32.5 percent to be split into share oil and "allocable profit oil." How share oil (which goes to CNOOC) and allocable profit oil is divided will be determined by the annual output of the area multiplied by an "x" factor which companies will submit in their bids. Winning bidders will receive 49 percent of the allocable profit oil as compensation, and CNOOC will get the other 51 percent.

The involvement of Western companies in China's petroleum industry illustrates some of the reasons why joint ventures have not taken off as fast as Beijing would like. Western firms fear that ambiguities in contracts together with China's imcomplete legal framework might excalate costs, hamper operations, or prevent them from cashing in on their share of oil. Another concern stems from the face their foreign firms will have to bear entirely the exploration expenses and risks. Judging by the model contract, Chinese officials want to use the first phase of exploration as a base for the People's Republic of China's own training and development. Foreign involvement in the second phase is intended to decrease and continue to do so, until exploration of the last third of the surveyed area proceeds without any foreign participation.

Some industry observers expect a full third of the model contract's provisions to come under negotiation. Companies can gain a competitive edge with their bid on "other considerations" whereby a financing offer or other contribution by the larger oil companies may be an important sweetener in Chinese eyes.

Joint Venture Regulation

The number of joint ventures could increase now that supplementary legislation dealing with the ambiguities of the July 1979 Joint Venture Law has been enacted. A spate of laws related to foreign investment and business have recently flowed from Beijing. They include Regulations on the Registration of Joint Ventures Using Chinese & Foreign Investment (1979), Regulations on Labor Management in Joint Ventures Using Chinese & Foreign Investment (1979), the Income Tax Law of the P.R.C. (1980), Interim Regulations for Control of Resident Offices of Foreign Enterprises in China (1980), Detailed Rules and Regulations for the Implementation of the Income Tax Law Concerning Joint Ventures (1981), and Detailed Rules & Regulations for the Implementation of the Individual Tax Law (1981).

The Joint Venture Tax Law defines taxable income in a joint venture as the net income in a tax year after deduction of costs, expenses and losses. The income tax rate on joint ventures, except those exploiting natural resources, is 33 percent, including a local surtax of 19 percent. A 10 percent income tax is levied on repatriated profits, while profit shares reinvested in China for five years or more entitle the investor, upon approval of tax authorities, to a refund of 40 percent of the income tax paid on the reinvested amount.

Joint ventures may, upon approval of tax authorities, be exempted from income tax in the first profit-making year and allowed a 50 percent tax reduction in the next two years which may be carried forward for five tax years.

Joint ventures are also granted preferential treatment in the levying of taxes. First, equipment and other materials which foreign participants in joint ventures need to import, for investment abroad with cash of their registered capital for the running of enterprises, can be applied for exemption from import duties and unified tax. If equipment or material is later sold in the domestic market, it is necessary to make up for the amount exempted.

All raw materials, spare parts, or packing materials imported for the manufacture of exported goods are exempted from import duties and the unifed tax. However, tax is levied on the byproducts turned out in production and for goods that were slated for export but instead were sold in the domestic market—for whatever reasons. Some exported merchandise produced by joint ventures which earns relatively little foreign exchange can be exempted from the unified taxation.

There is no national standard for charges for land used by joint ventures. It is decided by the provisional, municipal, and autonomous regional governments where the joint venture is located, and varies according to the kind of project being undertaken and the size of the Chinese investment in the land/project. In remote areas where industry is lagging behind, or in those industries in which investment profits are low, the charges for land to be used by the investor can be accordingly reduced. Investment in Special Economic Zones (SEZs) will be given preferential treatment in many respects. For example, production equipment, raw materials and other items can be imported duty free with tax rates set at 15 percent with special exemptions or reductions available under certain conditions. Profits and wages of foreigners may be repatriated under special foreign exchange regulations that have not yet been issued.

Countertrade at the Subnational Level

While China's readjustment policies have reduced state allocations to local Chinese enterprises, Beijing has extended to all the provinces some of the autonomy enjoyed by the Special Economic Zones (SEZs) in Guangdong and Fujian in order to better attract foreign investment. Both Guangdong and Fujian have the authority to conclude compensation trade contracts of up to $5 million without prior approval of central government organs. China's three largest cities, Beijing, Shanghai, and Tianjin, can approve contracts under $3 million. The ceiling for other ministries is only $1 million.[9]

The approval ceilings are only guidelines and by no means stringently adhered to. Some contracts below the ceiling require approval, and some contracts above the ceiling do not require a green light from higher authorities. Development of natural resources, however, always requires approval from Beijing.

In August 1980, detailed regulations were adopted governing trade in the three SEZs in Guangdong Province. The regulations set up a Provincial Administrative Committee to plan the development of the SEZs and to review and approve individual investment projects, including thoise involving countertrade. It is not clear, however, at this point in time, whether these regulations will be extended to other zones or seperate regulations will be forthcoming.

Municipal or provincial governments look upon countertrade as a means to earn foreign currency without having to draw on scarce foreign currency allocations. Countertrade can also supplement government assisitance provided to manufacturing plants slated for upgrading, or can increase the number of plants being refurbished such as AMF did in supplying machinery and technology for tennis ball manufacturing.

Those negotiaitons involving countertrade may begin at the local levels, but are usually concluded in Beijing. However, increased local autonomy in China due to decentralization will make it important to cultivate new contacts on the provincial and municipal levels while still maintaining contacts in Beijing. Large-scale contracts will still require approval from MOFERT.

Negotiating Countertrade

Given China's variable and sometimes unwritten legal system, foreign parties must negotiate highly detailed contracts which clarify as many ambiguities as possible and specify standards of quality. If possible, the stipulation that payment is contingent upon satisfaction of those standards should be written into the contract. Contract proposals should be drawn up in clear, straight-forward language that can be translated into Chinese with relative ease.

Prior to 1980, third-party arbitration clauses were rarely included in compensation trade contracts because of Chinese inexperience with arbitration. Since then, arbitration has been negotiated in some cases in the country of the party that did not fulfill their part of the agreement, or a third country, such as Sweden or Switzerland.

The Chinese usually refuse to grant exclusive marketing rights to Western firms, but are eager to have their products marketed abroad, so in contrast to East European countries,

China will allow a foreign firm to take an active role in insuring quality control. For example, Nike, the athletic shoe manufacturer, concluded a compensation agreement in which it took total responsibility over quality control, bypassing third party inspection by the highly regarded China National Import and Export Commodities Inspection Corporation (CHINSPECT). Still, quality control remains a big problem in China. There are many instances of sub-standard products being turned out under compensation arrangements. Compliance with quality control standards is expecially important in cases where production is beyond the technical capabilitites of the Chinese partner.

In negotiating the Western export clause of a countertrade agreement, the Chinese insist on a description of the Western party's contractual obligations relating to equipment, technology, and services to be provided. They strive whenever possible for a cooperative work formula that makes room, for the most significant contributions possible of Chinese equipment, manpower, and management to the project. On the other hand, the Western import contract is kept simple and brief. Either no penalty provisions are included, or such provisions appear in vague language.

At the insistence of the Chinese, many negotating sessions have, in effect, become free technical seminars. The People's Republic of China has a strong commitment to acquiring only the most up-to-date technology. The Chinese involved in the purchasing process are likely to be extremely well versed in all relevant technological details and they expect the Western negotiators to be equally conversant in technological matters. It is, nonetheless, up to the foreign party to convince the Chinese of the desirability of the technology to be acquired.

Why Countertrade is Limited

Problems of an economic nature have prevented the desired investment in compensation, processing, and joint-ventures that China wishes. Chief among these difficulties is that of finding a suitable factory in China to serve as a reliable, long-term business partner. Among the key problems encountered by executives are:

- Chinese enterprises seem to pay insufficient attention to consumer satisfaction
- Factories selected by Beijing ministries for joint-venture often lack infrastructure
- Chinese factories sometimes tolerate hazardous levels of pollution
- Managers of Chinese enterprises have very little authority
- In China all management decisions must be cleared with a factory's communist party committee, and the local industrial bureau responsible for drawing up and supervising the factories annual plan
- The management ground rules under which Chinese enterprises operate are in a constant state of controversy and flux.

Restructuring and readjustment has forced the Chinese plant manager to assume greater decision making powers at a time when the allocations of funds, centrally-determined production and raw materials have all been cut back. Unaccustomed to the concepts of supply and demand and risk/benefit, he fails to understand the full complexities of countertrade. He tends to view it as a way to shift risk factors to the Western exporter who is expected to provide capital, equipment and technology for the plant's modernization and to secure needed outlet markets.

These circumstances suggest that Western companies negotiating compensation arrangements have to familiarize themselves with the limitations and needs of their local counterparts. The Western firm might have to structure its proposal to include varied fallback options which would appeal to the limited risk/exposure sought by the Chinese plant manager, and which he would be confident he could justify to the higher authorities charged with approving the transaction.

Inadequate means of resolving interagency disputes prolong negotiations and hinder countertrade agreements from being reached. To streamline bureaucracy and improve trade relations, China created MOFERT, the Ministry of Foreign Ecomonic Relations and Trade. MOFERT will assume the authority formerly vested in the Foreign Investment Control Commission (FICC) to give final approval to offshore oil contracts. MOFERT will also supervise the China Council for the Promotion of International Trade (CCPIT) and provide guidance to the China International Trust and Investment Corp. (CITIC). CITIC was set up to channel foreign funds into Chinese projects (via joint-venture, countertrade agreements, and wholly-owned foreign operations) that promise to earn a profit. Since the establishment of CITIC in 1979 many municipally-sanctioned organizations such as the Shanghai Investment & Trust Corp. (SITCO) were established with similar mandates.

The Foreign Trade and Aid Affairs Division within MOFERT'S Treaties and Law Department is now drafting an omnibus foreign trade law covering compensation and countertrade. In addition, within the Finance Investment Administration, the Compensation Trade Division is the Chinese organization specifically responsible for compensation and countertrade.

Another major culprit is Chinese regulation, or lack thereof. For example. a maximum of only 30 percent of compensation trade output for domestic sales is allowed[10] One of the most successful compensation trade deals with an American firm has eluded this condition, however: Coca Cola's Beijing bottling plant sells almost its entire output domestically.

Westerners fear technology infringments because China is not a member of the Convention of Paris for the Protection of Industrial Property (Paris Convention), and has only recently passed a patent law, which will go into effect in April, 1985. Also, the Chinese are determined to have final say over joint ventures' operation on Chinese soil, as evidenced by their reservation of the right to appoint venture chairmen. Questions as basic as the securing of utility service and raw materials, the determination of what constitutes a profit and how products will be distributed cannot be resolved by the ventures board acting alone. Prospective foreign participants in joint venture will relate to state (at national, provincial, and local level) and to party apparatuses.

FOOTNOTES

1. Pompiliu Verzariu, "An Update on Countertrade with China," *Business America* (January 11, 1982), p.8.
2. *The China Reporter* (July 1981), p. 5.
3. Stephen Markscheid, "Compensation Trade: Keeping Deals Simple is No Easy Task," *China Business Review* 9, no. 1 (January-February 1982), p. 51.
4. James B. Stepanek, "Direct Investment in China, "*China Business Review* 9, no. 5 (September-October 1982), p.22
5. Ibid., p. 25.
6. Ibid., p. 25.
7. Ibid., pp. 20-21.
8. Ibid., p. 24.
9. Stephen Markscheid, "Compensation Trade: Keeping Deals Simple is No Easy Task, " *China Business Review* 9, no. 1, (January-February 1982), p. 51.
10. Ibid., p. 52.

AGREEMENT
between
THE GOVERNMENT OF THE UNITED STATES
and
THE GOVERNMENT OF JAMAICA
for the
BARTER OF BAUXITE
for
AGRICULTURAL COMMODITIES

AGREEMENT FOR THE BARTER OF
AGRICULTURAL COMMODITIES FOR BAUXITE

This Agreement is hereby entered into this 25th day of February 1982, by and between the Government of Jamaica represented by the Bauxite and Alumina Trading Company Ltd. (hereinafter called BATCO) and the Government of the United States represented by the Commodity Credit Corporation, an agency and instrumentality of the United States within the Department of Agriculture (hereinafter called the "CCC").

WITNESSETH:

Whereas, BATCO desires to enter into a barter arrangement with CCC under which BATCO agrees to sell to CCC 400,000 Long Dry Tons (LDT) of metal grade bauxite; *Whereas,* CCC desires to enter into a barter arrangement with BATCO under which CCC agrees to sell to BATCO 7,238 metric tons of nonfat dry milk and 1,905 metric tons of anhydrous milkfat;

Now therefore, CCC and BATCO agree as follows:

PART A
BAUXITE PROVISIONS
ARTICLE 1: PURPOSE

This Agreement represents a portion of a total transaction between the Government of the United States of America and the Government of Jamaica for acquisition of

1,600,000 Long Dry Tons (LDT) of metal grade bauxite for the National Defense Stockpile. The principal purpose of this Agreement is to define the terms and conditions under which BATCO will sell 400,000 LDT of metal grade bauxite to CCC and the terms and conditions under which CCC will sell 7,238 metric tons of nonfat dry milk and 1,905 metric tons of annydrous milkfat to BATCO. The balance of the bauxite (1,200,000 LDT) will be covered in an agreement between the United States General Services Administration (GSA) and BATCO, which agreement will also contain provisions covering the transportation costs for the 400,000 LDT of bauxite covered by this Agreement. The total amount of bauxite to be acquired by CCC and GSA is 1.6 million tons, all of which is to be delivered prior to September 30, 1982.

ARTICLE II: MATERIAL

2.1 *Material*
　　BATCO will furnish the management, labor, facilities, materials, tools and equipment and do all things necessary and/or incidental to performance of the work described below:

Item 1- Provide 400,000 LDT of Grade 2 metal grade bauxite conforming to the chemical and physical requirements of National Stockpile Purchase Specification P-5b-R, dated December 15, 1981 (referred to herein as "Specification"), except that in Article II, Paragraph A, the following is deleted:

　　　　Ferric Oxide　　　　Max: 20.0
　　　　Titanium Dioxide　　Max: 2.5

and the following is substituted:

　　　　Ferric Oxide　　　　Max: 22.0
　　　　Titanium Dioxide　　Max: 3.0

and Article II, Paragraph B, is deleted in its entirety.

Item 2- Deliver the material listed in Item 1 to the U.S. Government Storage Track No. 10 which is located on the Reynolds Metals Company facilities, Gregory, Texas.

Item 3- Build, trim and shape the pile of material delivered under Item 2 to conform to the following requirements:

a. Toes of the piles shall not extend beyond the prepared pad on Storage Track No. 10.
b. Outside slope of the pile shall average 30 degrees, but must not exceed 35 degrees.
c. The stockpile shall be built in lifts of a maximum of three feet per lift. The haul trucks will be dumped and dumped material graded with a dozer to form the lift. This method should achieve a density of at least 81 pounds per cubic feet.
d. A berm four feet high shall be provided around the top edge. The bauxite used for forming this berm shall be moistened, compacted and formed up on the inside face to a maximum angle of repose.

Item 4- Provide a sampling platform located adjacent to the scale used for weighing the bauxite. The platform shall include a ramp or catwalk in order to provide the sampler access to the bauxite in the trucks. The sample shall be taken after the truck gross weight is recorded and before the material is unloaded. The platform and access ramp shall be constructed so as to accommodate various size trucks, and still provide safety for the sampler while being suitable for the purpose of sampling. A drawing of the platform shall be supplied to GSA for comment prior to construction. The platform shall be operational prior to commencement of deliveries.

Item 5- Refurnish and maintain existing weighing station adjacent to the storage site. The scales shall be certified by a recognized scale company or State Weights and Measures Authority, at least every three (3) months or after major repairs to the scale.

ARTICLE III: DELIVERY OF THE MATERIAL

3.1 *Schedule*
Deliveries of the material shall begin on or about July 15, 1982, and be completed by September 30, 1982. A minimum of 150,000 LDTs to a maximum of 250,000 LDTs shall be delivered within each 30-day period beginning with the first delivery date.

3.2 *Destination*
Material will be delivered to U.S. Government Storage Track No. 10, at Reynolds Metals Company facilities, Gregory, Texas.

3.3 *Notice*
BATCO shall notify CCC, or its authorized representative (for Part A of this Agreement, the authorized representative shall be the General Services Administration, hereinafter called "GSA"), in writing not less than ten (10) working days prior to commencement of initial delivery. GSA shall be notified in writing five days prior to any forseeable and subsequent reinstatement of delivery.

ARTICLE IV: INSPECTION, SAMPLING, ANALYSIS, WEIGHING AND ACCEPTANCE

4.1 *Lot Size*
For the purpose of weighing, inspection, sampling, and analysis, a lot shall constitute 10,000 Long Wet Tons consecutively delivered.

4.2 *Inspection*
Inspection of the bauxite shall be performed or witnessed by a GSA representative at Gregory, Texas.

4.3 *Sampling and Analysis*
GSA will sample the bauxite at Gregory, Texas. Sampling and sample preparation shall be at the direction and expense of GSA. Sampling shall be accomplished as close as possible to the time of weighing of the bauxite at Gregory, Texas. Representative samples shall be taken from each lot. Samples taken shall be for the purpose of determining conformance of the lot to the requirements of the Specification. Procedures and methodology for the laboratory testing shall be those described in Exhibit A-2.

4.4 *Moisture Content Determination*
One portion of the sample taken for moisture determination will be delivered to Reynolds Metals Company. One or two portions of the GSA sample shall be used for moisture content determination. The GSA sample shall be dried at a temperature of 140 degrees centigrade for

not less than eight hours or to constant weight. The loss of weight shall be regarded as moisture. The percentage of moisture in the sample shall be subtracted from the net weight of the lot as determined in Paragraph 4.6 below, and the resulting dry weight shall be used as the basis for payment. The moisture determination of the GSA analysis shall be final on all deliveries and not subject to umpire.

4.5 *Umpire Laboratory Procedure*

BATCO may request that a sample be sent to umpire for chemical analysis of any compound failing GSA test analysis. The umpire laboratory shall be mutually acceptable to both BATCO and GSA. The average of the umpire analysis results and the results of either GSA or BATCO analysis, whichever is closer to the umpire results, shall be final and govern. For individual lots not in conformance with the Specification, only compounds that failed to meet the Specification requirements may be analyzed by the umpire. The cost of the umpire will be for the account of the party whose analysis is the farthest from umpire's results. If both are of equal difference from the umpire, the cost will be shared equally.

4.6 *Weighing*

Weighing shall be performed by an official weighmaster mutually acceptable to GSA and BATCO at the Reynolds truck scales located as close as possible to the storage site. Weighing shall be at the expense of GSA. Every truck shall be gross weighed prior to delivery of the bauxite to the storage area. The tare weights of the trucks shall be established periodically as directed by GSA. A complete record of weights by scale weight tickets shall be made for each vehicle for each load hauled. Weight certificates listing truck weight data in tabular form shall be issued by the weighmaster. When a completed lot of material has been weighed, a certified weight certificate shall be signed by the weighmaster and attested to by the GSA representative.

4.7 *Acceptance*

4.7.1 If the analysis of the GSA sample indicates that the bauxite complies with the requirements of the Specification when considered on a weighted average basis with all previous deliveries, the lot shall be accepted.

4.7.2 If any lot fails to comply with the requirements of the Specification when considered on a weighted average basis with all previous deliveries, acceptance shall not be made for such lot until (by subsequent lots) the weighted average of all lots delivered shall comply with the requirements of the Specification.

4.7.3 If after 80 percent of the material has been delivered to the site, the weighted average analysis as defined in 4.7.1 does not comply with the Specification, all further deliveries shall cease until BATCO can show that the remaining 20 percent of the material will be of such quality as to bring the weighted average analysis of the site into compliance with the Specification.

4.7.4 The Notice of Inspection, GSA Form 308-A, shall be issued by GSA after receipt of reports on analysis, weighing, and physical requirements on one or more lots. Acceptance or notice of noncompliance of the material tendered shall be made by GSA on Form 308-A.

ARTICLE V: CONSIDERATION AND PAYMENT FOR THE BAUXITE

5.1 *Unit Price and Amount*
BATCO will be paid as follows for the bauxite delivered to CCC.

Description	Quantity	Unit Price	Total Value
Bauxite	400,000 LDT	U.S. $32.50 Per LDT	U.S. $13,000,000

5.2 *Transportation, Handling and Delivery to the Pile*
BATCO will be paid by GSA for the transportation, handling and delivery to the pile of the bauxite purchased by CCC at the rates provided in Article VI, paragraph 6.2, and Article X of the Memorandum of Agreement. Between the Government of the United States and the Government of Jamaica for the Acquisition of Bauxite.

5.3 *Payment*
Payment for the value of the bauxite delivered to CCC,

excluding the cost of transportation, handling and delivery to the pile, as provided in paragraph 5.2, shall be paid for by CCC by delivery to BATCO of an equivalent value of agricultural commodities as specified in Articles VII and VIII.

5.4 *Barter Account*

Upon delivery to and acceptance of the bauxite by GSA, the value of the bauxite accepted shall be credited to a "barter account" for BATCO. The value of each lot will be credited to the account upon determination of acceptance by GSA, as demonstrated by the issuance of a GSA Form 308-A. The "barter account" will be liquidated as specified in Article XII, by applying to the account the value of the agricultural commodities delivered to BATCO in accordance with Part B of this Agreement.

5.5 *Invoices*

5.5.1 An invoice shall be submitted weekly by BATCO to GSA covering the quantity of material to be delivered in the following week. The format shall be one acceptable to GSA.

5.5.2 *Fixed Price*

The unit price of the bauxite as provided in paragraph 5.1 is inclusive of all costs of performance, including costs and cost escalations not known or not contemplated at the time this Agreement was signed, and includes (without in any way limiting thereto) all costs and costs escalations related to material, labor, transportation to the vessel, and testing, as well as Jamaican customs, duties, taxes, assessments, licenses and permits. The unit price of bauxite covered by this Agreement is firm and fixed and not subject to revision.

PART B
AGRICULTURAL COMMODITY PROVISIONS
ARTICLE VI: CONTRACT QUANTITY

CCC agrees to sell, and BATCO agrees to purchase, 7,238 metric tons of nonfat dry milk (5,184 metric tons of medium heat and 2,054 metric tons of high heat) and 1,905 metric tons of anhydrous milkfat.

ARTICLE VII: COMMODITY PRICE

7.1 *Nonfat Dry Milk*
The price of the nonfat dry milk shall be U.S. $1,100 per metric ton, FAS Gulf ports, plus storage charges of U.S. $10 per metric ton for deliveries of nonfat dry milk made to Gulf ports after August 31, 1982. Delivery shall be evidenced by the date of the dock receipt.

7.2 *Anhydrous Milkfat*
The price of the anhydrous milkfat shall be U.S. $2,625 per metric ton, FAS Gulf ports. No storage charges shall apply to deliveries of anhydrous milkfat.

ARTICLE VIII: DELIVERY SCHEDULE

8.1 *Nonfat Dry Milk*
   8.1.1 CCC shall deliver the nonfat dry milk to BATCO FAS Gulf ports in accordance with following schedule:

Delivery Month (1982)	Medium Heat (MT)	High Heat (MT)
MAY	594	250
JUNE	650	100
JULY	650	284
AUGUST	650	284
SEPTEMBER	650	284
OCTOBER	650	284
NOVEMBER	670	284
DECEMBER	670	284
TOTAL	5,184	2,054
GRAND TOTAL		7,238

   8.1.2 In consideration of CCC's agreement to furnish nonfat dry milk manufactured within 90 calendar days from date of delivery to Gulf ports, CCC has the option to vary the quantities between medium heat and high heat nonfat dry milk each delivery month. However, CCC shall endeavor to deliver nonfat dry milk in accordance with the quantities of medium heat or high heat called for by the delivery schedule. CCC will adjust shipments in July, October and December so that the cumulative quantities of medium heat and high heat delivered will agree with the cumulative amounts called for by the delivery schedule.

8.2 *Anhydrous Milkfat*

CCC shall deliver the anhydrous milkfat to BATCO FAS Gulf ports in accordance with the following delivery schedule:

Delivery Month	Quantity (MT)
JULY 1982	250
AUGUST	250
SEPTEMBER	250
OCTOBER	230
NOVEMBER	230
DECEMBER	230
JANUARY 1983	230
FEBRUARY	235
TOTAL	1,905

8.3 *Notice to Deliver*

At least 21 days prior to the final date that CCC is to have the nonfat dry milk and anhydrous milkfat at port, BATCO shall furnish CCC with a notice to deliver listing the vessel name, estimated time of arrival and port, quantity of nonfat dry milk and anhydrous milkfat scheduled to be lifted, and stating whether the shipment is to be containerized or unitized, such as on pallets and stretch-wrapped. The notice shall be sent to the Kansas City Agricultural Stabilization and Conservation Service (ASCS) Commodity Office.

8.4 BATCO shall be responsible for all expenses after delivery by CCC of the nonfat dry milk and anhydrous milk to FAS Gulf port, including any expenses for failure of the vessel to lift all or part of the shipment as scheduled, pier or warehouse storage, rail, truck and/or barge demurrage, reinspection and deterioration. In the event CCC fails to deliver all or part of the quantity scheduled to be delivered each month, CCC shall be responsible for all expenses resulting from such failure including, but not limited to, dead freight and demurrage.

ARTICLE IX: QUALITY AND QUANTITY DETERMINATIONS

9.1 *Nonfat Dry Milk*

9.1.1 The nonfat dry milk shall be U.S. Extra Grade and shall meet the United States Standards for Grades of Nonfat Dry Milk (Spray Process), in effect on April 1, 1973, except that the moisture content must be no more than 3.7 percent. (Exhibit B - 1)

9.1.2 The nonfat dry milk shall have been manufactured in the United States within 90 calendar days from date of delivery to Gulf ports. The date of delivery to port will be evidenced by the date of the dock receipt.

9.1.3 The nonfat dry milk shall be produced in a plant meeting the USDA requirements contained in the "General Specifications for Dairy Plants Approved for USDA Inspection and Grading Service." (Exhibit B - 2)

9.1.4 Inspection and testing procedures for the nonfat dry milk to determine the grade and weight shall be in accordance with USDA General Instructions for Sampling NDM dated July 13, 1970, as revised (DA INST. NO. 918-30) and USDA Methods of Laboratory Analysis for Nonfat Dry Milk dated November 30, 1972 (DA INST. No. 918-103-1) (Exhibit B - 3).

9.1.5 BATCO shall have the right of reinspection of the nonfat dry milk at the U.S. port of export and the right to reject any nonfat dry milk which does not meet the terms and conditions of this Agreement.

9.2 *Anhydrous Milkfat*

9.2.1 The anhydrous milkfat shall have a flavor similar to bland, unmelted, unsalted, uncultured, fresh cream butter; when heated to approximately 140 F, be clear; and have a uniform light yellow to golden color. It shall be free from objectionable foreign flavors and odors, such as rancid, scorched, stale, oxidized or metallic. The anhydrous milkfat shall be free from lumps or large crystals, be smooth with the interior free of air bubbles and contain no antioxidants. In addition, the anhydrous milkfat shall meet the following analytical requirements:

(a) Milkfat - not less than 99.8 percent

(b) Moisture - not more than 0.15 percent

(c) Free fatty acids - not more than 0.3 percent (calculated as oleic acid)

(d) Peroxide value - not more than 0.1 milligram equivalent per kilogram of fat

9.2.2 The product shall be produced in a plant meeting the USDA requirements contained in the "General Specifications for Dairy Plants Approved for USDA Inspection and Grading Service". (Exhibit B-2)

9.2.3 Inspection and testing procedures for the purpose of determining the quality of the anhydrous milkfat shall be in accordance with USDA Methods of Laboratory Analysis for Moisture, Fat, Salt, Curd and PH dated November 30, 1972 (DA INST. NO. 918-101-1). (Exhibit B - 4)

9.2.4 The anhydrous milkfat must meet the required specifications and standards published in the Federal Register, Vol. 40 No. 198 of October 10, 1975. (Exhibit B - 2)

9.2.5 BATCO shall have the right of reinspection of the anhydrous milkfat at the U.S. port of export and the right to reject any anhydrous milkfat which does not meet the terms and conditions of this Agreement.

ARTICLE X: PACKAGING AND MARKING

10.1 *Nonfat Dry Milk*

10.1.1 *Packaging Description*

The nonfat dry milk will be packed in 50 pound (22.68 kilos) sacks constructed of 3 layer kraft paper and a loose - inserted 4 mil-low density food grade polyethylene liner. Sacks may be sealed by sewing horizontally along the upper edge without sewing the polyethylene liner, or the sacks may be sealed with heat. If bags are sewn, exposed threads will be covered with paper to prevent insect and dust penetration into the powder. The loose-inserted polyethylene liner will be gathered in the form of a goose neck and tied.

10.1.2 *Packaging and Markings*
Sacks containing the nonfat dry milk shall be marked to show the following:
(a) Name of product.
(b) Name and location of manufacturing plant or plant number.
(c) Month and year manufactured.
(d) Manufacturer's lot number.
(e) Marked net weight of 50 lbs.
(f) The sacks containing high heat nonfat dry milk will have a clearly visible red marking on the outer layer of each sack. The medium heat nonfat dry milk will not have these special distinctive markings.

10.2 *Anhydrous Milkfat*
10.2.1 *Container Description*
The anhydrous milkfat shall be packed in new 55 gallon nonreturnable steel drums. The drums shall be Type II, liquid tight, 18 gage or heavier closed-head cylindrical steel, with double seamed chimes, flat heads, integral chime reinforcement, expanded side wall consisting of a series of parallel circumferential beads meeting the requirements of Federal Specification PPP-D-1152 or PPP-D-729 (Exhibit B - 5). Steel cap seals shall be applied to each closure in accordance with PPP-D-729 or PPP-D-1152 (Exhibit B - 5). The drums shall be lined with a Food and Drug Administration approved food-grade liner recommended for contact with anhydrous milkfat.
The drums shall contain anhydrous milkfat weighing approximately 440 pounds net (200 kilos). The drums will be vacuum sealed, or a

nitrogen blanket may be applied to eliminate air in the drum. The drums containing anhydrous milkfat will be transported to Gulf ports and stored at port without refrigeration.

10.2.2 *Labeling and Marking*
The following information shall be indicated on the exterior of the drum:
(a) Name of product
(b) Date of manufacture (day, month, year)
(c) "Keep Refrigerated"-(32 F to 40 F)

ARTICLE XI: DOCUMENTS REQUIRED

11.1 *Nonfat dry milk*
11.1.1 CCC shall furnish to BATCO an inspection and grading certificate issued by the U.S. Department of Agriculture showing the manufacture date, weight, quality and origin of the nonfat dry milk. The inspection and grading certificate will show the nonfat dry milk to be extra grade, to have been manufactured in the United States within 90 calendar days from the date of delivery to Gulf ports, and that the moisture content is no more than 3.7 percent. The inspection and grading certificate will be the only document required to be presented by CCC evidencing the quality, weight, origin and date of manufacture of the nonfat dry milk.
11.1.2 CCC will furnish to BATCO a copy of (a) any over, short or damage report for each shipment; (b) a dock receipt; and (c) a consignee receipt.
11.1.3 BATCO will furnish to CCC one copy of the signed on-board ocean bill of lading showing the ultimate destination of the nonfat dry milk as Jamaica.
11.2 *Anhydrous Milkfat*
11.2.1 CCC shall furnish to BATCO an inspection and grading certificate issued by the U.S. Department of Agriculture showing the laboratory analysis, manufacture date, weight, the place of manufacture of the anhydrous milkfat and a

health statement that reads - "The anhydrous milkfat was manufactured in a plant inspected and approved by the U.S. Department of Agriculture as operating under sanitary conditions and the anhydrous milkfat was considered suitable for human consumption at the time of inspection and laboratory analysis". The inspection and grading certificate will show that the anhydrous milkfat was manufactured in the United States and meets the specifications required by this Agreement. The inspection and grading certificate will be the only document required to be presented by CCC evidencing the quality, weight and origin of the anhydrous milkfat.

11.2.2 CCC will furnish to BATCO a copy of (a) any over, short or damage report for each shipment; (b) a cook receipt; and (c) a consignee receipt.

11.2.3 BATCO will furnish to CCC one copy of the signed on-board ocean bill of lading showing the ultimate destination of the anhydrous milkfat as Jamaica.

11.3 *Transmittal of Documents*

CCC shall furnish BATCO, or its designated agent, with an invoice and a copy of each required document promptly after each shipment. BATCO shall notify the Kansas City ASCS Commodity Office of its designated agent to which the documents are to be sent promptly after the signing of this Agreement.

ARTICLE XII: PAYMENT FOR THE AGRICULTURAL COMMODITIES

12.1 Payment to CCC for the FAS value of the nonfat dry milk and anhydrous milkfat delivered to and accepted by BATCO shall be paid for by BATCO by delivery to CCC, in accordance with Part A of this Agreement, of a quantity of bauxite equivalent in total value to the total FAS value of the nonfat dry milk and anhydrous milkfat delivered. CCC will establish a "barter account" in which the value of exports of nonfat dry milk and anhydrous milkfat will be applied against the value of the bauxite delivered to CCC in accordance with Part A of this Agreement.

12.2 If the total value of the nonfat dry milk and anhydrous milkfat delivered to BATCO exceeds the value of the bauxite received by CCC, BATCO shall make payment to CCC for such excess value in U.S. dollars.

12.3 If the value of the bauxite delivered to CCC exceeds the total value of the nonfat dry milk and anhydrous milkfat delivered to BATCO, CCC shall make payment to BATCO for such excess in U.S. dollars.

ARTICLE XIII: EXPORT REQUIREMENTS

13.1 BATCO shall export the nonfat dry milk and anhydrous milk delivered by CCC only to Jamaica. The nonfat dry milk and anhydrous milk shall not be reentered by anyone into the United States nor shall BATCO cause the nonfat dry milk and anhydrous milkfat to be transshipped to any other country.

13.2 The sale by CCC of the nonfat dry milk and anhydrous milkfat covered by this Agreement is made upon condition that BATCO complies with the export requirements of this Agreement. If the nonfat dry milk and anhydrous milkfat delivered by CCC is not exported or is reentered into the United States, the purchase price with respect to the quantity of nonfat dry milk involved shall be adjusted upward to the domestic unrestricted use price of $2,280 per metric ton and the contract price with respect to the quantity of anhydrous milkfat involved shall be adjusted upward to the domestic unrestricted use price for U.S. extra grade butter of $3,686 per metric ton, plus $988 per metric ton which reflects generally the processing charges paid by CCC to convert cream to anhydrous milkfat plus the cost of the drums in which the anhydrous milkfat is packed and the estimated shrinkage which occurs in processing cream into anhydrous milkfat.

13.3 The total amount of upward adjustment in the purchase price shall be paid by BATCO in U.S. dollars to CCC promptly on demand, plus interest on the upward adjustment in the purchase price at the rate of nineteen

(19) percent per annum from the date of signing this Agreement.

13.4 An upward adjustment of the purchase price for nonfat dry milk and anhydrous milkfat not exported, or which is reentered into the United States, will not be made if CCC determines that:

(a) The nonfat dry milk or anhydrous milkfat purchased from CCC was lost, damaged, destroyed, or deteriorated and the physical condition thereof was such that its entry into domestic market channels will not impair CCC's price support operations: *Provided*, that if insurance proceeds or other recoveries (such as from carriers) exceed the purchase price of the nonfat dry milk or anhydrous milkfat lost, damaged, destroyed, or deteriorated, plus other costs incurred by BATCO in connection with such nonfat dry milk or anhydrous milkfat prior to the time of its loss, the amount of such excess shall be paid to CCC; or

(b) The nonfat dry milk or anhydrous milkfat was reentered into the United States without the fault or negligence of BATCO and was subsequently exported in accordance with the provisions of this Agreement.

13.5 If any quantity of nonfat dry milk or anhydrous milkfat is transshipped, or caused to be transshipped by BATCO to any country other than Jamaica, BATCO shall be in default and shall be subject to the applicable upward purchase price adjustment specified in Paragraph 13.2 of this Article XIII.

PART C
GENERAL PROVISIONS
ARTICLE 14: MANAGEMENT COMMITTEE

14.1 *Committee*

Promptly after the signing of this Agreement, the parties hereto shall establish a Management Committee to oversee the performance of this Agreement. CCC shall appoint to be members of such commitee an individual in the Department of Agriculture to represent its interests with respect to terms of this Agreement covering the anhydrous milkfat and nonfat dry milk and an individual in the General Services Administration to represent its interests with respect to the terms of this Agreement covering the bauxite. BATCO shall appoint two individuals to be a member of such committee. Each party shall also appoint an alternate member(s). The Management Committee will not be empowered to revise or amend this Agreement.

14.2 *Coordination*

Subject to requirements set forth in this Agreement, the Management Committee will coordinate efforts among the parties and resolve problems which may arise in the administration of this Agreement. Meetings may be called by either party upon seven days notice and will be held at the principal location of the non-requesting party. An agenda will be proposed for each meeting and distributed by the host at least three working days prior to the meeting. Minutes of each meeting will be published by the host within five working days after the meeting.

14.3 *Delegation of Authority*

14.3.1 CCC reserves the right to delegate to the GSA any and all authority to act as its agent in carrying out the terms and conditions of Part A of this Agreement as they relate to the shipment, handling and storing of the bauxite.

14.3.2 BATCO reserves the right to delegate to Jamaica Commodity Trading Company, Ltd. any and all authority to act as its agent in carrying out the terms and conditions of Part B of this Agreement as they relate to the shipment of the agricultural commodities.

ARTICLE XV: DISPUTES

Any dispute arising under PART B of this Agreement concerning a question of fact or law which is not disposed of by mutual agreement between the parties hereto, shall be finally settled under the Rules of Conciliation and Arbitration of the International Chamber of Commerce by one or more arbitrators appointed in accordance with the rules thereof. The Agreement will be governed by the laws of the State of New York.

ARTICLE XVI: NOTICES

All notices required or permitted to be given under this Agreement shall be given in writing and by registered air mail or cable addressed to such party at the following addresses:

16.1 PART A - BAUXITE PROVISIONS
Jamaica Government
c/o The Bauxite and Alumina
Trading Company, Limited
5th Floor, 63 Knutsford Boulevard
Kingston, 5, Jamaica, W.I.
Telex: 2467, JABM JA

General Services Administration
Agent for Commodity Credit Corporation
18th & F Streets, NW
Federal Property Resources Service - D
Washington, DC 20405
Telex No. 89.2515

16.2 PART B - AGRICULTURAL COMMODITY
PROVISIONS
Commodity Credit Corporation
14th Street and Independence Avenue, S.W.
Washington, D.C. 20250
Telex: 8-9491
Telephone: (202) 382-9254 or 447-6301.

Jamaica Government
c/o The Bauxite and Alumina
The Trading Company, Limited (BATCO)
5th Floor, 63 Knutsford Boulevard
Kingston, 5, Jamaica, W.I.
Telex: 2467, JABM JA

Kansas City Agricultural Stabilization
and Conservation Service (ASCS) Commodity Office
P.O. Box 8510
Kansas City, Missouri 64114
Telex: 434126
Telephone: (816) 976-6140

ARTICLE XVII: FORCE MAJEURE

Neither BATCO nor CCC shall be liable for any failure
or delay in complying with their respective responsibilities
under this Agreement caused in whole or in part by force
majeure which shall include, but not be restricted to, acts of
God or of the public enemy, acts of the Government, fires,
floods, epidemics, quarantine, restrictions, strikes, freight
embargoes, and unusually severe weather; however, in every
case, the failure to perform must be beyond the control and
without the fault or negligence of the party to the Agreement
seeking excuse from liability.

ARTICLE XVIII: OTHER PROVISIONS
(PART A ONLY)

18.1 *Applicable to Entire Part A*
The following clauses apply to Part A of this Agreement.
Wherever the word "contract" appears, it shall be
deemed to mean this Agreement. Wherever the word
"contractor" appears, it shall be deemed to mean
"BATCO".
  (i) Definitions, Clause 1, Standard Form 32 (copy
      attached)
  (ii) Assignment of Claims, Clause 8, Standard Form
      32 (copy attached)
  (iii) Examination of Records by Comptroller General,
      Clause 10, Standard Form 32 (copy attached)
  (iv) Disputes Clause, Clause 12, Standard Form (copy
      attached)
  (v) Use of U.S. Flag Commercial Vessels, Clause 57,
      GSA Form 1424 (copy attached)
  (vi) Pricing of Adjustments, Clause 24, Standard
      Form 32 (copy attached)

18.2 *Applicable to Work Performed in the U.S. Under Part A* BATCO shall include the following clauses in any subcontract work to be performed in the United States:
  (i) Clauses from Standard Form 32 (copy attached):
     15. Convict Labor
     16. Contract Work Hours and Safety Standard Act-Overtime Compensation
     18. Equal Opportunity
  (ii) Clauses from GSA Form 1424 (copy attached):
     59. Clean Air and Water
     62. Disabled Veterans and Veterans of the Vietnam Era
     65. Cost or Pricing Data Requirements
  (iii) Clauses (attached):
     Small Business and Small Disadvantaged Business Subcontracting Labor
     Surplus Area Subcontracting Program
     Women Owned Business Concerns Subcontracting Program

ARTICLE XIX: AMENDMENTS

Any amendments to this Agreement must be in writing and require the signature of both parties in order to be valid. Such amendments shall be expressly designated as amendments hereto and numbered consecutively.

ARTICLE XX: DURATION

This Agreement shall remain in effect for the period starting with the signature of both parties until the mutual obligations herein have been completed.

In witness whereof, this Agreement has been executed by and on behalf of CCC and BATCO by their respective duly authorized officers.

FOR THE GOVERNMENT OF THE UNITED STATES

BY_____

General Sales Manager
and Vice President, Commodity
Credit Corporation

Date_____

FOR THE GOVERNMENT OF JAMAICA

BY_____

Date_____

Appendix A
SAMPLE COUNTERTRADE CONTRACTS

General Agreement for Production of Metal Products in China

1. Sellers undertake to produce _____ (product for Buyers) with material from Buyers on processing fees basis. Designs, specification, quantity and rate or processing fees for such production will be stipulated in separate contracts as agreed upon by both parties.

2. Buyers undertake to provide Sellers with required processing equipment and equipment for production and maintenance of toolings for a total value of HK $_____ as per Appendix I attached.

3. To compensate the cost of equipment provided by Buyers, a special discount of _____ percent of invoice value will be deducted from the processing fees. such deduction will be effected from the first shipment of goods supplied by Sellers until the total value of equipment is fully reimbursed. Materials and dies are to be supplied by Buyers free of charge to Sellers.

4. All equipment to be provided by Buyers will be delivered in one or more shipments to arrive Shanghai latest by the end of 1978. Buyers will send technical staff to Shanghai to assist in installation and to render technical advice. Adequate quantity of materials, corresponding to the quantity of contracted production under this agreement with reasonable allowance of waste is to be delivered by Buyers to Sellers. First shipment of material should be delivered within 30 days after arrival of the equipment at Shanghai.

5. It is mutually agreed that the first lot of products to be processed will not be less than ____ (quantity) pieces each of Buyers' design no. _____ Specifications and quality of products will conform to Buyers' samples submitted. (Four sealed samples each are in possession of Buyers and Sellers for reference.) Finished products will be delivered to Buyers within 60 days after arrival of the materials at Shanghai.

6. Sellers hereby indemnify buyers from any loss or damage caused by deviation of quality or specification. Discrepancies resulted by contingencies beyond human control will be settled by means of mutual negotiation.

7. Sellers agree not to sell or supply any products under Buyers' design to any party other than the Buyers.

8. This agreement will have effect from _____ (date) for _____ years and the duration may be extended or amended by negotiation.

Draft of a Counterpurchase Agreement with the U.S.S.R.

Counterpurchases

1. In connection with the signing of the present Contract the parties have agreed that the Sellers will purchase from Soviet Foreign Trade organizations within the period of ____ _____ machines and/or equipment in the amount of _____, it being understood that the prices for the above machines and/or equipment will be of the world level.

2. The quantity and detailed specification of the machines and/or equipment as well as the prices, time and other conditions of the delivery must be agreed upon between the Sellers and the corresponding Soviet Foreign Trade organization not later than _____ from the date of signing the present Contract.

3. The Sellers will immediately notify the Buyers that the transaction has been concluded by sending to them a copy of the Contract, concluded with the Soviet Foreign Trade organization.

In the Contract there should be reference to the present Contract.

4. In case of non-fulfillment by the Sellers of the above obligation the Buyers have the right to deduct the sum, stated in Clause 1 of the present Article, from the Sellers' invoices. Should for any reason the stated sum not be deducted by the Buyers while paying the Sellers' invoices, the latter are to pay this sum at the first demand of the Buyers.

Bank Letter of Guarantee for a Counter Purchase Contract with Romania

BANK LETTER OF GUARANTEE
for fulfillment of contract Nr. _____ of RO-
MANIAN BANK FOR FOREIGN TRADE Bucharest

Messrs. ROMCHIM, Bucharest and Messrs. _____
have concluded on the _____ the Frame
Contract Nr. _____ through which Messrs.
_____ oblige themselves to buy Romanian
commodities according to Chap. I, Art. 3 and 4 and to Chap.
IV. par. 1 and 2 as follows:

Chap. I — Art. 3 "_____"
— Art. 4 "_____"

Chap. IV (par. 1 and 2)
"_____
_____"

In case of nonfulfillment of the obligations stipulated in

the Frame Contract Nr. _____ according to Chap. II of the aforementioned Frame Contract, Messrs. _____ are obligated to pay a penalty guaranteed by a bank letter of guarantee, that is:

Chap. II — "_____
_____"

According to these stipulated above, we oblige ourselves irrevocably to pay in favor of Messrs. ROMCHIM up to the amount of _____ any sum requested by you invoking Chap. II reproduce above, at your first and simple demand without any other proof except your declaration that Messrs. _____ have not complied with obligations foreseen in Chap. II of the Frame Contract Nr. _____ concluded with Messrs. ROMCHIM.

By virtue of this letter of guarantee we will immediately effect the payments, deliberately renouncing at the benefit of the division and discussion, without having the right on our part of opposing the payments requested, or to invoke another objection or any other formality of any kind on the part of Messrs. _____ or on our part, not to invoke currency restrictions of which Messrs. _____ could prevail, and without being necessary for you to have recourse against Messrs. _____ or to Arbitration or to any Tribunal.

The validity of this letter of guarantee expires 30 days after the time limit foreseen in Chap. I art. 4 of the Frame Contract Nr. _____ for purchasing the Romanian commodities, but can be automatically extended, without any formality with the delays agreed by the partners of the above mentioned Frame Contract.

After the obligation under this letter of guarantee has been performed, this letter of guarantee shall be returned to us.

_____
(Bank)

Draft of a Counterpurchase Contract with Romania

FRAME CONTRACT

concluded on the _____ 197X between _____ and ROMCHIM, Bucharest, Bd., Dacia 13.

Chapter I

1) ROMCHIM and Messrs, _____ have concluded the contract Nr. _____ for the supply of _____ amounting to _____

2) Further to the above conclusion, Messrs. _____ _____ oblige themselves to purchase Romanian commodities mutually agreed upon, directly or through third firms, under competitive conditions to be established from case to case.

3) The value of Romanian commodities agreed upon represents ____% of the contract value, that is _____ _____ out of which

4) Messrs. _____ oblige themselves to buy and pay the Romanian goods foreseen under Point 3) above before _____

Chapter II—Guarantee

In case of failure of Messrs. _____ to fulfill their obligations in contractual time, or if they fulfill them only partially, the company shall pay to ROMCHIM a penalty of ____% on the non-fulfilled partial value of the obligation. As a guarantee of the penalty payment Messrs. _____ _____ will remit in favour of ROMCHIM a bank letter of guarantee (according to the attached draft) issued by a corresponding bank of the Romanian Bank for Foreign Trade.

The receipt of the aforementioned bank guarantee letter conditions the acknowledgement on the part of Messrs. ROMCHIM of entering into force of the contract Nr. _____

Chapter III—Artibration—Art _____ of the contract Nr. _____

Chapter IV—Final provisions

The contractual parties agree upon that only those export contracts concluded with the Romanian exporting enterprises can be taken into consideration, as counter-parties, which stipulate precisely a clause that "the export contract constitutes a counter-party to contract Nr. _____"

Only the values of the goods contracted, delivered and payed after the coming into force of the contract Nr. _____ _____ will be deducted.

The values deducted are only the FOB and/or franco border of the exporting country values.

Irrespective of their value, or object, no contracts will be taken into consideration without the above mention.

Messrs. _____ and ROMCHIM shall keep record of the export operations contracted according to this Frame Contract.

The parties shall quarterly compare their records.

This Frame Contract is an integral part of the contract Nr. _____ and enters into force at the same time as the contract Nr. _____

ROMCHIM
Bucharest

Bank Guarantee for an Actual Counterpurchase Contract with Bulgaria

BANK GUARANTEE

In agreement with the
instructions of the Company _____
we give the following guarantee to
TECHNOIMPORT, Sofia:

We, the _____ Bank, have been advised that the Company _____, seller, and the FTO TECHNOIMPORT, buyer, have concluded Contract No. _____ for the delivery of _____

With Contract No. _____, the Company _____ _____ obligates itself, one month after the effective date of the contract, to give TECHNOIMPORT a bank guarantee in the amount of _____ as guarantee to TECHNOIMPORT, in the event that the Company _____ or the firms _____ empowered by it, do not buy or pay for the goods which are to be purchased from the Bulgarian exporting organizations, in the following values by year, as specified in Contract No. _____ being determined.

Year	Value
1976	_____
1977	_____
Total Value:	_____

In fulfillment of the above obligations of the Company _____ we, the _____ Bank, irrevocably, unconditionally without reservations and independently of the intervention or demands of _____ or third parties, take upon ourselves, at your first request, to pay the sums demanded by you to your account with the Bulgarian Foreign Trade Bank, up to the sum of _____ allocated by year as follows:

Year	Value
1976	_____
1977	_____
Total Value:	_____

For the payment of the sums in the present bank guarantee you shall send us an invoice, describing the amount of the obligation which was not met by the Company _____ and the manner in which the penalties payable by the Company _____ are calculated.

The present bank guarantee goes into force on _____ and is reduced proportionally with fulfillment of the obligations mentioned above, or is lessened by payment of penalties on your behalf, and is terminated on _____, when it is to be returned to us, if by that time you have made no request for payment of penalties. /Date/.

Bank _____

Draft of an Actual Counterpurchase Contract with Bulgaria

CONTRACT NO. ____

Relating to Contract No. ____ concluded between the Company _____, seller, and the FTO TECHNOIMPORT, buyer.

1. In connection with Contract No. ____ the seller ____
_____ obligates himself in a period of _____ from the effective date of the Contract, on his own or through other parties, to purchase for resale without any restrictions machinery or equipment of his choice from the export list of the indicated Bulgarian organizations _____, in the value of _____

2. The Contract for purchase of machinery and equipment shall be concluded directly between the Company _____ or other parties authorized by this firm, _____ and _____ _____ The purchase obligation for machinery and equipment is to be fulfilled as follows:

Year	Value
1976	_____

1977 _____

Total Value: _____

Any change in the amounts is permissible only by mutual agreement, and only if the above total value remains under all circumstances unchanged.

If such a mutual agreement is reached, the bank guarantee and penalties noted in this contract will be changed accordingly for the corresponding year.

3. The prices and all other conditions for the purchase of Bulgarian machinery and equipment are determined on the basis of international prices and conditions.

4. Contracts concluded by the Company _____ _____, or other empowered firms, with the Bulgarian exporting organizations mentioned above, shall contain a clause which indicates that they are to be concluded on the basis of Contract No. ____ between the FTO TECHNOIMPORT, as seller, and _____ _____, as buyer, dated ____

5. It will be considered that the Company _____ has fullfilled its obligations under this contract for the purchase of machinery and equipment, if by the end of each year all monies due for that year are received by the Bulgarian Foreign Trade Bank. The Company _____ will regularly and promptly notify the FTO TECHNOIMPORT, through the Bulgarian Foreign Trade Bank, Sofia, about the fulfillment of these obligations, that is, regarding contracts concluded with Bulgarian exporting organizations and regarding payments made pursuant to these contracts.

6. If the Company _____ does not meet its obligations for the purchase of Bulgarian machinery and equipment, and does not make the payments called for in Paragraph 5 of this contract, the Company _____ will pay penalties, paid to TECHNOIMPORT, at the rate of ____ percent of the unpaid value, payable by the end of the respective year. The penalties, if these should occur, are to be paid to

the FTO "TECHNOIMPORT" within one month following the year in which the contractual obligations were not fulfilled. At the end of each year, TECHNOIMPORT will present the Company _____ _____ with a bill covering the value of the penalties.

7. One month after the effective date of this contract, and not later than the date of payment by TECHNOIMPORT to the Company _____ of the amount specified in paragraph ____ of Contract No. ____ dated _____, TECHNOIMPORT will transmit a bank guarantee, issued by a first class _____ bank, correspondent of the Bulgarian foreign Trade bank, in accordance with the text of Appendix No. 1 of the present contract. The amount of these bank guarantees will be _____ in effect until _____, or one month after the fulfillment deadline of the counterpurchase obligations.

8. If the mentioned Bulgarian exporting organizations cannot deliver to the Company _____ , or to the other firms _____ authorized by that company, machinery and equipment according to the terms of the present contract as prescribed in paragraph 2, the parties will agree on the possibility of postponing, depending on market conditions, the purchase of this machinery and equipment for the next year or years, up to the last year foreseen for this transaction.

In that year or in those years, when the Company _____ did not meet its purchasing obligations for reasons described in this contract, the Company _____ will be relieved of the obligation to pay penalities for the corresponding year or years. The Bulgarian exporting organizations shall confirm in writing to TECHNOIMPORT that they have not fulfilled their contractual obligations, or the Company _____ shall give a statement of a court of arbitration confirming the Bulgarian exporting organizations' lack of performance related to these paragraphs.

9. In the case of dispute the stipulation of the court of arbitration of contract No. ____ dated _____ as seller, and TECHNOIMPORT as buyer, applies. Insofar as a higher enforcement clause is introduced into this same Contract, then it shall come into effect.

10. The present Contract goes into force automatically from the effective date of Contract No. ____ mentioned in paragraph 9 above.

11. The present Contract was concluded in Sofia, in ____ _____ copies for each party.

Sofia, on the _____

TECHNOIMPORT
(Signature)

The Seller
(Signature)

Appendix No. 1 to
Contract No. ____

Directive on Implementation in the Linkage of Government Import Purchases with Non-Petroleum Exports (Jakarta, April 8, 1983)

I. GENERAL

1. This directive is in keeping with the essentials of the decision concerning The Linkage of Government Import Purchases with Non-Petroleum Indonesian Exports, issued by the Minister State Secretary in his capacity as Chairman of the Team for the Guidance of Government Procurement of Goods and Equipment, No. R-079/TPPBPP/I/1982 of January 21, 1982. Hereunder The Linkage of Government Import Purchases with Non-Petroleum Indonesian Exports will be referred to as "Linkage".

2. By Government purchases is meant purchases and procurement undertaken by any Government Department, Non-Departmental Government Agency or State Enterprise funded by the State Budget (APBN) and/or Export Credit.

3. a. Government Departments, Non-Departmental Government Agencies and State Enterprises subject to linkage are required to fulfill the stipulations of Presidential Decree No. 10/1980 concerning the Team for the Guidance of Government Procurement of Goods and Equipment, Presidential Decree No. 14A/1980 as well as Presidential Decree No. 18/1981, the implementation of which are coordinated by the Minister/State Secretary in his capacity as Chairman of the Team for the Guidance of Government Procurement of Goods and Equipment (i.e. the "Kepres 10 Team").

b. The Minister/State Secretary determines (menentukan) the purchase and procurement of goods required by the Government, in his capacity as Chairman of the Team for the Guidance of Government Procurement of Goods and Equipment.

4. Subject to Linkage are all purchases and procurement (contracts) in which the import component has a value more than Rp. 500 million.

5. Those who offer bids must submit a linkage document, i.e. a Letter of Undertaking, signed by the chief executive officer of the firm or by another officer whose designation has been evidenced by a power of attorney sent to the Department of Trade (Linkage Work Committee).

6. Exempted from linkage are:

a. Purchases funded by "soft" credit, e.g. from the World Bank, the Asian Development Bank and the Islamic Development Bank.

b. That component of a foreign supplier's contract which consists of domestic costs, such as services, domestic goods or taxes and duties.

c. Services utilized by Government agencies related to the work performed by professional experts, such as accountants, lawyers, surveyors, or consultants, as well as the costs for patent fees and the like.

d. Purchases undertaken within the framework

of joint ventures between foreign firms and State Enterprises.

(Note: Specifically for procurements in connection with contracts for construction, the amount subject to Linkage is that amount stipulated for the import of goods and materials. This amount must be clearly indicated in the documents accompanying the bid.)

7. Indonesian exports which qualify for linkage are products of agriculture, industry and mining, with the exception of petroleum and natural gas. The Department of Trade will periodically issue lists of goods qualifying for Linkage, as well as the names of qualified exporters and commodity associations. The value of goods exported in Linkage must be the same as the value of the Government import purchase (FOB).

8. Foreign suppliers who win tenders purchase or arrange for the purchase of Indonesian non-petroleum exports with one firm, or with several affiliated or connected firms.

Third parties in other countries may serve to implement the purchases if permission is granted by the Department of Trade.

9. The foreign supplier chooses one or more goods to be purchased from Indonesia and then negotiates and signs the contract(s) in the customary manner.

10. The purchase by a foreign supplier must constitute an amount in addition to the total for sales usually transacted. Supervision of this is carried out by the Department of Trade, in cooperation with the commodity associations and Commercial Attaches overseas.

11. Indonesian exports involved in Linkage must go to the country of the supplier. If the foreign purchase by the Government is supplied by firms in more than one country, then the goods involved in linkage may go to the country of the firm winning the tender or to the country of origin of the goods procured.

Export to a third country is only allowed if that country is not a normal market of the Indonesian goods involved and if the export of the goods does not disturb already existing channels in that country for marketing Indonesian products.

12. The value of transactions is calculated in U.S. Dollars, or other convertible currencies.

13. The contract between an Indonesian exporter and a foreign supplier may not constitute "future buying" as an effort by the supplier to stabilize his position or by the Indonesian exporter to hedge against price fluctuations.

14. The implementation of the export of non-petroleum Indonesian goods must take place by stages and in an orderly manner during the life of the contract for Government purchase, and must be completed before the end of the purchase contract.

15. A foreign supplier who wins a tender but is not active in trade and therefore unable to fulfill his obligations in countertrade may transfer that responsibility to a third party who is deemed bona fide by a bank or other institution. The Department of Trade may agree to or refuse the designation of a third party in this regard.

16. The winner of a tender must assume full responsibility for his obligation to buy non-petroleum Indonesian goods. In the event that the obligation to export Indonesian goods is not fully discharged by the time of the completion of the contract for Government procurement, then the winner of the tender, or the third party designated, is subject to a penalty in the amount of 50 percent of the value of the remainder of the goods not exported.

II. 1. The document for Linkage is the Letter of Undertaking which is considered a tender document and a stamp for Rp. 25 must be affixed.

2. Through the channel of the Government Department, Non-Departmental Agency or State Enterprise which handles the tender (hereunder referred

to as the Tenderer), the original of the Letter of Undertaking is forwarded for evaluation to the Department of Trade, addressed to,

Secretary Linkage Work Committee
Jl. Ml. Ridwan Rais No. 5, Lantai IX K, 30
Gedung Department Perdagangan, Jakarta

3. The result of the evaluation is then communicated to the Tenderer and to the Team for the Guidance of Government Procurement of Goods and Equipment/State Secretary.

4. The participant in a tender who is declared to have won by the State Secretary/TPPBPP, must communicate the following information to the Department of Trade through the Linkage Work Committee: the values of the goods involved (FOB); the country of the supplier or affiliate, together with the period of time for the completion of the contract as stated in Annex A to the Letter of Undertaking.

5. After Annex A has been accepted by the Department of Trade, then the award is made by the Tenderer to the bidder.

III. Imports to be Considered Additional ("on top")
1. Imports by the winner of the contract must be an increment (i.e. "additional" or "on top").
2. "Additional" is to be interpreted in terms of the total imports by the company which wins the bid. The basis of calculation will be the total of imports during the year 1981. For projects beginning in 1984, the basis will shift to the average for the period of three years before.
3. If the company has not previously imported goods from Indonesia, the imports affected will then be considered to be additional.
4. As data for these calculations, the firm winning the bid is requested to supply reports on its imports in 1981.

Commercial attaches in foreign countries are requested to compile reports on the imports of those firms involved.

IV. Evidence of Export

1. The foreign supplier who wins a tender is required to have commenced the regular purchase of Indonesian exports within six months after receiving the award and to have reported the purchases to the Linkage Work Committee, together with the Export Certificate (PEB), Bill of Lading, Invoice and L/C.

2. The Department of Trade will monitor compliance with countertrade requirements on the basis of the PEB's from the company involved and has the power to refuse or accept the company's report on purchases based on the results of its monitoring.

The Department of Trade will provide confirmation of results of monitoring the implementation of the countertrade transaction within two weeks after receipt of the materials.

3. The name of the firm winning the tender or its affiliate in the purchase of Indonesian goods must be noted at item 10. of the PEB form. If the company has designated a third party and that designation has been approved, the name of the third party must be entered at item 10a. on the PEB form.

4. A foreign company which wishes to participate in a tender involving the linkage of countertrade, may begin to make purchases and orders for Indonesian goods *before* the decision on awarding the contract, providing the Department of Trade is informed.

Woodward & Dickerson

Singapore Pte. Ltd

MAIN OFFICE:	TOWER 1202, 12TH FLOOR DBS BUILDING	TELEX: RS 25257
937, HAVERFORD ROAD.	6, SHENTON WAY,	CABLES: WOODWARD
BRYN MAWR, PA. 19010	SINGAPORE 0106.	TELEPHONE: 2223588
U.S.A.	MAXWELL ROAD P.O. BOX 2791	
	SINGAPORE 9047.	

29th May 1982
HV/tbt/443/82

Department of Trade And Cooperatives
Republic of Indonesia
Directorate General For Foreign Trade
Jalan Aboul Muis 87
Jakarta
Indonesia

c/o
Staf Bina Perusahaan Negara
Sektor Pertanian
Jalan Cut Mutia No. 11
Jakarta
Indonesia

RE: LETTER OF UNDERTAKING

We refer to your invitation to Bid (Bid number 46/DAGRI/ II/82) closing date 28th May, 1982 and our offer submitted herein through Tjipta Niaga, Indonesia, Jakarta.

If Woodward is selected as a supplier of Muriate of Potash, Woodward hereby irrevocably undertake from the date of award of the Contract relating to such tender and receipt of full and satisfactory Letter Of Credit covering such Contract:

1) To purchase, or to cause to be purchased by one or more of our affiliated companies in the U.S.A. or elsewhere or by third parties located in such country acceptable to you, Agricultural and/or Industrial Products Contained in Books A.1 and 1.2, each entitled "List of Indonesian Export Commodities available for additional exports in 1982.", published in January 1982 and March 1982, respectively, by the Department

Of Trade And Cooperatives (Hereinafter the "PROD-UCTS") from one or more of the Commodity Associations or Exporters named in Books B.1 and B.2, each entitled "List of Indonesia Commodity Associations and Exporters", published in January 1982 and March 1982, respectively, by The Department Of Trade And Cooperatives (Hereinafter the "EXPORTERS") in an amount at least equal to US$4,164,000.00 (Representing 48,000 metric tons of Muriate Of Potash in Bulk, FOB U.S.S.R. ports).

2) To use the Products, or to resell the Products for use, or to cause the Products to be used or resold, in the U.S.A., unless with your specific authorization which shall not be unduly withheld, we are permitted to use the Products, or to resell the Products for use, or to cause the Products to be used or resold, in any other country.

3) To purchase the Products, or to cause the Products to be purchased, within eighteen (18) months from the date of receipt of a Letter Of Credit covering the award of such Contract in full.

4) To submit, or to cause to be submitted, to The Department Of Trade And Cooperatives such evidence of the shipment of Products purchased pursuant to this undertaking as well as permit the Department Of Trade And Cooperatives to monitor compliance herewith.

In connection with our irrevocable undertaking contained herein, this will confirm our understanding that:

A) The commercial terms, including those relating to price and delivery, in respect of each purchase of Products from an Exporter shall be negotiated by us or by other purchasers thereof at the time of actual purchase.

B) The amount of each purchase to be applied towards our obligation hereunder shall be equal to the invoiced purchase price of the Products purchased, excluding, however, any shipping costs included in such invoice and any taxes or customs duties charged in connection therewith.

C) The amount of each such purchase (If measured in a currency other than the currency in which our obligation hereunder is measured) shall be applied against our obligation hereunder at exchange rates (As quoted by Bank Indonesia) prevailing at the date of the Exporter's invoice issued in respect of such purchase, and

D) If we or our affiliated companies in the U.S.A. or elsewhere have traditionally purchased Products from Indonesia Exporters, our undertaking contained herein shall be viewed as representing a commitment over and above such traditional level of purchases, it being the spirit and intention of such undertaking that purchases of Products hereunder shall be in addition to such traditional level of purchases, and

E) If the Contract relating to the above-described tender should be prematurely terminated, our undertaking contained herein shall also terminate without/further obligation on our part, and

F) If, during the course of performance of our obligations contained herein, we should be of the view that sufficient Products are either not available in Indonesia or are not of suitable export quality or internationally competitive in price, you shall, at our request, review with us the actual circumstances at the time and shall consider, but without obligation, modifying the requirements contained herein (Including, without limitation, an extension of the time during which our obligations contained herein must be satisfied).

If we fail to comply with our undertaking contained herein, we hereby agree to pay to you as liquidated damages an amount equal to 50% of the difference between the total value of Products actually purchased pursuant to this under-taking and the foreign currency amount referred to in paragraph number 1 above.

In connection with our undertaking contained herein, we hereby represent and warrant to you that:

(I) We have full power and authority and legal right to enter into this undertaking and to perform and observe the terms and provisions hereof.

(II) We have taken all necessary legal action to authorize, execute and deliver this undertaking.

(III) This undertaking constitutes our legal, valid and binding obligation, and

(IV) No law, rule or regulation or contractual or other obligation binding on us is or will be contravened by reason of our execution and delivery of this undertaking or by our performance and observance of the terms and provisions hereof.

This undertaking shall be binding upon our successors.

Very truly yours,
WOODWARD & DICKERSON SINGAPORE PTE. LTD.,

HORST VINKE
Managing Director

_____, 198__

(Address of Tenderer)
(Please refer to code no. C/P)

Dear Sirs:
We refer to _____ tender No. _____
_____ issued on _____, 198 ___, by (insert name
of Indonesian Department, Agency or Corporation issuing
tender) (the "Tender") and to your tender document submitted
in response thereto and the Letter of Approval No. _____
issued on _____ , 198 ___ by the Minister/State Secretary
acting as the Chairman of the Government Supervising Team
for the Government Procurement.

We acknowledge receipt of your Letter of Undertaking
of _____, 198 ___ a copy of which is attached
hereto and initialled for identification by the Department of
Trade and Cooperatives.

In accordance with the provisions of paragraph number
1 of such Letter of Undertaking, we confirm the following:

1. The foreign currency value of all equipment, materials
and products to be supplied by you from non-Indonesian
sources pursuant to the terms of the contract relating to the
tender shall be _____.

2. The countries referred to in such paragraph shall be
_____ and other countries provided that your
counter purchase shall not cause any friction in the respective
destination, nor to cause any friction with existing trade activities by Indonesian traders.

3. Affiliated companies which may purchase Indonesian agricultural and industrial products in satisfaction of your obligation under such Letter of Undertaking shall be _____
_____ .

4. The Counter Purchase obligations contained in such Letter of Undertaking must be satisfied by you on or before

_____ (insert date of final satisfaction) unless, pursuant to paragraph 4.f. thereof, such date is extended.

Your signature in the space marked "Agreed" below shall be conclusive evidence of your agreement to be bound by the terms of your Letter of Undertaking of _____, 198 _, as supplemented by the provisions hereof.

(TENDERER)   Very truly yours,
                              DEPARTMENT OF TRADE
                              AND
                              COOPERATIVES

By _____   by _____

                              _____,198 _

Department of Trade and Cooperatives
Republic of Indonesia
Directorate General for Foreign Trade
Jalan Abdul Muis No. 87
Jakarta
INDONESIA

Attention
Dear Sirs :

We refer to tender of _____ No. _____
_____ dated _____ and to the related counterpurchase Letter of Undertaking dated _____ _____ and annex A Letter, ref. No. _____

_____ dated _____ code no. CP /_____
_____ (such Letter of Undertaking and annex A Letter hereinafter collectively referred to as the "Letter of Undertaking").

We attach hereto copies of "Pemberitahuan Ekspor Barang" (PEB) forms and related Bills of Lading evidencing shipment of the following commodities/goods from Indonesia :

Description   FOB Value

We hereby represent and warrant to the Department of Trade and Cooperatives that such shipments comply in all respects with the Letter of Undertaking, and we therefore request your confirmation that the above-stated FOB value of such shipment may be applied in (partial) (full) satisfaction of the counterpurchase obligations evidenced by the Letter of Undertaking.

Assuming full application of such value, we understand our remaining counterpurchase obligations to be US$ _____.

_____ Very truly yours,

_____

Summary of
AGREEMENT FOR BUSINESS-TECHNICAL COOPERATION
between
Control Data Corporation (CDC), Minneapolis, Minnesota
and
Central Industrial for Electronics, Technology for Computers (CIETC), Bucharest, Romania

WITNESSETH

WHEREAS, the governments of United States of America and Socialist Republic of Romania had concluded on November 25, 1976 a long-term agreement on economic industrial and technical cooperation which identifies as an area of particular interest the development of economic, industrial and technical cooperation between firms, companies and economic organizations of the two countries in the computers and data processing domain; and

WHEREAS, the parties entered into a Technological Interchange and Cooperation Agreement dated September 30, 1976, (hereinafter referred to as the "Technology Agreement") to further the development and exchange of technology; and

WHEREAS, both parties are interested and willing to extend their existing relationship into a long-term oriented Business-Technical Cooperation with respect to certain data processing products, systems, and services; and

WHEREAS, CIETC is interested in acquiring state-of-the-art technologies and know-how related to data processing products, systems, and services and CDC is prepared to furnish CIETC such technologies and know-how and to grant licenses for the use, manufacture and sale of certain data processing products, systems, and services; and

WHEREAS, the main objective of this Business-Technical Cooperation is to establish CIETC with the indigenous expertise and capability required to successfully configure, manufacture, test, install and support data processing products and systems and to provide data services in Romania and identified export markets; and

WHEREAS, CDC desires to enter into a program with CIETC of cooperative development, production and marketing of certain of its data processing hardware, software and services for the Romanian market and such other markets where

CIETC's goodwill and marketing capabilities may prove to be advantageous;

NOW, THEREFORE, in consideration of the foregoing and the mutual covenants and conditions hereinafter contained, the parties hereto agree as follows:

Article 1. *Scope*

1.1 The "Business-Technical Cooperation" established by this Agreement shall mean cooperation, in accordance with the terms of this Agreement, in the following areas:

(a) Planning - the joint specification of future Products;

(b) Research and development - the joint preparation and introduction of new Products;

(c) Manufacturing - the assembly, test and integration of certain products and systems in Romania;

(d) Marketing - the sale of certain products, systems, and services in the Romanian economy and agreed upon export markets;

(e) Logistics - the establishment of a service and maintenance network in Romania and agreed upon export markets as well as the training of personnel.

Article 2. *Business-Technical Cooperation*

2.1 The Cooperation will be carried out pursuant to existing agreements or separate agreements, the terms and conditions of which will be negotiated between the parties. It is the intent of the parties to extend where appropriate the Technology Agreement to future joint ventures. Furthermore, it is intended that such agreements will include one or more of the following:

(a) an agreement for the establishment of a joint venture for the marketing of certain Data Services for the Romanian market and agreed upon export markets;

(b) an agreement for the establishment in Romania of a Data Services Applications Software Research and Development Center;

(c) a multiple procurement agreement for the sale by CDC of computer systems to or in conjunction with CIETC;

(d) an agreement granting CIETC the right to manufacture, use and sell certain CDC mainframes;

(e) a master agreement including sale by CDC and/or assembly by CIETC of peripheral equipment;

(f) an introduction into ROMCD of new products through technology transfer from either CDC or CIETC;

(g) agreements for specific projects of cooperation in research and development;

Article 3. *Joint Business Committee*

3.1 In order to carry out the purposes of this Cooperation there is hereby established a Joint Business Committee which will consist of eight representatives, four of whom will be appointed by each of the parties to this Agreement. The Joint Business Committee shall seek to enhance the business relationship between the parties through the establishment of strategy statements and policy guidelines essential to the conduct of business between the parties. Further, the Joint Business Committee shall assist the executive management of the various cooperative ventures which have been or may be established between the parties to this Agreement (hereinafter referred to as "Venture") by helping to identify problems and facilitate solutions and in other ways as may be requested, without modifying any governing principles as established in the individual agreements.

3.2 Each of the parties shall inform the other party no later than four weeks following the effective date of this Agreement of the names of its official representatives on the Joint Business Committee.

3.3 The Joint Business Committee will meet as often as may be required but ordinarily not less than two (2) times per year.

3.4 A Chairman will be elected by the members of the Joint Business Committee. The Chairman will serve for a period of one year.

3.5 A Secretary/Liaison Coordinator shall be appointed by the Chairman for a term coincident with that of the Chairman.

3.6 The Secretary/Liaison Coordinator shall take written minutes of all meetings of the Joint Business Committee in which all decisions shall be recorded and shall ensure appropriate follow-up.

3.7 Each of the parties shall bear the expenses incurred by their own representatives on the Joint Business Committee.

Article 4. *Implementation of Cooperation*

4.1 The parties agree that this Cooperation will be implemented in phases. The highest priority in the first phase will be the establishment of a Data Services Joint Venture. It is the intent of the parties to conclude an agreement for the establishment of a Data Services Joint Venture within twelve (12) months from the effective date of this Cooperation.

Article 5. *Effective Date*

5.1 This Agreement shall become effective on the date when all of the following events have occurred:

(a) it has been approved by the appropriate CIETC management authority;

(b) it has been approved by the appropriate CDC management authority;

(c) it has been approved by the appropriate agencies of the government of Romania; and

(d) it has been approved by the appropriate agencies of the government of the United States.

5.2 Each party shall immediately notify the other party of the occurrence of an event listed above with regard to that party or its government or of the fact that no such approval may be required.

Article 6. *Term of Agreement*

6.1 This Agreement shall run for a period of ten (10) years from the date on which it becomes effective unless sooner terminated as hereinafter provided.

Article 7. *Proprietary Information*

7.1 The parties agree that all proprietary information, whether written or oral, which may be transmitted by either party to the other pursuant to this Agreement shall be held in confidence. Neither party shall make any use of any proprietary information obtained from the other party pursuant hereto except as authorized in writing by such other party.

7.2 To the extent possible, proprietary information shall be transmitted in writing and shall be clearly marked as such.

7.3 Each party shall be obligated to hold proprietary information disclosed to it under the terms of this Agreement in confidence.

7.4 During the term of this Agreement and upon its termination each party shall return to the other party upon request any proprietary information or materials belonging to such other party.

7.5 The provisions of Article V of the Agreement on Trade Relations between the United States of America and the Socialist Republic of Romania done on April 2, 1975 will also be observed by the parties.

Article 8. *Obligations Undertaken*

8.1 By signature of this Agreement, each of the parties undertakes to negotiate in good faith with the intent of entering into one or more of the separate agreements referred to in paragraph 2.1 above.

Article 9. *Miscellaneous*

9.1 Each party reserves the right to negotiate and to enter into agreements with third parties concerning matters within the scope of this Agreement.

9.2 This Agreement shall in no way modify any existing agreements between CIETC and its affiliated organizations and CDC and its affiliated companies.

9.3 Each party agrees that it will abide by all applicable export laws of the governments of Romania and the United States.

Article 10. *Assignment*

10.1 Neither party may assign or transfer any rights or obligations deriving from this Agreement without the prior written consent of the other party.

Article 11. *Arbitration*

All disputes of any kind arising out of this Agreement or in connection with it and which cannot be settled by common accord shall be submitted to arbitration under the Rules of

Conciliation and Arbitration of the International Chamber of Commerce then in effect.

Article 12. *Language*

12.1 This Agreement shall be executed by the parties hereto in both an English and a Romanian version.

New York City, New York, U.S.A., April 17, 1978

TRADING HOUSES WITH COUNTERTRADE CAPABILITY

Austria

Allgemeine Finanz- und
    Waren-Treuhand AG
Schottenring 12
A-1013 Vienna
Telephone: (0222) 63-36-06
Telex: 747-87

Agentur fur Export,
    Import, Transit GmbH
Marokkanergasse 8
A-1030 Vienna
Telephone: (0222) 72-58-69
Telex: 131-030

Austost Handels- und
    Treuhand-GmbH
Fleishmarkt 1/III
A-1010 Vienna
Telephone: (0222) 3-33-31
Telex: 133-394

Bank Winter and Co.
Singerstrasse 2
A-1010 Vienna
Telephone: (0222) 63-46-41
Telex:

Centro Internationale
    Handelsbank AG
Tegetthoffstrassel
A-1010 Vienna
Telephone: (0222) 524-5100
Telex: 136-990, 136-996

Centropa Handels- GmbH
Seilerstatte 15
A-1010 Vienna
Telephone: (0222) 52-51-48
Telex: 113-498

F.J. Elsner & Co.
Kohlmarkt 11
A-1011 Vienna
Telephone: 52-67-71
Telex: 133-166

Evidenzburo fur
    Aussenhandels-geschafte
    (EFAG)
Brucknerstrasse 4
A-1040 Vienna
Telephone: (0222) 65-13-06
Telex: 133-166

Finanzierungs-,
Compensations-und
Handels- GmbH (FCH)
Fleischmarkt 1/III
A-1010 Vienna
Telephone: (0222) 63-33-32
Telex: 131-748

Ing. W. Hamerschlag & Co.
KG
Renngasse 10
A-1010 Vienna
Telephone: (0222) 63-88-41
Telex: 074-712

Handelsverkehr GmbH
Tuchlauben 8
A-1040 Vienna
Telephone: (0222) 63-96-86
Telex: 740-08

Ladislav G. Harmath
Handels-agentur-Import
Export
Lassallestrasse 2
A-1020 Vienna
Telephone: (0222) 24-21-70
Telex:

International Equipment
Systems Janosek &
Hanschitz GmbH
Obere Donaustrasse 71
A-1020 Vienna
Telephone: (0222) 33-16-69
Telex: 075-030

JLC-Chemie, Chemische
Industrie Lasnausky &
Co.
Praterstrasse 42
A-1020 Vienna
Telephone: (0222) 26-25-51
Telex: 076-578

A. Johnson & Co. Wien
GmbH
Taborstrasse 13
A-1020 Vienna
Telephone: (0222) 6-65-56
Telex: 134-208

Jurimex
Handelsgesellschaft-
Export-Import
Wiedner Hauptstrasse 17-8
A-1040 Vienna
Telephone: (0222) 65-57-97
Telex: 013-926

Krainz & Company KG
Herrengasse 6-8
A-1010 Vienna
Telephone: (0222) 63-23-34
Telex:

Meyer, Ritter & Co. GmbH
Stubenring 6
A-1010 Vienna
Telephone: (0222) 52-77-78
Telex: 151-5

Neocommerz Rohstoffe-,
Maschinen-und
Warenvertriebs- GmbH
Hietzinger Hauptstrasse
22, Ekazent
A-1130 ienna
Telephone: (0222) 82-83-68
Telex: 031-125

Polycommerz Warenhandel
Johannesgasse 12
A-1010 Vienna
Telephone: (0222) 52-46-16
Telex: 011-165

Quintus Export-Import
Handels-GmbH
Geyergasse 15
A-1180 Vienna
Telephone: (0222) 47-61-66
Telex: 512-06

Gebruder Schoeller OHG
Renngasse 1
A-1011 Vienna
Telephone: (0222) 63-56-71
Telex: 134-207

Transhispania Import &
Export GmbH
Silbergasse 9
A-1190 Vienna
Telephone: (0222) 36-42-07
Telex: 076-193

Unico Trading Handels-
GmbH
Jasomirgottstrasse 3
A-1010 Vienna
Telephone: (0222) 63-32-41
Telex: 136-385

Voest-Alpine Intertrading
GmbH
Schmiedegasse 14/IV
A-4040 Linz/Donau
Telephone: (0732) 3-83-31
Telex: 222-21

Weinberger
Handelsgesellschaft
Schwindgasse 20, P.O. Box
501
A-1041 Vienna
Telephone: (0222) 65-47-01
Telex: 011-786

Belgium

N.V. A. & A. de
Meulenaere & Co.
Werken
De Vladslostraat 33
B-8130 Zarren
Telephone:
Telex:

Belgafric
142A Avenue Louise
B-1170 Brussels
Telephone: (02) 48-55-21
Telex:

Devetra Trade
  Development Corp.
Chaussee de Charleroi 54
B-1060 Brussels
Telephone: (02) 538-8175
Telex: 211-65

Hugo Frei & Co.
Samberstraat 50-56
B-2000 Antwerp
Telephone: (031) 32-18-52
Telex: 315-88

N.V. Hibogan
President Building
Fr. Roosevelt Pl. 12-bus 22
B-2000 Antwerp
Telephone: (031) 33-53-61
Telex: 11-62

S.A. Intercontinentale de
  Compensation
1-3 Rue D'Egmont
B-1050 Brussels
Telephone:
Telex:

Interocean SA
Chaussee de la Hulpe 181
B-1170 Brussels
Telephone: (02) 673-9960
Telex: 217-67

N.V. Kreglinger
9 Grote Markt
B-2000 Antwerp
Telephone:
Telex:

Maas International NV
Klipperstraat 15
B-2030 Antwerp
Telephone: (031) 42-01-70
Telex: 348-71

Societe Cooperative
  (SOCSER)
Avenue Louise 534
B-1050 Brussels
Telephone: (02) 649-8068
Telex: 348-71

Societe Pachon
Galerie du Centre
Bloc 1, Rue des Fripiers
B-1000 Brussels
Telephone:
Telex:

Finland

Kaukomarkkinat OY
Kutojantie 4
SF-02610 Espoo 61
Tel: 52-37-11

OY Nino Lincoln & Co Ltd
Aleksanterinkatu 21 H
SF-00100 Helsinki 10
Tel: 124-624

France

ACECO
(Association pour la
  Compensation des
  Echanges Commerciaux)
28 avenue Hoche
F-75008 Paris
Tel: 563-0200
Telex: 640-912

COOPINTER
(Societe de Cooperation
  Internationale)
22 rue d'Aguesseau
F-75008 Paris
Tel: 266-6440
Telex: 650-475

Credi Lyonnais
Section "Contreparties" at
  the International Branch
16 rue du IV Septembre
F-75002 Paris
Tel: 295-1018
Telex: 612-400

Dreyfus Herschtel & Cie
3 avenue du Coq
F-75009 Paris
Tel: 280-6166, 874-0745
Telex: 280-513

Greficomex
58 avenue Marceau
F-75008 Paris
Tel: 720-0607
Telex: 613-365

Cie. Interagra
152-156 avenue de Malakof
F-75016 Paris
Tel: 502-1373
Telex: 630-038

Lafitte International
Rue Lafitte 21
F-75009 Paris
Tel: 523-4747
Telex: 290-290

Louis Dreyfus & Co.
6 Rue Rabelais
Paris 8
Tel: 225-70-85

J.A. Goldschmidt SA.
149 Rue Street Honore
Paris
Tel: 488-58-20

Merkuria SA*
133 Champs Elysees
F-75008 Paris
Tel: 723-5577
Telex: 611-688

Secopa SA*
22 rue d'Aguesseau
F-75008 Paris
Tel: 266-6440
Telex: 50-475

Societe Coprosid
54 avenue Marceau
F-75008 Paris
Tel: 723-3613
Telex: 611-983

SORICE
79-81 avenue Danielle
  Casanova
F-94200 Ivry-sur-Seine
Tel: 670-1182
Telex: 270-002

Sorimex
(Societe de Representation
  Internationale Import-
  Export)
F-92100 Boulogne-
  Billancourt
Tel: 604-9174
Telex: 203-758

Italy

Coe & Clerici SpA.
Via Martin Piaggio 17
I-16122 Genova
Tel: 5-48-91
Telex: 270-680

Compagnia Generale
  Interscambi SpA.
  (COGIS)
Corso Venezia 54
I-20121 Milan
Tel: 7742
Telex: 321-91

Novasider SpA.
Via San Francesco da
  Paola 17
I-10123 Torino
Tel: 51-26-06

Societa per l'Incremento
  dei Rapporti
  Commerciali con l'Estero
  (SIRCE)
Via Larga 23
I-20122 Milan
Tel: 87-70-87, 86-14-51
Telex: 310-288

Japan

C. Itoh & Co., Ltd.
Kitakyutaro - machi
Higashi-ku, Osaka

Marubeni Corp.
3, Moto - machi
Higashi-ku, Osaka

Mitsubishi Corp.
2, Marunouchi
Chiyoda-ku, Tokyo
Nissho-Iway Co., Ltd.
3, Imabashi
Higashi-ku, Osaka

Sumitomo Shoji Kaisha,
  Ltd.
5, Kitahama
Highashi-ku, Osaka

Netherlands

Handelsverdeer NV.
Westersingel 107
Rotterdam
Tel: 010-36-06-22

Hollandsche Bank-Unie
  NV.
Herengracht 434-440
N.-1002 Amsterdam
Tel: 020-29-92-22

Mueller International BV
Startbaan 5
NL-1185 XP Amstelveen
  (near Amsterdam)
Tel: (020) 47-04-81
Telex: 123-74

Philipp Brothers (Holland)
  BV
Prinses Irenestraat 39
NL-1077 MV Amsterdam
Tel: 46-12-11
Telex: 110-30

Transmedia BV
Rapenburgerstraat 109
NL-1011 VL Amsterdam
Tel: 25-57-96, 22-43-55
Telex: 132-23

Sweden

Sukab AB.
Burger Jarlsatan 2
S-10382 Stockholm
Tel: 23-47-95

Transfer AB.
Sundyberg 1
S-17220 Stockholm
Tel: 98-16-20

Switzerland

AFICO SA
Avenue de la Gare 52
CH-1001 Lausanne
Tel: 20-25-21
Telex: 259-70

Andre & Cie SA
7 Chemin Messidor
CH-1000 Lausanne
Tel: 20-11-11
Telex: 241-01

Arat S.A
17 Rue de la Dole, CH-1203
  Geneva
Phone: 45-76-11

Aussenhandel AG
Dufourstrasse 51
CH 8008 Zurich
Tel: 32-38-15
Telex: 523-59

Bank Für Handel und
  Effekten
Talacker 50
CH-8039 Zurich
Tel: 27-46-90

Codefeine SA
Rue Centrale 6
CH-1003 Lausanne
Tel: 20-17-61

Contraco Holding und
  Finanz AG
c/o Kaspar Marti
Chemin Du Cap 3
CH-1006 Lausanne
Tel: 28-71-22 Telex: 247-55

Siber Hegner Holding Ltd.
Bellerivestrasse 17
CH-8034 Zurich
Tel: 47-89-90
Telex: 556-46

Unitrac SA
PO Box 4033
Galaries Benj. Constant 1
CH-1002 Lausanne
Tel: 23-72-55/56
Telex: 241-68

United Kingdom

Alcon (Compensation
  Trading) Ltd.
Devlin House
36/37 St. George Street
London W1R 9FA
Tel: 499-2591, 491-2721
Telex: 895-4135

Anglo Austrian Trading
  Co. Ltd.
39 St. James Street
London SW1A 1JH
Tel: 493-1206
Telex: 282-62

Biddle Sawyer & Co. Ltd
(The Guinness Peat Group
  Ltd.)
32 St. Mary at Hill
London EC3 8DH
Tel: 01-623-9333

The Bowater Intl. Trading
  Co. Ltd.
46 Berkeley Square
London W1X 5DB
Tel: 629-7222
Telex: 281-22

Bremar Holdings Ltd.
Bremar House
27 Sale Place
London W2 1PT
Tel: 01-262-2271

Emerson Associated Ltd.
41/42 Berners Street
London W1 P3AA
Tel: 01-580-5441

M. Golodetz (Overseas) Ltd
Aldwych House
71/91 Aldwych
London WC2B 4HN
Tel: 242-8888
Telex: 235-67

Inchape International
  Trading Ltd
Iando House, 43
  Bartholomew Close
London EC 1A 7 HR
Tel: 01-606-0081
Telex: 88-6659

Leopold Lazarus Ltd.
(Part of the Lissauer
  Group, U.S.)
Gotch House
20-34 St. Bride Street
London EC4A4DL
Tel: 01-583-8060

Ralli Trading Finance Ltd.
46 Berkeley Square
London W1
Tel: 01-629-7222

Tennant Trading Ltd.
9 Harp Lane
Great Tower Street
London EC3
Tel: 01-623-7808

West Germany

Bafag AG
Lindwurmstrasse 11
D-8000 Munich 2
Tel: 23-60-51
Telex: 522-778-522-455

Comex
  Aussenhandelsgesellschaft
  GmbH
Immermannstrasse 40
D-4000 Dusseldorf
Tel: 3-61-71
Telex: 858-1806/07

Commerciale Link & Co.
Jülicherstrasse 17
D-5000 Cologne
Tel: 21-68-83

Contact
  Aussenhandelsservice
Bismarckstrasse 73
D-1000 Berlin 12
Tel: 313-6095
Telex: 183-682

Handelsverkehr GmbH
Rossertstrasse 2
D-6000 Frankfurt/Main
Tel: 71-71-71
Telex: 411-471

Industriehandel GmbH
(Handels und
  Industreausrustung
  GmbH)
Motorstrasse 20d
D-7000 Stuttgart
Tel: 4430
Telex: 723-305

Franz Kirchfeld GmbH KG
Königsallee 17
D-4000 Düsseldorf
Tel: 8-39-81
Telex: 858-1999

Marquard & Bahls & Co.
Kattrepelsbrücke 1
D-2000 Hamburg 1
Tel: 0411-339-741

Wilhelm Schulz KG
Martinistrasse 24
D-2800 Bremen 1
Tel: 32-58-68
Telex: 244-766
THV Handels und
 Verwaltungs GmbH
Neupfarrplatz 15
D-8400 Regensburg
Tel: 56-10-71
Telex: 657-37

United States

American IBC Corporation
770 Lexington Ave.
New York, New York
 10021
Tel: (212)486-1212

C. Itoh and Company
270 Park Ave.
New York, New York
 10017
Tel: (212)953-5495

Merban Corporation
State Street Plaza
New York, New York
 10004
Tel: (212)248-7800

Philipp Brothers Division
(Engelhard Minerals &
 Chemicals Philipp Corp.)
299 Park Avenue
New York, New York
 10017
Tel: (212)752-4000

Tower International
 Corporation
2750 Terminal Tower
Cleveland, Ohio 44113
Tel: (216)241-0266

Commercial Trading
 Imports, Inc.
(Control Data Corp.)
474 Concordia Ave.
St. Paul, MN 55103

Fallek Chemical Corp.
460 Park Avenue
New York, NY 10022
Tel: (212)943-4900

The East Asiatic Company,
 Inc.
110 Wall Street
New York, NY 10005
Tel: (212)943-4900

M. Golodetz & Co., Inc.
666 Fifth Avenue
New York, NY 10019
Tel: (212)581-2400

ICC International
720 Fifth Avenue
New York, NY 10019
Tel: (212)397-3332

International Ore and
Fertilizer Corp.
1230 Avenue of Americas
New York, NY 10020
Tel: (212)586-7800

International Commodities
Export Corp.
(ACLI International, Inc.)
110 Wall Street
New York, NY 10005
Tel: (212)747-1670

Kaiser Trading Co.
(Kaiser Aluminum &
  Chemical)
300 Lakeside Drive
Oakland, CA 94604
Tel: (415)271-2924

Philipp Brothers
(Engelhard Minerals

Chemical Corp.)
1221 Avenue of the
  Americas
New York, NY 10020
Tel: (212)575-5900

Welt International
1413 "K" Street
Washington D.C. 20016
Tel: (202)371-1343

Woodward & Dickerson,
  Inc.
937 Haverford Road
Bryn Mawr, PA 19010
Tel: (215)527-5200

Appendix C
COUNTERTRADE RISK INSURANCE

Companies, of course, seek insurance for countertrade deals as they would for any conventional commercial transaction. While penalty clauses cover losses in case of non-performance to some extent in countertrade deals, they do not perform nor are meant to perform the same function as commercial or political risk insurance which protects companies from substantial loss when contracts are unilaterally abrogated by a contracting party. Under counterpurchase arrangements, companies that take title to products before an exchange of goods is completed would be vulnerable to a non-performance outcome. These companies typically obtain insurance to secure such deals.

Political risk insurance for countertrade deals, called contract repudiation coverage, differs from similar coverage for conventional buy-sell transactions only in its somewhat greater complexity. This coverage, regardless of what kind of transaction it is being applied to, offers protection against arbitrary, capricious, and non-justified repudiation of any contract stemming from political events, such as government embargoes, civil war, government-enforced contract repudiation, etc. Coverage is offered in both directions, buying and selling, or in terms of countertrade, for delivery and counterdelivery.

Coverage does not extend to commercial reasons for contract non-performance nor does it cover production quality problems. To obtain commercial coverage, a separate insurance policy would be necessary; however, some of the companies that provide political risk insurance are highly specialized and do not offer other kinds of coverage.

Companies obtain political risk insurance to guarantee (counterpurchase) deliveries and also to cover pre-export financing, whether it be for two days or six months. Sometimes, counterpurchase is instituted at the suggestion of the insurance company as a precondition for receiving political risk insurance. This could occur, for instance, in sales to Latin America, where companies are often strapped for cash, especially hard currency. Before insurance for these sales is agreed to, the deals are restructured so that 100% of the goods sold is covered by a counterpurchase agreement.

Companies are eligible for political risk coverage if the deal does not span more than 2–3 years. For countertrade deals lasting longer than this, and many do, companies still have options ranging from restructuring the deal, to getting a bank to provide coverage, to taking on the risk themselves.

At present, the following companies offer contract repudiation coverage: Lloyds of London, AIG Political Risk Insurance of New York, Swett & Crawford of Texas, the American Foreign Insurance Association, Chubb & Son, and I.N.A. (Inamic Ltd.).

Appendix D
GOVERNMENT PROCUREMENT OF IMPORTS

1. Government procurement of imports which is linked to the export of Indonesian products other than oil and natural gas consists of that procurement which is financed from the State Budget and from export credits.

2. The compulsory linkage of Government procurement to export relates to purchases of Government and Non-Departmental Government Institutions and States Enterprises which are coordinated under Presidential Decree No. 10, 1980 (KEPRES No.: 10, 1980).

3. The following are exempt from such linkage:

   a. Procurement financed through consessional bilateral loans and credits from the World Bank, the Asian Development Bank and the Islamic Development Bank.
   b. Expenditures for domestically manufactured components which are included in the contract of the foreign supplier, including: service components, goods, taxes and duties.
   c. Services which are employed by various Government agencies, including those provided by foreign accountants, lawyers, surveyors, consultants, as well as the purchase of technology, patents, etc.
   d. Purchases of imports in the framework of joint ventures between state enterprises and foreign companies.

4. Export commodities linkage to procurement are agricultural commodities, industrial goods and other goods excluding oil and natural gas. The Department of Trade will periodically draw up a list of export commodities that are eligible for meeting linkage requirements for various countries or groups of countries. These lists will include the names of the exporters and commodity associations.

5. The foreign supplier is to purchase or arrange for the purchase of Indonesian export commodities through one or more companies that are affiliated or otherwise have a relationship with the foreign supplier. A company of a third party in another country acceptable to the Government may also become the executing agency thereof.

6. Foreign imports fulfilling linkage undertakings may select one or more commodities to be imported from Indonesia. The export value of the Indonesian linked commodities must be equal in value to the Government procurement from aboard taking into account the exceptions stated in point 3 above.

7. The value of the Indonesian export commodities and the value of the contract for the Government procurement are to be stated on an FOB basis. The price used in the calculation will be the price of the export commodity concerned at the time of signing the contract.

8. Foreign importers and Indonesian exporters will conduct negotiations directly and sign their trade agreement in conformity with normal practices, but inserting one additional clause concerning linkage undertakings. Copies of such contracts are to be submitted to the Department of Trade, for the attention of the Directorate General for Foreign Trade as well as to the Department or Government Institution making the procurement.

9. Purchases by foreign importers must be in addition to the total export transactions normally concluded with the country concerned. The department of Trade in cooperation with the commodity associations will monitoring the implementation thereof.

10. Commodities exported in fulfillment of linkage undertaking must be sold or used in the supplier's country of origin. In the case of Government procurement from overseas supplied from several countries, the linkage undertaking is to be effected with either the country that has won the tender and/or the country of origin of the procured goods.

11. Export to a third country can only be permitted if the third country has not yet become a market for the Indonesian export commodity concerned or by special permit of the Department of Trade.

12. Export transactions are to be made in United States dollars or other convertible foreign currencies, as long as such currencies are used by the supplier of the goods purchased by the Government.

13. Contracts concluded between the Indonesian exporters and the foreign importers are not to constitute a "future" buying arrangement designed to safeguard or "hedge" the position of the importer or the exporter against price fluctuations.

14. Indonesian export undertakings must be effected in stages during the contract period relating to the Government procurement and be completed prior to the termination date of the procurement contract.

15. The foreign supplier is responsible for the implementation of the contract for the export of the Indonesian commodity or commodities. The supplier will be liable

to a penalty amounting to 50 percent of the value of any unfulfilled export undertakings upon completion of a procurement contact.

*****

33 EXPORT COMMODITIES
THAT ARE LINKED
TO THE GOVERNMENT IMPORT

1. Rubber—176.000 ton—RSS, SIR
2. Coffee 52.000 ton—EK Special, Ek 1, 20–25% (for non-quota countries only)
3. White pepper—8.000 ton—ASTA, FAQ (for West European Market through UNIPRO)
4. Black pepper—6.000 ton—ASTA, FAQ (for American Market through CITC)
5. Tobacco leaf—2.000 ton (20.000 bales)—Besuki/NO (filler)
6. Manioc—150.000 ton—Pellet, Chip, Cube
7. Cement—500.000 ton—Portland cement, Clinker
8. Sawn timber—2.000.000 CuM—Indonesia Grading Rules, Malayan Grading Rules
9. Plywood—180.000 CuM—All sort of plywood
10. Other processed woods—20.000 CuM—blockboard, particle board, veneer, doors, rotary cut plywood lauan, dowels/mouldings, wood cement boards
11. Textile products—100.000 ton—Fabrics, yarn/twine, garments, batik (garment of category 6, 7 and 8 for non quota countries only)
12. Aluminium—8.500 ton—aluminium extrusion & fabrication, aluminium sheet
13. Asbest cement—30.000 ton—asbest cement, pipes water
14. Basketry—2.000 ton—basketry

15. Bauxite—500.000 m. ton—Al_2O_3, FeO_2, Free Moisture
16. Biscuit—2.000 ton—biscuit
17. Canned Fish—1.000 ton—Tuna in brine & in oil, Sardines in tomato sauce
18. Canned Fruit and Vegetables—5.000.000 tons— Canned pineapple, Fruit cocktail, Canned rambutan pineapple, Canned mushroom, Bamboo shoot
19. Cigars—2.000.000 sticks—cigars
20. Clove cigarettes—unlimited—Filter clove cigarettes, Plain clove cigarettes
21. Coffee roasted powder—5.000 ton—coffee powder, canned
22. Essential oil—1.500 ton—Vetiver oil, Citronella oil, Clove leaf oil, Cananga—oil, Patchouly oil, Sandalwood oil
23. Fruit juice—5.000.000 tins—Orange, Mango, Banana, Pineapple, Marquisa, Tetrapack, Zuurzak, Quora, Jambu pineapple
24. Glass—5.000 ton—Clear sheet glass, Tinted sheet glass, Figured sheet glass, Glassware, Bottle, Dinnerware, Corrugated carton box, Glasswall, Phamaceuticals, Glass container tumbler, Ampule, Vial
25. Granite—190.000 m.ton—Granite
26. Nickle—300.000 ton Ore, 4.000 ton Matte—Nickle ore, Nickle matte
27. Paper—20.000 ton—HVS, HVO, Writing, Printing, Craft liner, Corrugated
28. Pipes, steel—200.000 ton—Water pipe, Gas pipe, Oil pipe, Construction pipe, Furniture pipe
29. Rattan carpet—550.000 pcs—Rattan carpet
30. Rattan furniture—100.000 sets—Rattan Furniture
31. Tires—1.500.000—unit Automobile tires, Automobile tubes, Bicycle tires, Flaps, Motorcycle/Scooter/Minicar tubes & tires
32. Tinned corned beef—1.000 ton—canned beef
33. Tuna fish—1.000 ton—Tuna, Skipjack

SELECTED BIBLIOGRAPHY

Alford, William P. "Practical and Legal Problems of Doing Business with China." Federal Bar Association Convention. San Antonio, Texas (September 27, 1979).

Asante, Samuel K.B. "Restructuring Transnational Mineral Agreements." **The American Society of International Law** 73 (1979).

"Barter and Countertrade: A New Upsurge." **The Morgan Guarantee Survey**, October 1978.

"Big Slump in East-West Trade." **Dun's Review** III (April 1978).

Bispham, Thomas P. "Coal Mining Project Financings: Lenders' and Borrowers' Considerations." **Engineering Bulletin** 59 (April 1982).

Brown, Philip J. "Countertrade as a Weapon." Licensing Executive Society U.K. Summer Conference, Transcript. Worcester College, Worcester, England (July 1980).

Business International Institute. **The Future of Countertrade**. Seminar on New Developments on Doing Business with Eastern Europe, Vienna, October 1981.

"Capitalist Troubles for Eastern Europe." **Business Week** 2598 (August 13, 1979).

"CIA Eyes Growing Soviet Trade in Chemicals." **Chemical & Engineering**, January 15, 1979.

Cizauskas, C. **The Changing Nature of Export Credit Finance and Its Implications for Developing Countries**. Washington, D.C.: The World Bank, 1980.

Crawson, P.C.F. "The National Mineral Policies of Germany, France, and Japan." **Mining Magazine**, June 1980.

Davis, Robert. "Private Credits to Developing Countries." **The Bankers Magazine** 161 (May–June 1978).

DeMarines, Ronald J. "Analysis of Recent Trends in U.S. Countertrade." United States International Trade Commission Publication 1237 (March 1982).

Duncan, M.W. "Buy-Back Binge." American Management Association Countertrade Seminar, New York City (October 1978).

"East-West Trade: Opportunities and Problems." **Journal of Commerce**, October 6, 1978, pp. 1A–18A.

Farrell, Paul V. "Countertrade: A Special Kind of Buying and Selling." **Purchasing World**, November 1979.

Finley, E.C. "Countertrade: A Sophisticated Strategy for Increasing Exports." **Farm Chemicals**, June 1982.

Ford, Mark and Welt, Leo, eds. **Information Lagos**. Washington, D.C.: Welt Publishing Co., 1982.

"Foreign Trade: Barter is Back, Bigger than Ever," **U.S. News and World Report**, December 3, 1979.

Hill, David H. (President of Motors Trading Corp.) "Launching a Trading Subsidiary," American Management Association Seminar, New York, New York (June 1980).

Kaikati, Jack G. "The Reincarnation of Barter Trade as a Marketing Tool." **Journal of Marketing** 40 (April 1976).

Karr, Miriam and Zachariasz, Jerzy. "Countertrade Arrangements." Chase World Information Corp. (Date unavailable).

Leeper, R. "Project Finance—A Term to Conjure With." **The Banker**, August 1978.

Ludlow, H. "China's New Foreign Trade Structure." **China Business Review** 9, no. 3 (May–June 1982).

Mandato, Joseph; Skola, Thomas J.; and Wyse, Kenneth I. "Counterpurchase Sales in the GDR." **Columbia Journal of World Business**, Spring 1978.

"Marketing Opportunities in Communist Countries." **Business America**, Special issue, U.S. Department of Commerce, October 5, 1981.

Musharsky, Dieter E. "Steps in Contract Negotiations Possibly Involving Countertrade or Barter." American Management Association seminar, New York, New York (October 1980).

McVey, Thomas B. "Countertrade and Barter: Alternative Trade Financing by Third World Nations." **International Trade Law Journal** 6 (Spring–Summer 1980–1981).

"A New Barter System—One Way of Getting Payments from Turkey." **Briefing**, June 13, 1979.

Organization for Economic Cooperation and Development. **Countertrade Practices in East-West Proceedings**, Conference Transcript, Paris (November 1979).

_____.
East-West Trade: Recent Developments in Countertrade, Conference Transcript, Paris (1981).

"Opportunities for Bartering are Endless." **Infosystems**, September 1979.

Outters-Jaeger, Ingelies. "Synthesis Report." **The Impact of Barter in Developing Countries**. Paris: Organization for Economic Cooperation and Development, 1979.

Parkinson, Jack H. "The Automotive Industry Decree: Tooling Up for More Exports." **Business Mexico** (Date unavailable).

Radez, Richard E. "Opportunities in Project Financing." **The Banker**, July 1978.

"Raking in a Bundle in the Barter Business." **Business Week**, September 3, 1979.

Rasmussen, Thomas J. and Theroux, Eugene A. "China's New Tax Laws for Joint Ventures and Individuals." **China Business Review** 7, no. 6 (November–December 1980).

Spetter, Henry. "Countertrade Transactions in East-West Trade: Roles, Issues and Limitations." **Crossroads**, Winter 1979.

Trend, Dr. H.G. "Buy-Back Arrangements Threaten to End in an Economic Hang-over." **RAD Background Report 96 (Eastern Europe)**. Radio Free Europe-Radio Liberty, April 26, 1979.

United States Department of Commerce. **Selected Trade and Economic Data of the CPEs**. June 1979.

_____. **Communist Country Hard-Currency Debt in Perspective**. July 1980.

Verzariu, Pompiliu. **Countertrade Practices in Eastern Eu-**

rope, the Soviet Union, and China. United States Department of Commerce, 1980.

_____. "An Update on Countertrade with China." **Business America**, January 11, 1982.

Verzariu, Pompiliu and Stein, Daniel D. **Joint Venture Agreements in the People's Republic of China**. United States Department of Commerce, 1982.

Walsh, James. **Development-for-Import Arrangements**. United States Department of Commerce, Draft.

_____. **Countertrade: A Significant Widespread Type of Trading Arrangement**. United States Department of Commerce, Draft.

_____. "Countertrade: An Old Business Custom, A New Opportunity for Southwest Exporters." Meeting of Southwest regional branch, Academy of International Business, (March 1982).

Weigand, Robert E. "International Nonmonetary Transactions: A Primer for American Bankers." **Banking Law Journal**, March 1979.

_____. "Apricots for Ammonia: Barter, Clearing, Switching, and Compensation in International Business." **California Management Review** 22, no. 1 (Fall 1979).

_____. "Barter and Buybacks: Let Western Firms Beware." **Business Horizons**, June 1980.

Welt, Leo G.B. **Countertrade: Business Practices for Today's World Market**. New York: American Management Association, 1982.

Zorn, Stephen A. "New Developments in Third World Mining Agreements." National Resources Forum I, United Nations (1977).

INDEX

A

ACLI International, Inc., 106
Advance deposit, 104
Á forfait financing, 65, 66
Africa, 8
Agreements. *See* Bilateral
   clearing accounts
Albania, 68, 119
Algeria, 87, 95, 96, 114, 115,
   116
American Bureau of
   Collections (ABC), 117
AMF, 181
Annual plan. *See* Five-year
   plan
Arbitration, 129, 182
Argentina, 67, 79, 101
Asahan, Indonesia, 99
Association pour la
   Compensation des
   Echanges Commerciaux
   (ACECO), 79
Astgaldo Costruzione, 177
Australia, 67, 77, 98, 101, 102
Austria, 17, 21, 24, 53, 87,
   100, 129

B

Banco do Brasil, 108
Bangladesh, 101, 173
Bank of America, 71
Bank of China, 65, 67, 68, 173
Bank-to-bank credit lines, 60
Barter, 5, 8, 15, 16, 27, 39, 55,
   61, 74, 94, 96, 97, 102,
   115, 117, 144, 149, 173
   definition, 17–18
Belem, Brazil, 99
BHP, 98
Bilateral clearing accounts (or
   agreements), 5, 8, 25, 97–
   98, 117, 126–127, 138,
   155, 162
Bilateralism, 34, 75, 122
Billiton, 98
Bills of exchange, 63, 64
Bills of lading, 63
Brazil, 74, 76, 79, 96, 98, 100,
   101, 115
   countertrade practices, 107–
   109
   BEFIEX, 108
   Foreign Trade Department

Brazil (Cont.):
  (CACEX), 108
  Industrial Development
    Council, 108
  Ministry of Industry and
    Commerce, 109
Brezhnev, Leonid, 162
Brink's Inc., 73
British Aircraft Corp. (BAC),
  115
Bulgaria, 119, 124, 134, 143,
  145, 151
  countertrade practices, 130–
    134
Bumar, 57–58
Burma, 98
Buy-back. *See* Compensation
Buyer credits, 60, 61, 68
  definition, 66
Buying forward, 54

C

Canada, 67, 73, 77, 100
Cash-against-documents (or
  sight), 63
CE Lummus, 49
CE Trading, 49–53
Chase Manhattan, 71
Chicago exchange, 33
China. *See* People's Republic
  of China
China International Trust and
  Investment Corp. (CITIC),
  184
China Investment Bank, 67–
  68
China National Import and
  Export Commodities
  Inspection Corp.
  (CHINSPECT), 182

China National Offshore Oil
  Corp. (CNOOC), 177–178
China Southwest Energy
  Resources United
  Development Corp.
  (CSERUDC), 177
Chrysler, 112
Citibank, 71
Coca-Cola, 83, 184
Colombia, 96
Combustion Engineering
  Corp. (CEC), 49, 51, 83
Commercial banks (or
  Western banks), 18, 41,
  60, 61, 62, 63, 64, 65, 66,
  69, 70, 71, 94, 172
Commercial Credit
  Corporation, 54
Commercial Trading Imports
  (CT Imports), 53–56
Commercial Trading
  International (CTI),
  53–56
Commissions. *See* Discounts
Compensation (or buy-back),
  6, 15, 16, 39, 42, 49, 50,
  57, 58, 59, 61, 67, 68, 69,
  82, 91, 98, 110, 119–120,
  132, 133, 141, 144, 150,
  152, 155, 157, 161, 162,
  163, 164, 165, 166, 167,
  172, 173, 174–175, 176,
  177, 182, 184
  definition, 20–25
Completion agreements, 70
Continental Can Corporation,
  36
Contractual triangle, 39
Control Data Corporation, 53–
  56, 83
Control Data Technotec, 54
Control Data Worldtec, 54

Convention of Paris for the Protection of Industrial Policy (Paris Convention), 184

Cooperation agreements (or industrial cooperation), 22, 24, 56–58, 133–134, 144, 155, 164, 173
  definition, 24–25

Costa Rica, 79

Counterpurchase (or parallel barter), 6, 15, 18, 21, 59, 60, 96, 98, 102, 106, 115, 119, 123, 141–142, 147, 154, 162, 164, 165, 166, 167, 172

Countertrade:
  business and, 81–91
  China and, 171–184
  contracts, 39–47
  definition, 5–7, 15–16
  developing countries and, 93–118
  Eastern Europe and, 119–167
  financing, 59–72
  forms, 15–27
  government and, 73–79
  history, rationale, 8–14
  negotiations, 29–37
  obligations, 5, 32
  size of market, 7–8
  variables, 16–17

Countertrade contract, 39, 40

Credit programs, 40–41, 60, 61, 65, 66, 68

Cuba, 68

Current account. See Open account

Czechoslovakia, 64, 68, 123, 124, 151
  countertrade practices, 134–138

D

Daimler-Puch, 24

DAL, 160–161

DeBagtolis SpA, 177

Deliveries, 16, 24, 39, 41, 46, 164, 166
  barter, 18
  compensation, 20, 22, 23
  counterpurchase, 18, 20
  guarantees, 43
  reciprocal, 34

Detente, 9

Deutsche Aussenhandelsbank (DAB), 68

Development for import, 73, 77
  definition, 98–100

Direct foreign investment, 24, 66–67

Discounts (or commissions), 20, 27, 33, 36, 37, 50, 51, 81, 115, 132–133, 137, 138, 143, 148, 154, 159–160, 167, 174

Distribution, 46–47

Donaldson, Lufkin & Jenrette, Inc., 106

Double trap door, 31

Drafts, 63

Dubai, United Arab Emirates, 100

E

Economic Commission of Europe (ECE), 24–25

Ecuador, 96, 101

Egypt, 94, 96

Egypt Trading Company Act of 1982, 72

Elf-Aquitaine, 116

Ertzberg, New Guinea, 96
European-American Bank, 71
Evidence accounts, 5, 8, 84,
 135, 152, 159, 173
 definition, 25–26

F

Federal Republic of Germany,
 21, 23, 73, 74, 77, 87, 91,
 99, 100, 116
Fiat, 23
Financial guarantees (or
 guarantees), 18, 40, 64,
 65, 67, 68
 definition, 61–62
Five-year plan (or annual
 plan), 9, 30, 32, 56, 121,
 125, 144, 147, 152, 165
Ford, 112
Ford do Brasil, 108
Foreign debt, 9, 10, 93–94
 size, 9, 10–11, 67, 107, 109,
 131, 134–135, 139–140,
 144–145, 151–152, 156–
 157, 163, 172
Frame contract, 40
France, 8, 23, 67, 73, 77, 79,.
 87, 97, 99, 113, 116
 Mining Ministry, 96
Fujian Province, China, 180
Future-buying, 129–130

G

General Agreement on Tariffs
 and Trade (GATT), 76
General Electric, 83
General Motors Corp. (GM),
 83, 85, 112, 173

German Democratic Republic,
 68, 123, 124, 134, 137, 150
 countertrade practices, 139–
 144
Ghana, 96
Glass-Steagall Banking
 Reform of 1933, 72
Greece, 97, 116
Guangdong Province, China,
 174, 180
Guarantees. See Financial
 guarantees
Guyana, 99

H

Hermitage Museum, 55
Hong Kong, 174
Hungary, 17, 35, 57–58, 65,
 68, 73, 90, 119, 123, 134
 countertrade practices, 149–
 155
 Department for Exchange,
 Financial and Price
 Matters, 150
 Ministry of Foreign Trade,
 150

I

Ileseim, 149
India, 94, 96, 98, 99, 101, 115,
 173
Indonesia, 74, 79, 95, 96, 114
 countertrade practices, 105–
 107
 Department of Trade and
 Cooperatives, 105, 107
Industreanlagen-Import, 144
Industrial cooperation. See
 Cooperation agreements

Interag, 155
International Business
  Machines (IBM), 83
International Commodities
  Export Company, 106
International Monetary Fund
  (IMF), 67
Intrac, 144
Intragovernmental trade
  credits. *See* Official trade
  credits
Iran, 95, 96, 98, 99, 113, 115,
  116
Iraq, 95, 96, 97, 113, 115, 116
Israel, 102
Italy, 67, 115, 176–177

J

Jamaica, 14
Japan, 67, 73, 77, 98, 99, 100,
  115
  International Cooperative
    Agency, 99
  Overseas Economic
    Development Fund
    (OEDF), 99
Ji Chong, 175
Joint ventures, 10, 23–24, 59,
  61, 67, 68, 69, 96, 97, 98,
  102, 104–105, 119, 138,
  160, 172, 175–180, 182,
  183, 184

K

Kinsenda, Zaire (copper
  mine), 100
Kobe Aluminum Association,
  98

L

Lada, 23
Latin America, 8, 77, 97, 111
Ledger, 25–26
Letter of credit, 63, 129
  definition, 64–66
  irrevocable letter of credit,
    64
  sight letter of credit, 64
  standby letter of credit, 18,
    64
Letter of guarantee, 67
Letter of release, 129
Libya, 116
Licensing, 22, 25, 57, 58, 88,
  101, 119, 126, 138, 160
Limited recourse financing,
  64–65
Linkage, 19, 29, 41, 43, 105,
  124, 130, 138, 143, 160,
  172
  definition, 33–34
Lists, 35
London exchange, 33
London Inter-Bank Offered
  Rate (LIBOR), 68

M

Machimpex, 173
Machinoexport, 165
Manufacturer's Hanover
  Trust, 71
Manufacturing-for-export, 101
Marubeni, 98
Masinimportexport, 148
McDonnell Douglas, 73, 75, 88
Mercur, 149
Mesopotamia, 8
Mexico, 74, 76, 79, 98, 100,
  101, 102, 107

Mexico (Cont.):
  countertrade practices, 109–113
Middle East, 8, 96, 111
Mineroperu, 98
Mongolia, 68
Morgan Guarantee, 71
Motors Trading Corporation, 83, 85, 173

N

National Association of Credit Management, 117
National Bank of Hungary, 149
National Iranian Oil Company (NIOC), 115
Negative files, 129
New Caledonia, 96, 99
New Guinea, 96, 99
New Zealand, 101
Nigeria, 95
  countertrade practices, 103–105
Nike, 182

O

Obligation to purchase, 42–44
Occidental Petroleum, 113, 163
Official (or Intragovernmental) trade credits, 67
Offset, 5, 6
Offtake contracts, 70–71
Ok Tedi, 99
Olmer, Lionel, 76
Open (or current) account, 63

Organization for Economic Cooperation and Development (OECD), 21–22, 76, 97, 115, 119
Organization of Petroleum Exporting Countries (OPEC), 95, 96, 105

P

Pakistan, 96, 98
  State Trading Firm, 102
Parallel bank guarantees, 18
Parallel barter. *See* Counterpurchase
Penalties, 31–32, 43, 45, 46, 128, 142–143, 148, 155, 160
  definition, 44
People's Republic of China (or China), 8, 10, 11–12, 19, 22, 34, 49, 54, 56, 62, 65, 66–68, 77, 105, 114, 115, 171–184
  China Council for the Promotion of International Trade (CCPIT), 184
  Compensation Trade Bureau of the State Import and Export Commission (SIEC), 171, 184
  Finance Investment Administration, 184
  Foreign Investment Control Commission (FICC), 184
  Foreign Trade and Aid Affairs Division (of Mofert's Treaties and Laws Dept.), 184
  Ministry of Coal, 176

People's Republic of China
(Cont.):
Ministry of Foreign Economic
Relations and Trade
(Mofert), 175, 181, 184
Provisional Administrative
Committee (for Special
Economic Zones), 180
Pepsico, 35–36
Performance bonds, 18, 62
Pertamina, 114
Peru, 98
State Oil Agency, 114
Philippines:
Ministry of Trade, 87
Poland, 21, 24, 57–58, 64, 68,
90, 119, 122, 123, 124,
139, 154
countertrade practices, 155–
161
Ministry of Foreign Trade
and Maritime Economy,
160
Pricing formulas, 44–45
Processing arrangements, 174,
182
Production-sharing contracts,
113–114, 175
Indonesian model 114
Algerian model, 114
Project financing, 69–72
Promissory notes, 64, 65, 66
Protocol agreements, 31, 39,
42, 84, 124, 173
compensation, 21
counterpurchase, 19
definition, 40
Purchasing agents, 34, 35, 36

Q

Quality, 33, 42, 46–47

R

Range of goods, 33–34, 43
Release clauses, 41–42, 43
Reynolds, 98
Right to inspect, 45, 46
Rockwell International, 83
Romania, 64, 65, 68, 119, 124,
133, 134, 143
countertrade practices, 144–
149
Ministry of Chemical
Industry, 148
Ministry of Foreign Trade
Organizations, 149
Ministry of the Interior, 149

S

Saudi Arabia, 95, 116
Scandinavia, 102
Schroeder Bank, 71
Separation of contracts, 40–42
Shah of Iran, 115
Shangdong Province, China,
177
Shanghai Investment & Trust
Corp. (SITCO), 184
Shell Petroleum Co., 115
Shipping documents, 63, 64
Shushkov, Mihail, 162
Sight. *See* Cash-against-
documents
Singapore, 99
Slaini Costrurrorri, 177
SONATRACH, 114
South Africa, 100
South Korea, 88, 101, 115
Spain, 100
Special Economic Zones
(SEZs), 180

Sri Lanka, 94, 96, 98, 173
Standby bank guarantees, 62
Stankoimport, 165
Sudan, 94
Supplier credits, 60, 61, 68
    definition, 62–64
Sweden, 67, 87, 129
Swiss Franc, 26
Switch agreements (or switch
    trading), 5, 144, 149
    definition, 26–27
Switch trading. *See* Switch
    agreements
Switzerland, 129

T

Techmashexport, 165
Technology (or technology
    transfer), 16, 17, 19, 20,
    21, 39, 55, 57, 58, 74, 78,
    83, 88, 95, 109, 116, 119,
    121, 132, 134, 137, 138,
    139, 141, 147, 157, 161,
    164–165, 171, 172–173,
    175, 176, 177, 182, 183,
    184
Technology Services, 54
Technology transfer. *See*
    Technology
Technotrade, 176–177
Tera, 149
Togliatti, 23
Trading house, 20, 30, 33, 36,
    37, 47, 50, 51, 57, 144,
    149, 154, 160, 161, 166
    definition, 89–91
Trading subsidiary, 30, 49–56
    autonomous profit-making
    center, 83–86
    countertrade cooperative,
    87–88

Trading subsidiary (Cont.):
    countertrade purchasing
    organization, 87
    countertrade unit, 82–83
    direct countertrade
    organization, 86
    indirect countertrade
    organization, 86
Transferable obligations, 47
Transferable ruble, 26
Turam Corp., 117
Turkey, 98, 101
    countertrade practices, 117–
    118
Turn-key plants, 141, 144,
    155, 162, 164, 172

U

Union of Soviet Socialist
    Republics (Soviet Union
    or U.S.S.R.), 9, 21–22, 64–
    65, 66, 68, 74, 77, 119,
    155
    countertrade practices, 161–
    167
    Eleventh Five-Year Plan
    (1981–1985), 165
    Main Administration for
    Compensation Arrange-
    ments with the West
    (MACAW), 167
    Ministry of Culture, 56
    Ministry of Foreign Trade,
    167
    Office of Technical,
    Scientific and Economic
    Cooperation, 167
    Twenty-fifth Party Congress
    of the CPSU, 162
United Arab Emirates, 100
United Brands, 87

United Kingdom, 23, 67, 91
United Nations International
  Development
  Organization (UNIDO),
  175
United States, 53–54, 55, 67,
  71, 74–75, 76, 77, 87, 171
  Bureau of the Census, 58
  Department of Commerce,
    30, 76
  Department of Defense, 75
  Department of State, 76
  Department of the
    Treasury, 75, 76
  General Accounting Office
    (GAO), 75
  International Trade
    Commission (ITC), 75, 77
  Trade Representative,
    Office of, 75, 76
United States dollar, 26
Uruguay, 101

V

Venezuela, 115
Vietnam, 68

W

Weimar Republic, 8
Western Europe, 23, 54, 72,
  74–75, 77, 87, 116
World Bank, 10, 71

Y

Yugoslavia, 68, 74, 116, 139,
  151, 156

Z

Zaire, 100
Zentral Kommerz GmbH, 144
Zhe Zhen, China (coal
  mine), 177